Deductive Logic

in

Natural Language

Deductive Logic

in

Natural Language

by

Douglas Cannon

broadview press

National Library of Canada Cataloguing in Publication Data

Cannon, Douglas, 1946-
    Deductive logic in natural language / by Douglas Cannon.

(The Broadview library of logic and critical thinking)
Includes an index.
ISBN 1-55111-445-3

1. Logic. 2. Language and logic. I. Title. II. Series: Broadview library of logic and critical thinking.
P98.5.L63C35 2002   162   C2002-902038-7

Broadview Press Ltd., is an independent, international publishing house, incorporated in 1985.

North America:
P.O. Box 1243, Peterborough, Ontario, Canada K9J 7H5
3576 California Road, Orchard Park, NY 14127
Tel: (705) 743-8990; Fax: (705) 743-8353
E-mail: customerservice@broadviewpress.com

United Kingdom and Europe:
Plymbridge North (Thomas Lyster, Ltd.)
Units 3 & 4a, Ormskirk Industrial Park, Burscough Rd
Ormskirk, Lancashire L39 2YW
Tel: (1695) 575112; Fax: (1695 570120
E-mail: books@tlyster.co.uk

Australia:
St. Clair Press, P.O. Box 287, Rozelle, NSW 2039
Tel: (02) 818-1942; Fax: (02) 418-1923

www.broadviewpress.com

Broadview Press gratefully acknowledges the financial support of the Book Publishing Industry Development Program, Ministry of Canadian Heritage, Government of Canada.

PRINTED IN CANADA

For Mary Ellen

CONTENTS

Preface ix

Acknowledgments xv

Abbreviations xvii

I. Fundamentals
§1. Propositions and sentences—the basic units of logic and language 1
§2. Truth and (declarative) sentences 5
§3. Consistency and sets of sentences 8
§4. Validity and arguments 11
Exercises 19

II. Stories and Situations
§5. Reference and truth 22
§6. Meaning and truth 26
§7. Might have beens 31
§8. Truth with respect to a situation 37
Exercises 43

III. Establishing Inconsistency with Tableaux
§9. Obvious inconsistency 46
§10. Semantic tableaux: dividing and conquering 49
§11. Efficiencies in tableaux 58
§12. A tableau that closes 60
Exercises 66

IV. Extending the Tableau Technique
§13. Counter sets and validity 68
§14. Resolving reference 75
§15. Additional constructions 80
§16. When can a sentence be checked? 85
Exercises 91

V. Generative Grammar
§17. What we mean by a grammar 94
§18. Phrase-structure grammars; Phrase-markers 98
§19. Transformations 106
§20. Syntactic ambiguity 114
Exercises 120

VI. Logical Analysis of Complex Sentences
§21. "If's," "And's," or "But's": Conjunctions and sentence connectives 123

§22.	Rule-governed sentence connectives in tableaux	126
§23.	Transformations in logical analysis; Grouping	136
§24.	The reach of rules; Negated conditionals	143
§25.	Tableaux constructed by rules	149
	Exercises	154

VII. Logical Analysis of Simple Sentences: Identity and Other Relations

§26.	Designators and predicates	157
§27.	Properties and relations; Types of relations	161
§28.	The peculiar relation of identity	171
§29.	Tableau rules for identity	177
	Exercises	181

VIII. Logical Analysis of Simple Sentences: One-Word Quantifiers

§30.	Quantifiers in general	185
§31.	The simplest quantifiers: "everyone," "someone," and "no one"	189
§32.	Tableau rules for the simplest quantifiers	196
§33.	The simplest quantifiers in tableaux	204
§34.	"Anyone," quantifier scope, and anaphoric pronouns	210
	Exercises	215

IX. Quantifier Expressions and Syllogisms

§35.	The universal quantifier	218
§36.	Relative pronouns, and the existential and nihilistic quantifiers	228
§37.	Tableaux for syllogisms and other arguments	234
§38.	"Anyone" and logical equivalence	237
§39.	Things, times, and places	241
	Exercises	245

Appendix: Truth-Functional Logic

§40.	Review: Tableau rules for sentence connectives	248
§41.	Three levels of symbolization	250
§42.	Symbolic languages for algebra	252
§43.	Truth-functions and their computational tables	254
§44.	Truth tables and calculating truth-values	259
§45.	Constructing an arbitrary function; Normal form	270
	Exercises	274

For Reading and Reference	275
Index	280

Preface

This book explores the connection, dimly recognized since ancient times, between logic and grammar. The material in the book forms the basis of a logic course that I have taught for many years, largely to freshmen and sophomores at the University of Puget Sound. The course has been praised by students for improving their writing and for preparing them for law school admission. But under its influence many have moved to further study of logic and philosophy of language, and even into graduate study in linguistics.

The book presents an account of deductive inference in natural language, providing resources for assessing the logic of various grammatical constructions and for determining the meaning and reference of various expressions as they apply to given situations. It precisely defines the relations of logical consequence, mutual consistency, and logical equivalence among sentences of English, and the notion of a valid deductive argument expressed by sentences of English. And it develops techniques for recognizing when these relationships do and do not hold. Here the book makes use of theoretical and technical devices from standard symbolic logic, from generative syntax and binding theory, and from the pragmatics of indexical reference and incomplete descriptions, adapting and supplementing these devices with innovations of its own. Its focus throughout is on natural language—English in particular—and on grammatical structures that determine logical force. It also provides a theoretical framework for discussion of different kinds of ambiguity—syntactic and anaphoric, as well as lexical.

Whether propounded by philosophers, lawyers, theologians, mathematicians, or editorialists, deductive arguments are most often formulated in sentences of ordinary English (or some other natural language) perhaps embellished by specialized notations or expressions, as in mathematical proofs. And so this book defines and explains logical relations among such natural language sentences, and it does so directly. It does not symbolize sentences, or translate them into a formal language. It defines consequence, consistency, and equivalence for the sentences themselves, rather than for formulas that represent them.

The advantage of a direct approach is that a reader concentrates her attention on formulations in English, the medium in which she will ordinarily express those ideas whose logic is ultimately her concern. She thereby improves her expressive abilities, as well as her powers of analysis and evaluation. The account in the book gradually focuses in on various English phrase-classes and syntactic constructions of logical importance. These grammatical topics are treated as systematically as is permitted by the state of the art in linguistics and semantic theory and by the capacity of readers to grasp theoretical complications. By contrast, in treatments using formal languages, readers must focus on technical details that are of only derivative interest. It is widely acknowledged that, in the usual approach, it is the effort of symbolization that most challenges and refines a student's logical acumen. Nevertheless, most logic books treat the process of symbolization as an incidental task, best gotten through quickly, so that logical evaluation of the symbolic results— the real business—can proceed. No theoretical underpinning for symbolization is provided in these books, nor is any fuller understanding inculcated of the logical resources of natural language. The account here analyzes logical relations without an appeal to symbolic formulas. In doing so, it addresses the grammatical and semantic difficulties that a systematic method of symbolization would have to grapple with. A reader who later learns the symbolic approach will find these lessons immediately applicable.

As it remains within natural language for its treatment of logical relations, the books eschews the received conceptual basis for those relations, namely Tarski's theory of logical consequence. (That theory appeals to interpretations multiply imposed on an intrinsically uninterpreted formal system.) Thus an alternative conceptual basis is needed. That need is filled in Chapter II (§§ 7 - 8) where is sketched a definition of consistency of a set of sentences in terms of possible situations. Though no account of the ontology of situations is there attempted, a situation is deemed possible if it is described by an intelligible story. In order to settle the question of consistency, the sentences in a set must be disambiguated, and coreferential and anaphoric expressions within the set must be identified. Then the sentences are addressed to various possible situations, in each case raising the question whether the sentences are all true with respect to the given situation. Of course that

question will presuppose certain referential ties between the
referring expressions within the original sentences and the
characters, circumstances, and events in the situation under
consideration. Underlying these presuppositions are philosophical
issues as difficult as those of the metaphysics of situations, indeed at
least as difficult as widely controversial issues about referential
relations to actual circumstances and events. But here these issues
are suppressed in favor of the practical employment of this
conceptual apparatus. For the most part the book's techniques entail
constructing descriptions of relevant situations, thereby rendering
these referential ties obvious and uncontroversial.

The book flirts with philosophical perplexities in addressing
another matter worth mentioning here. In natural languages,
certain operations form complex sentences out of simpler ones,
giving rise to important logical relations. Every logician knows that
many, in fact most, sentence-forming operations are not truth-
functional. The typical logic book postpones consideration of such
operations to some later treatment of what are called alternative
logics. Of course, for all but a few students, that later treatment
never comes. Meanwhile, ordinary English sentences are forced into
a Procrustean bed of truth-functionality, and a technical theory of
these truth-functions is developed at more or less length. Students
either despair over the myriad cases left aside by the theory of truth-
functions, or else are caught up in its techniques as engaging, if not
very profound, mathematical exercises. In contrast, the techniques
of the book employ versions of the method of semantic tableaux
where neither truth-functionality nor bivalence of truth-values is
assumed. (Though a rule of double negation is offered, it is easily
withheld where its application would be problematic.) This
treatment lays the ground for a later consideration, by ongoing
students, both of the philosophical issues of intensionality and of the
standard truth-functional idealization. But it also provides technical
resources for those who will never study further, to handle live
instances involving "because", "since", and even "if . . then", with no
presumption of truth-functionality.

The book systematically investigates sentence constructions with
logical significance. It accounts for structural ambiguities and
enunciates tableau rules that advert to various constituents of
sentences and the phrase classes to which they belong. All of this
requires not only an account of English syntax, but reasonably
precise exercises to enable students to absorb that account. In
Chapter V this requirement is met with what is called the Standard

Theory by generative linguists—most fully set out in Chomsky's *Aspects of the Theory of Syntax* (1965). It must be emphasized that Chapter V does not represent current linguistic theory (no more than the Bohr atom represents the quantum conception of electron shells or the mechanics taught in freshman physics represents 20th-century developments).

In addition to employing the concepts and techniques of classic generative grammar, the account subsequent to Chapter V makes use of better behaved "transformational equivalents" as it subjects sentences of English to systematic analysis. Barely submerged with this strategy is the question of the relation between deep structure and logical form. This question was always an open one among logicians, and even in the heyday of transformations, the idea that semantic interpretation occurs only at the level of deep structure was not accepted without reservation among linguists. Yet the conviction that there must be some relationship between linguistic representation and logical force can hardly be resisted. It is enshrined in Chomsky's recent writings, as he attaches the label "LF"—for logical form—to the interface of the grammatical system "with systems of conceptual structure and language use." (*The Minimalist Program*, 1995, p. 131) The treatment below, especially in Chapters VI and IX, takes a moderate stance on these issues. It makes explicit what is taken for granted in all textbooks of symbolic logic as they address cases like "Either Martha or Mary saw George," or "Since George and Martha saw each other, Martha was seen by someone." But especially in its treatment of logical scope, the book emphasizes the difficulties that arise in cases like, "Everyone was seen by either George or Martha," and it calls the reader's attention to the need for a more subtle and deeply informed account of quantifier scope and semantic interpretation.

The later chapters of the book take up predicate logic. Chapter VII carefully distinguishes noun phrases that function as designators from other noun phrases, and introduces logical predicates by removing designators from declarative sentences. That leads to the notion of a relation, and the chapter treats the logic of those relations subject to rule-governed logical manipulation—those that are symmetric or transitive. It gives particularly full coverage to the relation of identity. Inferences involving identity are pervasive in ordinary reasoning, and particularly in mathematical derivations (substitution in algebra, "putting equals for equals"). And yet equality, qualitative identity, and what is called numerical identity, give rise to much confusion and many disputations. Thus a thorough account of them has as great as a practical value as any area of logic.

The treatment of quantifiers in Chapter VIII recognizes the wide variety of noun phrases that do not function as designators and calls attention to the complexity of inferences involving them. Among the various quantifiers, the simplest are the single words, "everyone," "someone," and "no one"; fully comprehensive rules are given for these. (Later in the book, the treatment is effortlessly extended to impersonal, temporal, and locational quantifiers, like "everything," "sometime," and "nowhere.") With the rule for the one-word quantifier "anyone," questions of logical scope become central. In Chapter IX the quantifier rules are generalized to handle some of the myriad quantifier expressions that can be formulated in English. (These are multiword noun phrases like "most philosophers," "two handsome women who have made fundamental contributions to ethics," and "nobody under the age of 18.") The book introduces innovative paraphrasing, using fully natural English formulations, where anaphoric and relative pronouns do the work that formal treatments assign to variables. Using that paraphrasing, three natural- language quantifiers are specified, and tableau rules are provided for each. These rules easily comprehend the realm of the classical syllogism, however generously conceived. More ambitiously, a careful intermingling of paraphrasing and rule-application enables the techniques of Chapter IX to handle inferences involving multiple quantifiers with relations, all the while remaining within the confines of natural language.

The book concludes with an appendix that relates the material in the middle chapters of the text to a more standard, symbolic treatment of truth-functional logic. However novel the book's emphasis on the logic of natural language, this appendix illustrates the easy transition to the formal logic that characterizes logic courses in most philosophy departments. Though not included in the appendix, the transition to the universal and existential quantifiers of standard predicate logic is equally easy. In fact, for most students, seeing quantifier expressions at work in natural language will make the quantifier and predicate notation of first-order logic seem more natural and less forbidding. Variables will rightly appear as distillations of flexible and pervasive expressive devices, which every student has unself-consciously mastered in his or her native language.

This book innovates for teaching effectiveness and even for philosophical illumination, and yet it facilitates entry by serious students into the mainstream of modern deductive logic and of contemporary linguistics.   Students can well proceed from the material here to subsequent study of the standard theory of first-order logic (and beyond).   Those who are intrigued by the sampling of syntactic theory can proceed to a presentation of "principles and parameters" syntax, with its alternative conceptions of phrase-structure, its much more capacious conception of transformation ("Move α"), and even its emphasis on the lexicon and its denial of multiple levels of representation (no "deep" and "surface" structure). And the inspired few can proceed further, to investigation of the true nature of logical relations, the question whether they do have their basis in linguistic principles, and the correct conception of logical consequence.   For all these endeavors, students are provided a sound and stimulating introduction by this treatment of deductive logic.

Acknowledgments

In many years of studying and teaching logic I have been influenced by a large number of powerful presentations of logical theory, some of which I have no doubt forgotten. Among the most memorable are well known logic textbooks by W.V.O. Quine, by Richard Jeffrey, by Benson Mates, and by E.J. Lemmon, as well as lectures, lecture notes, and unpublished material by Hilary Putnam, by George Boolos, and by Warren Goldfarb. The book from which this one most immediately descends is a small trade paperback by Wilfrid Hodges, entitled simply *Logic*. If that book had remained in print in the United States, perhaps this one would not have been written. On the side of linguistics I am most indebted to the voluminous writings of Noam Chomsky and to presentations of syntactic theory by John Lyons, by Howard Lasnik, and by Neil Smith. In retrospect I have come to recognize how greatly Quine's monumental *Word and Object* has influenced my treatments.

In conceiving and writing the book I have been encouraged, informed, and valuably upbraided by Lori Alward, Sylvain Bromberger, Richard Cartwright, Helen Cartwright, John Etchemendy, Hans Sluga, Scott Soames, and Cass Weller, and by my departmental colleagues William Beardsley, Paul Loeb, David Magnus, and Lawrence Stern. Seven anonymous referees, most of them for Broadview Press, provided stringent admonitions, expressions of high hope, and much helpful guidance. One or more chapters in draft were read and criticized by the late Gregory Harding, by Warren Goldfarb, by Robert Coburn, by Gregory Oakes, by Edward Richards, and by Heather Douglas—who also conceived one of the key ideas for my treatment of quantifier expressions. Colleagues at University of Puget Sound, particularly Geoffrey Block, Andrew Rex, and D. Wade Hands, gave essential advice toward securing publication. Among the fine staff of Broadview Press, Frances Brennan, Julia Gaunce, and Barbara Conolly have been especially supportive.

Because this book grew out of an undergraduate course, I am indebted to several hundred students who have more or less suffered through preliminary versions of the material and who have provided corrections, complaints, and first-hand responses as members of a representative audience. Equally there have been generations of teaching assistants, who have adjusted exercises, formulated answers, and freely advised on presentational strategies. Among them three will recognize their more specific contributions: Amy Hoard Kinsel, Rebecca Inscoe, and Joshua Epstein.

Mary Ellen Sullivan, to whom the book is dedicated and to whom I am luckily married, and our children, Mary, Sarah, and William Cannon, have been inundated with this material for much of their lives, so much so that their friends think them slightly odd. I could not have pressed on without their loyalty and confidence, and I have constantly depended on their logical acumen and their sure command of the English language.

For education, support, and affection accorded me by these people, I express my heartfelt gratitude. Each of them disagrees with something or other that I have continued to maintain, and so responsibility for what is asserted in the text remains, alas, with me.

By way of example and illustration the text incorporates copyright material—stylish lyrics from musical theater, all of which are literally quoted on the pages indicated below, in *Italics* or in *ITALIC SMALL CAPS*. I have received permission as follows, for which I am grateful.

Abbreviations

It is essential to the present account of deductive logic in natural language that all of our symbols be regarded as abbreviations of specific expressions of English, each understood in a particular (natural) sense.

Symbol	Abbreviated Expression	Page Introduced
¬	it is not true that	127
&	and (understood as without temporal force)	129
∨	or (understood inclusively)	130
. . . → - - -	if . . . , then - - - (that is to say, - - - if . . .)	127
↔	if, and only if,	134
=	is one and the same as	171
∀	no matter who you are (. . . you . . .)	220
	whoever he or she is (. . . he or she . . .)	220
	whatever it is (. . . it . . .)	244
	whenever it is (. . . then . . .)	244
	wherever it is (. . . there . . .)	
∃	there is someone (. . . who . . .)	231
	there is something (. . . that . . .)	243
	there is a time (. . . when . . .)	
	there is a place (. . . where . . .)	243
И	there is no one (. . . who . . .)	232
	there is nothing (. . . that . . .)	
	there is no time (. . . when . . .)	243
	there is no place (. . . where . . .)	

I: Fundamentals

In a fundamental—though not completely obvious—sense, the basic unit of language is what is called a complete **sentence**. On first glance this might not seem to be true, for there are two kinds of elements of which sentences are composed, and it would be natural to think that either of them is more basic. Of course I have in mind words and sounds. (Those who are strongly oriented toward the written language might be more comfortable if I said words and letters; for the time being we can accept either way of looking at it.) Sentences are made up of words. And words are made up of sounds. Clearly then sentences are not basic in the sense of being the smallest building blocks from which other linguistic entities are built up. It seems that what is basic about sentences needs some explanation.

For one thing, when we say something, whether it is to make an assertion, to ask a question, to request something of someone, or to say any of the myriad other kinds of things there are to be said, it is a sentence that we utter. While this might not be strictly or universally true, as when we answer a question with, "Yes,"—or for that matter, with, "Vanilla,"—exceptions clearly require special circumstances.

1

Many utterances that apparently fall short of being sentences, but nonetheless succeed in saying something, may be regarded as elliptical versions of recognizably complete sentences. Thus, when you say that someone is coming to dinner, and I reply, "Who?", my word might well be understood as short for, "Who is coming to dinner?"

For another thing, it is at the level of the sentence that meaning is primarily carried. (True, dictionary entries are for words. But how could it be otherwise: there are too many sentences.) When we consider individual words, even in context, it is not at all clear, in many cases, that the word in question itself has a meaning. Consider the word "sake" in, "For the sake of his honor, he accepted the challenge," or the word "way" in "Lefty and Ace throw a slider the same way." A similar point can be made with words that occur more frequently. What does "the" mean? Or, in such sentences as, "The leaves are brown," or, "The leaves are falling," what does "are" mean? In a passive voice sentence like, "The tree was struck by lightning," what does "by" mean? And, in a simple sentence like, "I do not know," what does "do" mean? Or consider the sentence, "It was in 1864 that the Confederation was agreed to." What does the pronoun "it" refer to? In each case the word makes a systematic contribution to the meaning of the sentence, but has no meaning in isolation. Since translation is supposed to preserve meaning, perhaps the point is best made there. Word-by-word translation of a given sentence may be awkward, difficult, or even impossible, while translation of the whole, freed from the word-by-word restriction, is easy or obvious. "Setzen Sie sich," means the same thing as "Please, sit down," though "sich" disappears without a trace and "please" and "down" come out of nowhere.

Finally, and perhaps most central for our purposes, it is with respect to sentences that questions of grammar arise. Whether noun and verb agree in number, whether the adjectives come in the right order, whether the verb form takes an auxiliary—all these are questions which apply at the level of the sentence. A paragraph, or even a chapter, may be more or less well organized. But a sentence that is badly organized is typically ungrammatical—a more serious failing. On the other side, a badly organized word is just no word at all, unless you count misspellings.

When we turn to questions of logic, the comparably fundamental unit is what philosophers call a **proposition**. It was John Stuart Mill who first introduced the technical notion of a proposition, and whether there really are such things has been a matter of dispute among philosophers of language. Despite such disagreement, the notion is quite close to common sense. An example of what Mill had in mind is found in the words of Abraham Lincoln, when he spoke in his Gettysburg Address of a nation dedicated to the *proposition* that all men are created equal. Another example, under a different name, is the Principle of the Conservation of Energy. Still another example of a proposition is the Pythagorean Theorem, and another, from a different field of discourse, is the Doctrine of the Trinity.

When John Stuart Mill formally introduced this notion, he identified propositions by three features.

(1) Propositions are the objects of belief.

(2) Propositions can be expressed in sentences.

(3) Propositions are susceptible of truth and falsity.

Thus Lincoln—and Jefferson, Rousseau, and Locke before him—believed the proposition that all men are created equal. After two centuries during which the relevant concepts were developed, physicists such as Joule and Kelvin came to believe the Principle of the Conservation of Energy; current physicists still do. And anyone who accepts Euclidean geometry believes the Pythagorean Theorem.

As for the second feature, the proposition that all men are created equal obviously can be expressed by a declarative sentence, in fact by the sentence,

<blockquote>All men are created equal.</blockquote>

A bit more work is required for the Principle of the Conservation of Energy, but a sentence that will do is,

<blockquote>The total energy in a closed system is conserved over time.</blockquote>

The Pythagorean Theorem, so described, does not wear its content on its sleeve, but when we consult an elementary geometry text, we again turn up a declarative sentence:

<blockquote>The sum of the squares of the sides of any right triangle is equal to the square of the hypotenuse.</blockquote>

As for the Doctrine of the Trinity, a familiar—if difficult—formulation is found in the sentence,

<blockquote>God is three in person, but one in substance.</blockquote>

Of course these are not the only sentences that express these varied propositions. The Pythagorean Theorem was first expressed by a sentence in Attic Greek, rather than one in English, and Latin was until recently the more usual vehicle for trinitarianism. Even in English alternative formulations readily come to mind.

Mill's third point was that propositions are susceptible of truth and falsity. This is borne out by the words to which Lincoln alluded, in the Declaration of Independence of the United States of America:

> We hold these *truths* to be self-evident, that all men are
> created equal . . .

You don't have to agree that the proposition is self-evident, or even that it, in fact, is true. The point is rather that it is the sort of thing that could be true, and that, if it is not true, then presumably it is false. If in geometry you proved the Pythagorean Theorem, you proved that it is true. And when Unitarians denied the Doctrine of the Trinity, they were asserting that the orthodox Christian doctrine is false. More needs to be—and will be—said about these matters of truth and falsity, but for now we are merely observing that Mill seems to have common sense on his side.

Diverse as they are in subject matter, the propositions that we have carried along as examples are misleading in one notable way. All four of them are important propositions—important enough to have names, to have been carefully investigated, to have conferences devoted to them and even wars fought over them. If we agree with Mill about the three features characterizing a proposition, we must recognize that lots of propositions are important in none of these ways. Such humdrum candidates come to mind as the propositions that Wednesday is in the middle of the week, that bread nourishes the body, that our subject is logic and language, and that Canada and the United States differ in their systems of health care financing. More ephemeral are the propositions that it snowed in Toronto on Christmas, that the Oklahoma City bombing trials drew to an end as the Unabomber trial began, and that, as you read this, you are sitting down. All of these examples qualify as propositions, in that all these have been believed (by someone or other), all are expressed by sentences, and all are the kinds of things that are true or false.

Having explained what propositions are, we must turn to what makes them fundamental for logic. The full answer can only emerge as we explore what logic is—by learning it. For now it is enough to recall that it is a kind of logical exercise—namely, a proof—that issues in the Pythagorean Theorem as a conclusion. And it is the Principle of the Conservation of Energy from which it follows that, when a car hits a tree, its kinetic energy must be absorbed by the tree, the car, and its occupants. And finally it is the proposition that all men are created equal that is inconsistent with assertions of black inferiority in some of Jefferson's political writings. The point is that recognizably logical properties—like being the conclusion of a proof, or following from another proposition, or being inconsistent with another proposition—apply to propositions.

It is no accident that the fundamental unit from the point of view of grammar corresponds to the fundamental unit from the point of view of logic. In traditional school grammar it is said that a sentence expresses a complete thought. It is natural to suspect that such a complete thought is precisely what we have been calling a proposition. Its very completeness is what enables it to relate logically to other complete thoughts.

TRUTH AND (DECLARATIVE) SENTENCES   §2

We said above, on Mill's behalf, that propositions are expressed by complete sentences. Actually this must be qualified in an essential way, for not all sentences do express propositions. It is only **declarative sentences** that have this capacity. School grammar typically distinguishes four kinds of sentence: declarative, interrogative, imperative, and exclamatory. The first, it is said, is used to make a statement; the second, to ask a question; the third, to give an order or command; and the fourth, to express a feeling of the moment. (Other terms have been used for declarative sentences; sometimes they are called "assertoric" sentences or even "indicative" sentences—though this latter term may mark a different distinction.) Making a statement—the characteristic use of a declarative sentence—seems pretty much the same thing as we have spoken of as expressing a proposition.

These characterizations are ponderous and not very illuminating, but providing more precise definitions would not be an easy task. It would probably require a fully developed grammatical theory of the sort we will consider in Chapter V. Still we can learn to categorize lots of sentences by looking at some examples. The sentences given in §1 were intended to illustrate the notion of a proposition, so we should expect all of them to strike us as declarative. They contrast with examples like,

> Who says that all men are created equal?

or,

Is it just men that are created equal?

These pretty clearly ask questions, questions of two different sorts. An obvious mark of the first kind is the presence of a "wh_" word; while the second kind typically involves a reversal of word order. Another contrast is with,

Don't you believe it,

or,

(1)   Stop using words in a prejudicial way.

These are imperatives, and can be recognized by the second-person "you"—sometimes left out—and again the alteration of word order. The fourth category is typified by one-word sentences:

Hallelujah!

and,

(2)   Ouch!

The last example helps us to recognize that the convictions we have about easy cases do not carry over to harder ones, and the traditional criteria in terms of the use to which the sentence is put do not help much. The sentence,

That hurts!

can be, and often is, used in exactly the same way as (2), namely to express a feeling of sudden or intense pain. Indeed, it is often uttered by way of exclamation. Nevertheless, there is some tug to categorize it as declarative. The tug becomes irresistible in the case of,

There is a throbbing pain in my upper-left wisdom tooth,

but Wittgenstein was moved by philosophical considerations to assimilate the latter to "Ouch" and deny that it expressed a proposition.

Another slippery slope begins with (1) above and continues through,

You must stop using words in a prejudicial way,

and,

You ought to stop using words in a prejudicial way,

to,

He ought to stop using words in a prejudicial way,

and finally to,

> Using words in a prejudicial way is something people ought
> never to do.

This last sentence seems to express a proposition of ethics, though preceding ones seem like different ways, varying in intensity and grace, of telling someone what to do. This very fact has led some philosophers to deny that there are any propositions of ethics.

A related difficulty arises with a sentence like the following.

(3)   With these words, I thee wed.

Though it has the form of a declarative sentence, (3) does not seem to express a belief—recall Mill's first characteristic—and it seems odd to call it true or false. Rather than describing how things are, it comprises an essential part of a ceremony, a ceremony in which a marriage is performed. For that reason, this kind of sentence has been called a **performative**. As in earlier puzzling cases, it contrasts with a third-person analogue that is **descriptive**:

> With those very words, she married him.

Interesting as these cases are, they complicate our original task, which was to identify those sentences that express propositions. We will have to settle for what we have dimly perceived. Declarative sentences can be distinguished from questions, commands, exclamations, etc., by their form: they have the ordinary word order and nothing left out. (This still leaves some hard cases involving "you.") Then among the declarative sentences, the descriptive ones can be distinguished from performative sentences by the uses to which they are characteristically put. None of this is very precise, but it goes back to our original conception of a proposition. A proposition can be the object of belief and must be susceptible of truth or falsity. So, a sentence expresses a proposition only if it makes sense to ask whether someone who uses it thereby formulates a belief, and to ask whether what she is saying is true. Thus, among sentences, it is only declarative sentences, and among declarative sentences, it is only descriptive sentences, rather than performatives, that express propositions.

The sentences that we have identified are the ones that express propositions or at least can be used to do so. Handling propositions is possible only through the medium of sentences that express them. The sentences can be uttered and heard, written and read. In fact they can be taken apart and rearranged. And so, in developing techniques for logic and grammar, it is sentences that we will work with.

Whatever other purposes it is assigned, logic is concerned primarily with the pursuit of truth. We analyze and compare sentences precisely because the propositions they express may be true, or false, and we want to know which. These notions of truth and falsity have challenged philosophers and logicians for centuries. We will not take time now to try to understand them better, much less to define them. For now we will simply work with them, taking ourselves to understand these notions adequately, as they apply to propositions.

Since it is sentences that we will be manipulating, it will be convenient, however unconventional, to apply these notions of truth and falsity to the sentences themselves. It is obvious how we should do so. We will say that **a sentence is true** (or **false**) just as the proposition that it expresses is true (or false). Sentences that do not express propositions will not qualify as either.

§3   CONSISTENCY AND SETS OF SENTENCES

Once a man said the following. All who heard him agreed that he was being illogical.

Whoever sells drugs makes victims of his customers and ruins their lives. Such scum should all be locked up and the keys thrown away. My son is a good kid though. When his friends give him money for the cocaine he gets them, he is just helping them to have a little fun. It is outrageous that the police have put him under arrest.

Before we consider this example more closely, let's mention a few more cases that, speaking colloquially, we would call illogical. We would say that it is illogical to be afraid of lions and tigers under your bed, but also to think that if only you shut your eyes, they will go away. It was illogical of Aesop to suppose that a frog inflated itself until it burst like a balloon. When Donald Duck mounts a fan on the deck, hoping to move his becalmed sailboat, he is being illogical. It's illogical to believe that Wiley Coyote would hang unsupported in the air just as long as he didn't look down, and it's illogical to expect that your printer will work very well every day of the year, but not on the day your term paper is due, unless of course you knock on wood.

These ideas are childish or fantastic, wildly implausible or even—in some sense—impossible. That is why we call them illogical.   No one with a lick of sense would accept them for a moment.   At the very least, none of these suppositions are true.   For all that, they will not turn out to be contrary to logic in the account that we give of it.

Take the lions and tigers under your bed.   It's not true that there are any.   In an earlier day, you found that out by bravely looking. Now you know without looking.   But you can't expect reassurance from your logic book.   Using the ideas from §2, we can say that the proposition expressed by the sentence,

There are lions and tigers under my bed,

is not true, and derivatively that the sentence itself is not true.   It is false.   Once we found this out by looking.   How we know now is not easy to explain.   But we do not expect logic to tell us.

Perhaps it will help to add some sentences.

> There are lions and tigers under my bed.
>
> Lions and tigers are found only in Africa and India.
>
> But, of course, my bed, and what is under it, are in neither Africa nor India; they are in British Columbia.

These, taken together, are also illogical.   No one with any sense would suppose that they are true, at least not all of them.   In this case, unlike the earlier one, logic can help.   These three sentences, taken together, are **inconsistent**.   That is to say, this **set of sentences** is inconsistent.   They can't all be true, because they contradict each other.   You could tell a story incorporating the first sentence, or even one incorporating the first two sentences.   But you couldn't tell a story incorporating all these sentences, at least not one that would be intelligible to a discerning listener.   It wouldn't just be fantastic: it wouldn't make any sense at all.

We can confirm the point by considering another set of sentences.

> There are lions and tigers under my bed, lying on the floor.
>
> Lions and tigers are no less than ten inches tall, even as cubs, even lying down.
>
> But, of course, my bed is only six inches off the floor.

Again this set of sentences is inconsistent.   It's not just that they are not all true.   We don't need to look under the bed or do any measuring.   They couldn't all be true; you couldn't even tell an intelligible story where they were all true.   And this is something we will look to logic to explain.

The notion of inconsistency that we are beginning to recognize is a logical notion. To believe things that are mutually inconsistent is to be illogical in a quite strict sense, a sense in which to believe things that are fantastic, childish, superstitious, or wildly implausible, is not to be illogical.

Contrast this notion of inconsistency with other ways in which the word is used.

I voted for a Labor MP because I support Labor policies.

But I voted for the Likud Presidential candidate because he has been a military leader.

This Israeli voter may be inconsistent in her voting behavior, but the sentences are not inconsistent. They may well both be true.

When Dolly raced by in her BMW, Clancey waved.

When the Mayor raced by in her Cadillac, Clancey saluted.

When Mom raced by in her Accord, Clancey stopped her for speeding.

Clancey may be inconsistent in his enforcement of the traffic laws, but the sentences are consistent. The story they tell could be true.

Now let's return to our outraged father. He is being illogical not simply because he favors his son. He is inconsistent not just because he wants the law enforced selectively. The things he says, what he apparently believes, cannot all be true. The reason is that the following sentences form an inconsistent set:

Whoever sells drugs ruins his customers' lives and should be imprisoned.

My son sells drugs to his friends harmlessly.

He should be left alone.

The notions of consistency and inconsistency will be central to our study of logic. They characteristically apply not to sentences alone, but to sets of sentences. Whether the individual sentences in such a set are true or not ("There are lions and tigers under the bed") may be beyond the reach of logic. But logic can determine whether the set as a whole is consistent or not. And if it is inconsistent, the sentences comprising it can't all be true. It would be illogical to think they were.

We have seen that consistency of sets of sentences is a matter for logic to address. But there is another matter that is central to logic. Logic may be characterized as the study of correct reasoning. When you draw conclusions for yourself, you are reasoning. And often you reason with others, perhaps in the way of trying to persuade them of something you already believe.

Despite the hopes of many investors, the stock market will not rise this year. It's bound to stagnate, or even to drop further. It will not rise unless demand for high-tech products rebounds. But Japan's economy cannot recover without a substantial increase in consumer spending by the Japanese people. And high-tech demand is bound to molder if the economies of Japan and other Pacific-rim nations do not recover. The people of Japan will not give up their frugal ways and increase their spending on consumer products. Put your money in land.

This is an example of an **argument**. It is a discourse set out for the purpose of persuasion. Expressed in it, there is a particular proposition for which the argument provides support. Whoever formulated the argument wanted to convince the audience that the stock market would either stay at its current level or fall. The sentence,

(1)   The stock market will not rise this year,

expresses this problematic proposition. That sentence is called the **conclusion** of the argument. Despite the name, it does not appear at the end of the argument. Rather it expresses what you are supposed to conclude as you read the argument. The point of the argument is to induce you to draw this conclusion. In fact, the conclusion often appears at, or near, the beginning of an argument as it is ordinarily presented. There is an obvious rhetorical explanation for this. In setting forth an argument, the arguer is trying to get the audience to accept the conclusion. Setting it out first draws attention to it, brings it up for consideration, right away. Providing support for it, or giving the audience reason to accept it, can come in good time.

An argument is intended not just to convince, but to convince rationally. It is intended to provide good reason for accepting the conclusion. It does so by way of other propositions from which the conclusion follows logically, or from which it at least can be reasonably inferred. Sentences expressing these other propositions, formulated in the presentation of the argument, are called the **premises**. In order to lay open an argument for logical scrutiny, we do well to identify the premises and the conclusion, and to eliminate repeated or extraneous passages. Our earlier argument appears as follows when set out in this **conventional style**.

(2)

The stock market will not rise this year unless demand for high-tech products rebounds.

Japan's economy cannot recover without a substantial increase in consumer spending by the Japanese people.

Demand for high-tech products will molder if the economies of Japan and other Pacific nations do not recover.

The people of Japan will not give up their frugal ways and increase their spending on consumer products.

The stock market will not rise this year.

In the conventional style, a line serves to separate the conclusion from the premises. It can be read "Therefore," because it indicates that what is below the line is supposed to follow from the premises, which have been listed above the line.

Typically the premises of an argument are stated explicitly, but the effect of stating them varies from case to case. Let us presume that the aim of the argument is indeed to persuade the audience of the conclusion by offering rational support for it. The most effective kind of premise will be a statement whose truth is already recognized by those to whom it is addressed. Many listeners could be expected to agree that Japan's economy has not been strong in recent years. Stating this in an argument has the effect merely of calling attention to it, of putting the listener on notice that this is one among the propositions that are invoked in support of the conclusion. In other cases, the premise might not be one that the listener has recently had in mind. It is a fact that overall values in the Tokyo stock market had a serious decline in 1991. A premise stating this fact would have the effect of reminding an audience of something that they are likely to accept as true once they recall it. In still other cases, the audience might not have any prior knowledge of the proposition in question at all. Nonetheless, in hearing it stated, they may accept it on the basis of the authority of whoever advances the argument. This particularly results when the proposition has reference to some bit of personal information relative to the arguer. For example, if I assert that I sold a block of stock in a Hong Kong corporation at a loss, the audience will probably take my word for it.   There is nothing implausible about the claim—and who, after all, should know better than I do what I have lost in stock sales? But it is not only personal information on which speakers are taken to have special authority. Perhaps the arguer is an expert on purchasing practices in Thailand. If she says that Thai purchases of electronic components manufactured in Taiwan are particularly price-sensitive, the audience might well accept her assertion, simply on the basis of its being made by her, a recognized authority. To review, we have cases in which the premise is merely rehearsed, cases in which it is recalled, and cases in which it is authoritatively asserted. All such premises are likely to stand up, to do their part in providing the kind of support needed by the conclusion.

The premises in argument (2), none of which are obvious, comprise yet another kind of case. These are all statements that might be resisted, even when authoritatively asserted. Consider the second premise, a statement that is itself subject to controversy. Whether or not Japan's economy can recover without increased consumer spending is a matter on which even experts disagree. In advancing this proposition in support of the conclusion that the stock market will not rise, the arguer in effect asks the audience to set that controversy aside. When we evaluate the logic of the argument, our attention should focus not on the question whether we agree with the premise, but rather on whether this premise and the others together support the conclusion, that is, whether the conclusion does indeed follow logically from them. To use a time-honored expression, the premises should be regarded as "given," at least for the moment.

In advancing one or more premises that are controversial, as is the one about the recovery of Japan's economy, the arguer might acknowledge the controversy and employ either of two strategies. Once having established that the conclusion does follow from them, the arguer, under the first strategy, would go on to entertain controversy about these premises, one by one. In order effectively to persuade a listener that the stock market will not rise, by the means of argument (2), the arguer would have to provide rational support for the proposition that Japanese economic recovery depends on consumer spending, the claim that we noted as a premise in (2). To do so would be to propound another argument, one whose conclusion would be the sentence,

(3) Japan's economy cannot recover without a substantial increase in consumer spending by the Japanese people.

It may be because this task would be difficult in itself that it was set aside in propounding the original argument. The audience was asked to accept the controversial claim (3) "for the sake of argument," in order to take notice of what would follow about the future of the stock market, from this premise together with others. Chances are that the listeners' interest in the behavior of Japanese consumers will depend on seeing the relevance of that behavior to the stocks in which they have a stake.

It is important to note that the notions of premise and conclusion are entirely relative to the argument under consideration. We have a single sentence, namely (3), that serves both as a premise and as a conclusion. In argument (2), sentence (3) appears as a premise. Its purpose is to provide rational support for the conclusion of argument (2), namely sentence (1). In some other argument, one we never saw formulated, sentence (3) might well be the conclusion.

There is a second strategy that might be employed in the case of controversial premises like (3). The arguer might simply state the premises, in order to make explicit his own reasons for drawing the conclusion (here, that the stock market will not rise). Acknowledging the controversial character of the premises, the arguer may not hope really to change the minds of those he addresses. He hopes at least to draw attention to a structure of reasoning that would lead the listener to the conclusion if ever she were to come to accept the premises. Though his aim falls short of rational persuasion, where controversy reigns and convictions are uncertain, his argument can serve rational discourse in this more modest way.

All in all, we have cases in which the premise is rehearsed, is recalled, is authoritatively asserted, or is simply stated for the sake of argument. In studying the logic of an argument we need not care which kind of case is at hand. It is our business not to investigate the mysteries of consumer spending, but rather to ask whether the given premises do indeed provide rational support for the conclusion. They may do so to a greater or lesser degree.

A set of premises provides the greatest possible rational support for a conclusion when the argument is deductively valid. (We will just say **valid**.) By definition, an argument is valid if it is impossible for the premises to be true and yet for the conclusion to be false. Alternative ways of expressing this are that the conclusion follows logically, or follows necessarily, from the premises, or that the conclusion is a logical consequence of the premises, or yet again, that the premises entail the conclusion.

Where an argument is valid, no situation could possibly arise with respect to which the premises are true but the conclusion is false. However wide your imagination, you cannot tell an intelligible story, even a fantastic or implausible one, in which the premises of a valid argument are true and the conclusion is false. Because such a situation is not possible, it would be reasonable to infer that the conclusion of the argument indeed is true, given that you accept the truth of the premises. In fact it would be irrational to resist such a conclusion. This captures the power of a valid argument rationally to persuade.

There are lots of arguments in which the conclusion would also be a **reasonable inference** from the premises, even though the argument is not valid by the strict standard set out above. Consider the following argument.

(4)

The beautiful heiress was found by her nurse, lying on her bed, her body cold and her joints stiff.

The girl's family was horror stricken and quickly arranged a funeral in their church, conducted by the priest who had been her confidant.

Her body was placed in a tomb by those members of her family that had died in earlier days.

The young Count, who had expected to marry her that very morning, visited her tomb in the evening and strew it with flowers.

The beautiful girl was dead.

Knowing the truth of the premises of (4), a reasonable person might well draw the conclusion that the girl was dead. Nevertheless, the argument is not a valid one. Strictly speaking, the conclusion does not follow logically from the premises. It is *possible* for the premises to be true even though the conclusion turns out not to be true. A situation could arise with respect to which the premises were true and yet in which the girl is not dead, and thus with respect to which the conclusion is false. In Chapter II we will see a way of recognizing the possibility of such a situation by imagining a story of the required sort. So long as the story is intelligible, even if it is fantastic or wildly implausible, the requisite situation will be possible and the argument will not be valid, by our strict standard.

It is this strict standard of validity that will be taken up in Chapter IV and thoroughly investigated in the second half of the book. But remember that we granted that it would be reasonable to draw the conclusion of argument (4). Even though not deductively valid, the argument represents a reasonable inference. The initial definition of validity given above will serve to distinguish merely reasonable inferences from arguments that are valid. Having our hands full with those that purport to be strictly valid, we will not systematically study arguments that are merely reasonable inferences. They comprise a great variety, and there is no discipline that treats them comprehensively. Even so, it will be worthwhile to illustrate their variety before leaving them behind, and to glimpse some of the various disciplines that help with them.

The following argument is a simple numerical induction. What is sometimes called inductive logic begins with inferences like this.

For each of the past ten years I have planted tomatoes in that location in early June. Each year the tomatoes have frozen before the fruit turned red.

If I plant tomatoes in that location in early June this year, the tomatoes will freeze before the fruit turns red.

It is easy to imagine that though the premises of this argument were true and though I stubbornly planted tomatoes in that favorite spot again, yet the tomatoes fully ripened and were picked before they could freeze. Perhaps global warming was underway. Or maybe there was just an unusually dry June, or a delayed autumn frost. It certainly would be possible for the conclusion to be false even though the premises were true. Even so, we do accept the conclusion as a reasonable one. In fact, my persistence in the face of such bad results would seem quite unreasonable. Despite the apparent appeal of such inductive reasoning, the philosopher Nelson Goodman called attention to a deep difficulty involving even simple numerical induction. He called this difficulty the New Riddle of Induction.

A little more complicated is a statistical argument like the following one, which would be illuminated by the science of statistics.

Forty-five percent of the voters polled supported the Reform Party. The voters that were polled were representative of the province of Alberta as a whole in those characteristics that influence voting.

Approximately forty-five percent of the voters of Alberta support the Reform Party.

For the voters polled to be representative of the larger population is for them to constitute what statisticians call a fair sample. A good deal of statistical theorizing is devoted to characterizing that notion. But there is no presumption that the conclusion follows necessarily given that the polled voters were representative. The failure of a statistical prediction does not in itself show that the sample was not fair.   It is in the nature of statistical reasoning that it is only a matter of probability that the statistics of even a fair sample will project accurately onto the whole population.   Even though the premises are true, it is possible that no voters in Alberta at all—other than the ones polled—support the Reform Party. It's just highly unlikely.

Probabilistic arguments are the subject of the mathematical theory of probability.

> The probability that the ear a random kernel grew on was pollinated by allergic corn is .01.
>
> The probability that the kernel carries the allergen, given that the ear it grew on was pollinated by allergic corn, is .25.
> _____
> Around .25% of the corn carries the allergen.

Note that the conclusion of this argument does not itself incorporate the notion of probability. It goes from a probability to an actual percentage of the population. This is one reason that the argument is not a deductively valid one. This percentage is only the most likely one, given the premises; it is not guaranteed. What about the argument whose conclusion does incorporate probability?

> The probability that a random kernel carries the allergen is .0025.

This conclusion can be derived from the premises by way of the mathematical theory. Whether that shows that the argument itself is deductively valid turns on a central philosophical question about the nature of mathematics.

Argument (4) is neither a simple numerical induction nor any kind of statistical inference.   On its face it does not even involve probabilities in the mathematical sense—though we say colloquially that any other conclusion would be quite improbable. Sometimes an argument like (4) is called an inference to the best explanation.   It does sound right to say that the girl's being dead is the best explanation for all of the circumstances described in the premises. And precisely because other explanations are possible, the argument is not deductively valid. Except for the unhelpful remark that other explanations seem unlikely, it is not easy to say what makes this conclusion the best explanation, why it is a better one than others.

Here are two more arguments that fall into the general category of inferences to the best explanation.

Four percent of the voters in Palm Beach county voted for Buchanan.

The county is dominated by Jewish Democrats.

Gore's name was opposite Buchanan's on the ballot.

Many ballots marked for Buchanan were intended for Gore.

My cat was accidentally locked indoors over the weekend.

I have a brand new chair, whose legs were smooth before I left.

When I came home, one of the chair legs had numerous vertical scratches, each from six to twelve inches long, each about 1/32nd inch deep.

My cat has been scratching the chair leg with his claws.

The controversy that gripped Florida (and the United States as a whole) late in the year 2000 showed that reasonable people could disagree about the first of these inferences. Alternative explanations were given of the unusual percentage of Buchanan voters in Palm Beach county. And some shrugged off the anomaly as just a fluke, as having no explanation. But many people thought the conclusion that Gore supporters had mismarked the ballot offered the best explanation, and that was the reason they drew it. Choosing among such competing claims would no doubt be aided by an understanding of political science. What counts as an adequate explanation, and what explanation is best, in the arena of political behavior quite likely differs from what counts as a good explanation in chemistry or in abnormal psychology. Perhaps the ability to distinguish reasonable inferences from those that are unreasonable is the product of an entire education, rather than a technique to be learned in a special branch of logic. Of course there is no textbook on the fortunes of furniture in its interactions with cats. And so, even though book learning helps, it is not sufficient for choosing the best explanation.

By contrast the study of deductive arguments is a specialized discipline, one with concepts and techniques all its own, but one that turns out to be applicable to every area of inquiry, to every topic of reasoned discourse. Perhaps it compares to arithmetic in that respect. There are special techniques for calculating, but numerical calculations are relevant to ever so many endeavors and inquiries. Philosophers have thought that deductive logic is at least as widely relevant.   In this chapter we have begun to define its proprietary concepts along with those of the allied discipline of linguistics.   We will go on to develop techniques that draw on both disciplines— techniques for assessing sets of sentences for consistency and for assessing arguments formulated in English for deductive validity.

Exercises for Chapter I

1.   Which of the following sentences could express propositions? Why or why not?

     a.   Can you pick up a paper on your way home from work?

     b.   Meet me at the library at one o'clock.

     c.   George knows when the committee will meet.

     d.   I hereby name this ship, *Rights of Man*.

     e.   Smashing a bottle of champagne against its bow, the elegant lady intoned those words and thereby named that ship, *Rights of Man*.

     f.   I promise to pay you back at the end of the month for the dinner you bought me.

     g.   What a magnificent performance!

     h.   Bravo!

     i.   Wasn't that a magnificent performance?

     j.   The diva performed the death scene magnificently.

2.   Of the following examples, choose four with which you are familiar. In each case, formulate a declarative sentence of English that expresses the indicated proposition.

     a.   what North American schoolchildren have traditionally been taught about Columbus

     b.   the equation for the area of a circle

      c.   the Law of Supply and Demand

      d.   the *Titanic*'s telegraphic message, dot-dot-dot-dash-dash-dash-dot-dot-dot

      e.   the defining doctrine of Islam (i.e., the first Pillar of Wisdom)

      f.   Descartes' *cogito*

      g.   the clause of the Meech Lake Accords regarding Quebec

      h.   the central claim of Copernicanism

      i.   the conclusion of the Warren Commission on the assassination of President Kennedy

      j.   the verdict of the Athenian jury on the case of Socrates

3.   Which of the following sets of sentences are consistent? (Don't let your imagination fail you with respect to which situations are possible.)

      a.   Tom, Dick, and Harry are all climbing Mt. Rainier. Tom doesn't like to climb. Dick is afraid of climbing. Harry never climbs.

      b.   Either Citlaltépetl or Popocatépetl will erupt during the 22nd century. Though its current eruptions will continue during this century, Popocatépetl will be dormant for the following hundred years. Citlaltépetl's volcanic activity has stopped for good.

      c.   Seventy percent of the inhabitants either speak English or speak French. Fifty percent of the inhabitants speak English. Twenty percent of the inhabitants speak German. Forty percent of the inhabitants speak French.

      d.   William Clinton, who was born in Arkansas, has been President of the United States. Jean Chrétien, who was born in Quebec, has been Prime Minister of Canada. The constitution of France, which will not be changed in our lifetimes, requires that the President of France be born either in France or in a current or former colony of France. Nonetheless both Clinton and Chrétien will someday serve as President of France.

4.   Rewrite each of the following as an explicit argument, in the conventional style. Some of the premises have not been made explicit. Complete what is partially stated or state what is implicit, as is required by the context in each case.

      a.   Either George or Frank is guilty of cheating since their answers on the last algebra exam were almost identical and that cannot be just a coincidence.

b.   The moon must not be a celestial object, for if it were, its surface would have to be perfectly smooth. But if it were smooth, there would be no varying shadows on it. Such varying shadows have been observed recently through these new telescopes.

c.   The Korean airliner must have had a radar malfunction; otherwise it would never have strayed over Russian territory.

d.   I fear that the Europeans will reject the euro and demand to return to their national currencies. In the past, new currencies have been accepted only when the more familiar currencies either are the issue of discredited governments or have lost their value through inflation.

5.   For each of the examples in #4, say whether the argument is valid or merely a reasonable inference.

II: Stories and Situations

In Chapter I we talked about truth. We took note of whether various propositions—and the sentences that express them—are actually true or not. To use a familiar example, the actual situation in which we find ourselves is truly described by the sentence, "A new millennium has begun." (That sentence expresses the true proposition that a new millennium has begun.) In §7 below we will turn to talking about stories that are not actually true, but might have been. And we will consider other situations than the one we are in, situations in which other propositions would be true, situations which would best be described by other sentences. For now we should recall the relationship between sentences and propositions. Declarative sentences (with some exceptions) are used to express propositions, and we call a sentence true just insofar as the proposition that it expresses is true. Labeling a sentence true (or false) in this way would work best if there was a particularly simple correspondence between sentences and propositions, namely that there could be no more than one proposition expressed by any given sentence. We already noted that the converse cannot be counted on, that there is not exactly one sentence that expresses a given proposition. Remember that the Pythagorean Theorem has variously been expressed in Attic Greek and in English and that even in English different formulations of the theorem will amount to the same thing.

Since we wish to think of declarative sentences as inheriting truth and falsity from the propositions that they express, we here should focus on the former question: Can a given sentence express different propositions? In this section and in §6, we will see examples of sentences that can. In such instances, supposing that one of the propositions is true while another is false, no determinate truth value will be inherited by the sentence in question. Despite this inconvenience we still want to take advantage of sentences, to write and rewrite them, to take them apart and combine them together. Since we also need to take note of whether the sentences are variously true or false, and this will depend on what proposition is expressed, we will be obliged to take special measures to guard against confusion.

In many instances, what proposition is expressed by a given sentence depends upon the circumstances in which the sentence is uttered or written (or even upon the circumstances in which it is heard or read). A particularly striking example is the simple English sentence,

I am here now.

When this sentence is used, reference is made to the person speaking and to the place and time of utterance. In fact it is an essential feature of words like "I" and "you" that what they refer to depends on who is speaking and who is listening. What "now" and "here" refer to depends on when and where they are used. "There" and "then" require contextual cues—perhaps a gesture, perhaps a look, perhaps a place or a time already under discussion. Listeners easily catch such cues and understand the reference, variable as it may be. Considerable efficiencies result from employing words like all of these, though they complicate our task as logicians. Because they are indexed to speaker, listener, time, and place, we call these words **indexicals**.

To pursue ideas about reference using indexicals, contrast these two sentences:

(1)   I am writing.

(2)   You are reading.

If we take the sentences seriously, understand them really to be making assertions, not just to be displayed as examples, we will recognize that the propositions that they express are both true. In sentence (1), the indexical "I" refers to the author of this book; as sentence (1) was being written, it expressed the proposition that that individual was at that time writing. Since he was indeed writing at that time, the proposition was, and remains, true. Sentence (2), as it is being read, refers to whoever is doing the reading; it expresses the proposition that the reader—you—are at this time reading. Again that proposition is a true one.

Matters change fast though if these same sentences are uttered by you as you are reading, if they are uttered, that is, not just by way of reading aloud but rather by way of your making assertions yourself. The indexical "I" in (1) then comes to refer to you, and the proposition expressed by the sentence—as used by you—is false— because *you* are not writing. Patently, in the case of a sentence containing indexicals, whether what is expressed by the sentence is true or false depends on who or what is referred to by those indexicals.   When indexicals are present, the same sentence expresses different propositions on different occasions; it may be that some of these propositions are true and some false.

It is not only indexicals that vary in their reference from time to time. The sentence,

> The President of Russia is renowned for having made a
> defiant speech atop a tank,

appearing in a newspaper published in 1998 was true. But the same sentence appearing in a current newspaper would not be true at all. The explanation is obvious. The phrase "the President of Russia," as earlier used, referred to Boris Yeltsin. As used now, it refers to Vladimir Putin. In speaking of someone's political history, who is being referred to makes all the difference between truth and falsity. In fact who is referred to makes the difference as to what proposition has been expressed. The proposition expressed in the earlier newspaper was a true one and that expressed by using the sentence now is not true.

The phrase, "the President of Russia," is a more or less formal title. As such it varies in its reference from epoch to epoch, but it doesn't much depend on peculiarities of the conversation or discourse at hand. Perhaps more typical are phrases quite similar to it in form that behave almost like the indexicals "there" and "then." In relating an anecdote a speaker might repeatedly use phrases like "the woman in the BMW" or "the policeman she passed," repeatedly using each one to refer to the same woman and the same man. In understanding these phrases, we would not—without being filled in—know exactly what woman and what man were under discussion. During some telling the woman in the BMW might in fact be in view, and a gesture or other indication would be enough to call the listener's attention to her. For the duration of the conversation those indications would serve to keep the reference secure. But clearly on another occasion the very same phrase would refer to an entirely different woman, indicated by a different gesture. On this occasion sentences containing these phrases would express different propositions than they did earlier. And the sentences would differ in their truth values depending on whether the woman in question on the latter occasion did or did not do as alleged. In fact these descriptive phrases behave very much like what grammarians call third-person pronouns, those pronouns other than "I" and "you." The point is that just as we referred to the woman as "her," we could refer to her somewhat more securely as "the woman in the BMW." In both cases the reference depends on pointing or other gestures, on the role of the woman or the car in the current conversation, or perhaps merely on the prominence in our current perceptual situation of the woman in the car or of the car zooming by. Indexicals with descriptive content ("the green car," "the BMW with a woman driving") we will call **descriptive indexicals**, contrasting them with pure indexicals like "it."

In summary then, what is referred to in a sentence containing indexicals or descriptive indexicals depends on circumstances of use and on contextual cues. What proposition is expressed by the sentence depends on what is referred to. Since it is the proposition that fundamentally is true or false, the truth or falsity of the sentence may vary as it expresses different propositions, in consequence of variations in the circumstances in which it is used.

We saw that it is not uncommon for a phrase or several phrases in a family to occur repeatedly in a conversation or a discourse. So these several expressions might appear and reappear:

> the woman in the green car
>
> the woman in the car
>
> the woman
>
> she

The usual thing is for the single reference of all these recurring phrases to have been fixed early on and to remain secure throughout the discourse. Just how long the reference stays fixed, or what is the same, just what stretch of talk or text counts for these purposes as a discourse may not be quite clear. Often it is a paragraph. But what is clear is that within such a discourse a recurring phrase will refer each time to the same thing. And, as illustrated by the italicized examples below, a repeated sentence, or a variation using another phrase from the family, will repeatedly express either a truth or a falsehood.

The woman in the green car sped by. As *the woman in the car sped by*, the policeman looked up. Because *the woman sped by*, he was forced to give chase. In fact the policeman regretted that *she sped by*. If he clearly saw that *the woman in the green car sped by*, he had no choice but to give her a ticket.

According to an old saying, it is the exception that proves the rule. A case in point is the greeting given a new monarch by the cheering crowd.

The King is dead. Long live the King!

They cheer almost tongue in cheek, because what they say is incoherent under normal conventions. In this exceptional case the title, "the King," is used in the second sentence to refer to a different man than in the first. Of course the title has been passed, and it is just this passing that the crowd remarks upon and celebrates.

§6   MEANING AND TRUTH

None of the sentences or phrases discussed so far are properly called ambiguous. The reference of the given word or phrase, and the proposition expressed by the given sentence, depend on the circumstances under which these expressions are used. The truth-value varies accordingly. But in each case these variations, and our understanding of them, depend precisely on the meanings of the expressions in question. The most striking case is the first-person pronoun: to know the meaning of the English word "I" is precisely to know the procedure for determining what it refers to, varying as it does across various occasions of use. But similarly, knowing how descriptive phrases like "the woman in the BMW who passed the policeman" work involves knowing that something special about the particular occasion of use will enable you to identify the woman, the car, and the man under discussion.

Ambiguity is a quite different phenomenon. A sentence is **ambiguous** if it can be understood in more than one way. The sentence,

(1)   Green blackberries are red,

at first strikes us as incongruous, even self-contradictory. On second thought we realize that, properly understood, it is true. Two different propositions (perhaps even more) can be expressed by the sentence, corresponding to two different ways of understanding it. Since the colors are incompatible, one of the propositions that can be expressed is false. Since blackberries in an unripe state in fact are colored red, the other proposition is true. Under the usual circumstances, any particular use of an ambiguous sentence is intended to express only one of the propositions in question. If the circumstances do not make it clear which one, perhaps an alternative—unambiguous—sentence should have been used. On the other hand, an ambiguous sentence, under some circumstances, achieves a literary or comic effect—in a pun or a *double-entendre*.

For our purposes, it is important to distinguish different kinds of ambiguity. **Lexical ambiguity** results when one or more words in the sentence have different senses or meanings. Typically such a word has multiple entries in a dictionary, recording and defining the multiple senses. In (1), the word "green" could mean a particular color, or it could mean unripe. Either meaning could sensibly apply to a piece of fruit. Someone might argue that even the word "blackberry" is ambiguous as between any berry that is black and a particular kind of berry that in fact is very dark purple.

Structural ambiguity is more interesting. Even when the senses of all of the words in a sentence are fixed, there may remain different ways of understanding it.

Martha will apply to graduate in December.

Are we to understand that Martha expects to finish with her requirements and be awarded her degree in mid-year? Or is it that the application is being made in December, for a more typical late-spring ceremony? The meanings of all of the words remain the same. What changes is the relationship of the phrase "in December" to other parts of the sentence. This is a matter of the structure of the sentence as a whole. A more complicated case is the well-known example,

Violet spends her summers at a pretty little girls' camp.

Again the differences are matters of structure, sometimes indicated with connecting hyphens: pretty-little girls'-camp versus pretty-little-girls' camp.

If we think of pretty little-girls or pretty little girls'-camps as well, we recognize a complication. In some cases of structural ambiguity there seem to be subtle lexical ambiguities as well. To confirm the point, let's shift to another example.

<blockquote>She is going to see The Godfather another time.</blockquote>

In this ambiguous sentence, is it that she is going to see this landmark movie that she has already seen, perhaps already seen more than once? Or rather is it that she is going to see it not now, but later? The answer does not depend so much on the meaning of "another time" as on whether she will see it for another time or whether she is going at another time. Even granting this, some will insist that "another time" varies between meaning "again" and meaning "another period of time." This insistence does not undercut the notion of structural ambiguity. It just reveals that lexical uncertainty frequently arises in company with structural ambiguity, and perhaps is a mark of the general phenomenon, remarked in Chapter I, that words do not have their meaning in isolation, but rather as a function of their occurrence in sentences.

Some structural ambiguities have logical ramifications. Questions of consistency and validity will turn on how structural ambiguity is resolved in each of the next several examples.

<blockquote>We will invite either Jane or Nancy and Ronald.</blockquote>

<blockquote>Partridge will be nominated and Quayle will be his running-mate only if Rooster withdraws.</blockquote>

Are we committed to inviting Ronald whatever we decide about the women? The answer depends upon which structure we assign to the sentence. Have we predicted Partridge's nomination without qualification? Or does the condition about Rooster apply to our convictions about the entire ticket? Again the answer depends on a structural distinction; all of the words stay fixed in their meanings whichever way it goes.

In reading Chapter I, perhaps you looked twice when you encountered,

<blockquote>Her body was placed in a tomb by those members of her family that had died in earlier days.</blockquote>

Were you to believe that her dead relatives placed the girl in the tomb? Not if you believe that the dead are forever incapacitated. The two beliefs would be inconsistent. On a second look you realized that whoever laid her in the tomb—they go unmentioned—placed her body by the bodies of her dead relatives. Again the ambiguity is one of structure, but it gives the word "by" an ambiguity all its own. In Chapter V we will give a full analysis and explanation of this kind of case. We will learn why the ambiguity of "by" is itself essentially structural. For now, it is enough to note that in one of its uses "by" can be paraphrased as "next to." But, in the other use there is no synonym; the word plays the peculiar structural role of marking out the agent, a role which no other word can play.

An interesting series of cases that also invites fuller treatment begins with,

(2)   I can't seem to remember her.

Pretty clearly this sentence is unambiguous, and synonymous with,

        It seems that I can't remember her.

Remarkably, a very similar sentence sounds odd at first.

(3)   You must not seem to remember her.

This clumsy sentence becomes more intelligible when we imagine an intrigue in which you are set up to encounter one of your co-conspirators in a public place. As the plan goes, she will be introduced to you by a third party. Of course it is crucial that you not betray the conspiracy:

        Seeming to remember her is something you must not do.

Only when we go to a third-person case and change the time perspective, and thus the tense, do we get a truly ambiguous sentence.

        He couldn't seem to remember her.

We can interpret this sentence in parallel to (2) above. If so, it is equivalent to,

        It seemed that he couldn't remember her.

Alternatively we can give it the more remote interpretation we found for (3). Doing so gives us this equivalent.

        Seeming to remember her is something he couldn't do.

Working with these sentences brings out the subtlety and complexity of so-called natural languages, like English.

A special kind of structural ambiguity is **anaphoric ambiguity**. The following passage is from Plato's *Meno* (Grube translation, at 72a):

> There is virtue for every action and every age, for every task of ours and every one of us—and Socrates, the same is true for wickedness.

What is the reference of "the same"? Does the passage mean that there is virtue for wickedness, as there is for every action, etc.? Or rather does it mean that there is wickedness for every action and every age, etc.?

A more mundane example of anaphoric ambiguity can be drawn from a narrative. With the context removed, we can't tell which way the bullet flew.

> As the agent realized that the spy had a gun, she shot him.

The question might arise why we should call this a matter of ambiguity, since what is indeterminate seems not to be the structure of the sentence, but rather what the words "she" and "he" refer to. This is discussed below, but note now that the pronouns reach back in the sentence to earlier phrases whose reference is determinate. The question is which phrase is reached by which pronoun. Described that way the structure does seem to be varying. And when the sentence is variously rephrased, the ambiguity disappears. Compare this rephrasing,

(4)   As she realized that the spy had a gun, the agent shot him.

to this one,

(5)   As the agent realized that she had a gun, the spy shot him.

They are confusing to grasp precisely because from one rephrasing to the other, the shooter and the shot trade places, and genders.

Having introduced a technical term to categorize this special kind of ambiguity, we can use the sentences that make it vivid to explain what anaphora and anaphoric reference are. Suppose we're driving down a highway known for radar traps and a BMW overtakes us, going ninety. I say to you, "She's going to get a ticket." The reference of "she" is to the fast driver, and you know because of the salience of the BMW and its driver in these circumstances. This is a clear case of an indexical reference. For a contrasting example simpler than (5), consider,

> The spy fired because she feared the agent.

However visible she is to the agent, the spy is not visible, and thus not salient, to us. We know nonetheless that "she" refers to the spy. It is a case not of indexical reference, but of anaphoric reference. In **anaphora**, a pronoun, or other expression, reaches back to an earlier phrase, sometimes called its antecedent. It is the job of the antecedent phrase to secure its own reference, whether by circumstances of its use or some other means. Then the anaphoric expression inherits that reference. In (4) and (5) the reference of "she" is anaphoric as well, but in each of them the pronoun reaches forward in the sentence.

There is a special kind of logical mistake that arises in connection with ambiguity, and even with indeterminate reference. An **equivocation** is an invalid argument that appears to be valid because of an ambiguity in one or more of the sentences with which the argument is expressed. Sometimes the mistake is intentional, or at least works to the advantage of the arguer. After all, we might unjustifiably be persuaded of some conclusion by an argument that appears to be valid.

By intelligence we understand whatever is measured by the standard battery of IQ tests. So the tests show that students from fashionable suburbs are more intelligent than other students. But everybody knows that intelligence contributes to doing well in college. So students from fashionable suburbs are more likely than others to do well in college.

At the outset the word "intelligence" has been given a meaning different from the vaguer and more complex ordinary notion of intelligence, and it is with that meaning that the second sentence is true. But in the third sentence the clause, "intelligence contributes to doing well in college," is lexically ambiguous. The argument trades on this ambiguity. It is only in one sense—the ordinary sense—that "everybody knows" that the clause is true. But it is only in the other sense that it provides support for the conclusion. Here we are unjustifiably persuaded of the conclusion of an argument that appears to be valid because it equivocates on the term "intelligence."

MIGHT HAVE BEENS   §7

In Chapter I we identified notions of consistency and inconsistency in a logical sense. These notions apply not to the execution of policies or to people's conduct, but rather to sets of sentences. We now want to develop the logical notion of consistency in terms of what we will call a possible situation. The root idea of a possible situation is the idea of what might have been so, whether or not this might-have-been is likely, or sensible, or even possible at all, given other things that we know to be so. Envisioning such possibilities involves the exercise of the imagination. We picture to ourselves combinations of circumstances or events that may be far from what we have actually witnessed or experienced, far from what we take to be possible under the constraints of finances, of available resources, of established evidence, and sometimes even of common sense. We often explore such distant possibilities in narrative. It is a commonplace that stories take us from the here and now, open new vistas, and introduce us to undreamt-of possibilities. We will take advantage of this exploratory function of stories, but we want to do so in a way that serves the logical notion of consistency. However unconstrained our story telling, we want to keep it within the bounds of intelligibility. Sometimes an elaboration or fuller telling of a story renders intelligible what might at first have seemed unintelligible. But in other cases it is an elaboration of what has already been said that reveals that it was not really, despite first impressions, fully intelligible after all. We will encounter cases of both kinds.

For now let's make these ideas concrete by considering a narrative that is familiar, but one that tests the boundaries of intelligibility. We choose a well-loved Christmas story.

THE NIGHT BEFORE CHRISTMAS
by Clement C. Moore

'Twas the night before Christmas,	(1)
when all through the house	(2)
Not a creature was stirring, not even a mouse!	(3)
The stockings were hung by the chimney with care,	(4)
In hopes that St. Nicholas soon would be there.	(5)
The children were nestled all snug in their beds,	(6)
While visions of sugarplums danced in their heads.	(7)
And mamma in her kerchief, and I in my cap,	(8)
Had just settled our brains for a long winter's nap—	(9)

When out on the lawn there arose such a clatter,   (10)
I sprang from my bed to see what was the matter.   (11)

Away to the window I flew like a flash,   (12)
Tore open the shutters and threw up the sash.   (13)

The moon on the breast of the new-fallen snow   (14)
Gave a luster of midday to objects below.   (15)

When what to my wondering eyes should appear,   (16)
But—
        a miniature sleigh, and eight tiny reindeer;   (17)

With a little old driver so lively and quick   (18)
I knew in a moment it must be St. Nick!   (19)

More rapid than eagles his coursers they came,   (20)
And he whistled and shouted and called them by name: (21)

"Now, *Dasher* ! Now, *Dancer* ! Now, *Prancer* and *Vixen* !   (22)
On, *Comet* ! On, *Cupid* ! On *Donder* and *Blitzen* !"   (23)

"To the top of the porch, to the top of the wall!   (24)
Now, dash away, dash away, dash away all!"   (25)

As dry leaves that before the wild hurricane fly,   (26)
When they meet with an obstacle, mount to the sky,   (27)
So up to the housetop the coursers they flew,   (28)

With the sleigh full of toys—and St. Nicholas too.   (29)
And then in a twinkling I heard on the roof,   (30)
The prancing and pawing of each little hoof.   (31)

As I drew in my head, and was turning around,   (32)
Down the chimney St. Nicholas came with a bound.   (33)

He was dressed all in fur from his head to his foot,   (34)
And his clothes were all tarnished with ashes and soot.   (35)

A bundle of toys he had flung on his back,   (36)
And he looked like a peddler just opening his pack.   (37)

His eyes—how they twinkled!   (38)

His dimples—how merry!   (39)
His cheeks were like roses, his nose like a cherry.   (40)

His droll little mouth was drawn up like a bow,   (41)
And the beard on his chin was as white as the snow.   (42)

The stump of a pipe he held tight in his teeth,   (43)
And the smoke it encircled his head like a wreath.   (44)

He had a broad face and a little round belly   (45)
That shook, when he laughed, like a bowlful of jelly.   (46)

He was chubby and plump—a right jolly old elf,   (47)
And I laughed when I saw him, in spite of myself.   (48)

A wink of his eye and a twist of his head   (49)
Soon gave me to know I had nothing to dread.   (50)

He spoke not a word, but went straight to his work,   (51)
And filled all the stockings   (52)
          —then turned with a jerk,   (53)

And laying his finger aside of his nose,   (54)
And giving a nod—   (55)
          Up the chimney he rose!   (56)

He sprang to his sleigh, to his team gave a whistle,   (57)
And away they all flew like the down of a thistle.   (58)

But I heard him exclaim, ere he drove out of sight: (59)
"Happy Christmas to all,   (60)
          And to all a good night."   (61)

However fantastic "The Night Before Christmas" may be, we understand quite well the events that have been described in it. It's not that the story might have been true in the realistic sense that for all we know the narrator was describing something that happened to him. Rather it might have been true in the larger sense that if the world were very different than it is, with reindeer having different capabilities than they do and effects being brought about very differently than they actually are, under those circumstances these events might have occurred. Since we see no fundamental reason that the world might not have been different than it is in just those

ways, we conclude that indeed the story might have been true. The
key signal here is the intelligibility of the story. When we understand
a story, as we do this one, and conclude that it might have been true,
we can say that the story describes a **possible situation**. The situation
it describes is a possible one not in the sense that for all we know the
story *is* true, but rather in the sense that the story *might have been*
true—if the world were very different than it is—even though we
know very well that the story is not true, in fact, that it is quite
fantastic.

As an exercise of the imagination, Clement Moore's fantasy can
help us with the logical question whether the following sentences are
consistent with one another.

He was outside the house a few minutes ago, but now he is inside.
All of the doors have remained closed.
Only one window has been open, and the narrator has been looking out of it the whole while.
No one has entered through that window while he has been looking.

With reference to the narrative situation of "The Night Before
Christmas," the clauses of the first sentence (can naturally be taken
to) express the proposition that St. Nicholas was outside of the
narrator's house as the story began, but that at the current
moment—say, just after the narrator drew in his head—St. Nicholas
was inside the house. The proposition so expressed is true in the
fantasy as narrated. Similarly, the fourth sentence expresses the
proposition that while the narrator has been looking out his open
window, no one has entered into the house through it. All four of
these sentences are faithful to the narrative, in that the propositions
that they express are all true in the fantasy situation. Since it is also
true in the fantasy that St. Nicholas easily moves up and down
chimneys, we do not find it disturbing to acknowledge that we accept
all four of these propositions. There is a suspension of disbelief that
opens us to the pleasures of fantasy. In that special way, we believe
all of these propositions as elements of the fantasy situation, or at
least we pretend to believe them. The story is an intelligible one, and
for our logical purposes we can use it to make manifest the
consistency of a set of sentences that might at first have struck us as
inconsistent.

Sharp readers of Sherlock Holmes are fond of pointing out an
inconsistency across the many stories that Conan Doyle wrote and
published about his fictional detective. The lapse is regarding Dr.

Watson's war wound. In some of the stories it is described as a
wound in his shoulder. In others, the wound shifts to Watson's leg.
What is wrong with this? Why is this inconsistency a failing in
Doyle's story-telling? Even though these stories are fictional, they are
supposed to describe situations that might have happened. In fact,
taken together, the stories are supposed to describe one grand
situation, persisting and developing over time, that might have
happened as a whole. This is why Doyle has to find some plausible
way of resurrecting Holmes after he has gone over the Reichenbach
Fall. It won't do for him simply to reappear, hale and hearty, in the
next installment.

To return to Watson's war wound, we can see what the problem
is by setting out another set of sentences. The first two express
propositions more or less explicit in two of Doyle's stories. Taken as
referring to Watson, the third is implicit in Doyle's account of Dr.
Watson in all of the stories. And the fourth is something that goes
without saying, expressing a true proposition about whosoever's body
parts, in this case those, again, of Watson.

> Watson had a wound in his shoulder.
>
> Watson had a wound in his leg.
>
> He had exactly one wound.
>
> His leg is entirely distinct from his shoulder.

When we spell them out, we see that these sentences are inconsistent
in the logical sense of Chapter I. We can't really make sense of a
situation that they purport to describe. Though there are situations
with respect to which each of the sentences is true, there is no
(possible) situation with respect to which they all are true. But aren't
they all true with respect to the developing situation in the Sherlock
Holmes stories? The reply is that the situation described in the
stories is not really a possible one. Intelligibility is the telling notion
here. If a narrative is to describe a possible situation, it must be fully
intelligible. (How many wounds did you say Watson had?) And the
intelligibility of the narrative we take to be an indicatation of the
possibility of the situation. Many of us, when we first read Sherlock
Holmes' adventures, were carried along, feeling that we understood
the stories bit by bit as they unfolded. But the four sentences above
focus our attention on aspects of the narrative, some of them
unspoken, which wither under our scrutiny. What we thought was
intelligible turns out to be confused, and the situation as a whole no
longer seems possible. Thus, even though Doyle's stories of Sherlock

Holmes are much more realistic than "The Night Before Christmas," it turns out that the Christmas fantasy describes a possible situation, whereas the Sherlock Holmes stories, taken together, do not describe a possible situation.

We will take the intelligibility of a story to be a sign—though not an infallibly recognizable one—that the situation presented by the story is a possible one. The Sherlock Holmes stories seem quite intelligible to most readers. It is only the attentive reader who recognizes the slip and thus who finds the stories not thoroughly intelligible. Similarly, discernment of subtle inconsistency is not an easy task, and we will develop techniques to aid us in it, beginning with Chapter III.

TRUTH WITH RESPECT TO A SITUATION   §8

We have said that what might have been—a possible situation—can be articulated in a story. The appearance of intelligibility in a story, especially upon reflection, is our assurance that the situation is possible. But what about truth? Can we understand that notion in application to possible situations?

Truth in a situation cannot readily be defined, any more than truth itself can be. But let us reflect on the terms we found it natural to use in the previous section. The narration of a story proceeds with the articulation of a succession of sentences coming one after another. The propositions that these sentences express constitute the story. The idea is that, so long as the story is intelligible, a possible situation has been described. And the propositions expressed as the story is told are **true in the situation** described. (This is guaranteed by their constitutive relation to the story as a whole.) They would simply be true if the situation described were the actual situation, if the story as a whole were a true story.

Certain sentences are articulated in the telling of a story. But other sentences as well can have reference to the characters and events of the story. They may be used to discuss or to examine the story. They may be used to convey segments of it to other audiences. For these other sentences, not articulated in the original telling, it is crucial to recognize what proposition each sentence **expresses with respect to** the situation that has been developed. That is what we did above with the sentence, "He had exactly one wound." Though that sentence does not occur in the Sherlock Holmes narratives, we understood it with reference to those narratives. We understood it in particular to have reference to Dr. Watson. And so, with respect to the Sherlock Holmes situation as a whole, it expresses the proposition that Watson had, during the whole of the narrative, one and only one wound. Though that proposition is not expressed in so many words anywhere in the narrative, we understand it to be true in the Sherlock Holmes stories. And so, we conclude that the *sentence*, "He had exactly one wound," as we used it above, is true with respect to the situation of the Sherlock Holmes stories. In general, we want to say that a sentence is **true with respect to a situation** if the proposition that it expresses with respect to the given situation is true in that situation.

We must take care not to confuse the question whether a sentence is true with respect to a situation with the question whether a sentence is true *in* a situation. The clearest examples of the latter arise when a sentence is actually used by a character in a story. Then the sentence and its use are part of the story, and we can ask what proposition was expressed by the character who used the sentence and whether that proposition is true in the situation or not. Let's first take an example—not an optimal one for our purposes— from "The Night Before Christmas." In the fantasy, St. Nicholas uses the sentence, "On Comet." Since it is not a declarative one, the sentence does not express any proposition, but it is quite clear who St. Nicholas is referring to—or more precisely, who he is addressing— when he uses the name, "Comet." He is referring to one of his reindeer, a creature of fiction. To get a fuller understanding, let's switch to a Sherlock Holmes example. In *The Hound of the Baskervilles*, we have Dr. Watson saying,

Dr. Mortimer is a successful elderly medical man.

As Dr. Watson uses this sentence it expresses the proposition that this fellow Mortimer—he is the one who has left his walking stick behind at Holmes' and Watson's entry way—has had a long and successful career as a medical doctor. And, as Sherlock Holmes surmises and as events soon bear out, that proposition is false—in the story. We can say that it is false because, in the situation described in the first chapter, a walking stick is left by John Mortimer, who is young, rather shabby, and though a medical *officer*, not actually a medical doctor. It is the character, John Mortimer, whom the title "Dr. Mortimer" refers to as Watson uses it. And what Dr. Watson's sentence expresses about him is manifestly false. The important point is not as to truth or falsity, but as to the occurrence of the sentence *in* the situation itself. The sentence is not one formulated by us to say something about the Holmes-Watson situation, but rather is one formulated in that situation by Watson himself. And, as it happens, the proposition that Watson so expresses does not accurately reflect the situation that develops in the story.

Confusion is most likely to arise about sentences in a situation that are not explicitly quoted, but are imagined by us as we fill in the background, sentences that are only implicit in the telling of the story. "Once upon a time," we are told, there were people who spoke a language very much like our own, but when they counted, they said, "One, three, four, two, five, six, seven, eight, nine, ten." The question arises whether the sentence,

(1)   Two plus two is four,

is true or false in that story. Given the way the people in the story use counting words, the sentence is false. To be very clear about it, sentence (1) is false *in* the hypothetical situation, expressing as it does the (false) proposition that four plus four is three. But if *we* use sentence (1), whether with respect to this hypothetical situation or to any other, the proposition that it expresses is the familiar true proposition that two plus two is four. After all, in using sentence (1), which is a perfectly ordinary and familiar sentence of English, we use the words with the meaning and reference that it is customary for them to have in English, which after all is the language that we are speaking as we discuss the hypothetical situation. The situation that we have described is not a situation in which the proposition that two plus two is four is not a true one. In fact many philosophers declare that there is no possible situation in which that proposition is false; they declare that no matter what else might have been other than it actually is, it is not true that two plus two might have been other than four. We can embrace that doctrine in order to emphasize the contrast that we are drawing. Sentence (1) is not true *in* the hypothetical situation; though no one in the story actually has enunciated that sentence, we imagine, in effect, someone in the hypothetical situation using it with the meaning and reference that it has in their language, which is somewhat different from English according to the story that has been told. But sentence (1) is true *with respect to* the hypothetical situation. In the end, this confusing case enables us to highlight the important contrast for sentences, between truth in a situation and truth with respect to a situation.

An even different question would be whether a sentence used in the telling of a story is true. For example, the sentence,

> What to my wondering eyes should appear,
> But a miniature sleigh and eight tiny reindeer,

occurs in the telling of the story, "The Night Before Christmas." Waiving any perplexities about who the narrator is—Is it the person who recites the poem?—no doubt the sentence is not true. It is not really true that eight tiny reindeer appeared to the narrator, or to anyone else. That is part and parcel of the poem being a fantasy. Sometimes sentences as they are used in the telling of fictional stories do happen to be true. The sentence,

> When you are once out upon its bosom [that of the moor] you
> have left all traces of modern England behind you,

as used in the body of a Sherlock Holmes story does turn out to be true because even though the story is a work of fiction, it has a setting that in fact exists and was accurately described by Doyle. But the point is that our interest in a sentence which occurs in the telling of a given story lies in the proposition that the sentence expresses with respect to the situation described in the story. Almost all of the propositions so expressed are true (in the story situation) of course because in some sense they constitute the story and are the touchstone for what is true in the story and what is not.

Having drawn these contrasts, let us dwell on a new kind of example, one where we have already been given a set of sentences. We will envision a new situation and determine whether each of the sentences in the set is true with respect to the new situation. These sentences, familiar from Chapter I, will serve our purposes.

(2a)   The beautiful heiress was found by her nurse, lying on her bed, her body cold and her joints stiff.

(2b)   Her body was placed in a tomb by those members of her family that had died in earlier days.

(2c)   The beautiful girl was dead.

The situation we will address is that set out in Shakespeare's version of the story of Romeo and Juliet. Because two of these sentences are ambiguous, we first must be clear as to what we are taking the words to mean and what structures we are taking the sentences to have. We have already determined, for a case in point, how the structure of sentence (2b) is to be understood. As for (2a), we understand that it was her nurse that did the finding. And we specify that by "nurse" we mean not a trained medical attendant, but someone who suckles, or has suckled, an infant. Since we are considering these sentences as a set, we determine to hold fixed a commonality of reference among all of the phrases, "the beautiful heiress," "the beautiful girl," and "the girl," as well as all of the occurrences of the pronoun "her." To take some of these expressions to refer to one person and others of them to refer to another person would violate the conventions that enable us to follow a discourse consisting of several sentences in succession.   These conventions come to the rescue where the sentences, if taken in isolation, would be indeterminate of reference and hopelessly ambiguous.

All of these determinations must be in place before we address the sentences to a particular situation. Whatever propositions we take the sentences to express must reflect the structures we have settled on, the meanings we have understood, and the commonalities of reference that we have indicated. Keeping these understandings in mind, we can turn to the situation of Romeo and Juliet. Once we focus on that story, we naturally take "the beautiful heiress" to refer to Juliet herself. Even though Shakespeare never used it, the phrase aptly describes her. And mindful of another main character, one who had nursed Juliet as an infant, we naturally take "her nurse" to refer to Nurse. These latter determinations might well change if we addressed the sentences to a different situation or another story. But they, together with the earlier determinations, which we must hold fixed, are enough to determine what proposition is expressed by sentence (2a) with respect to the story of Romeo and Juliet. It expresses the proposition that Nurse found Juliet lying on her bed, cold and stiff. And this proposition is true in the story, as can be verified by consulting Act IV, Scene V. The upshot is that sentence (2a) is true with respect to the situation portrayed in Shakespeare's *Romeo and Juliet*.

We needn't treat (2b) in such detail. Suffice it to say that, with respect to this dramatic situation, it expresses the proposition that Juliet's body was entombed next to relatives of hers who had died earlier. This proposition being true in the play, sentence (2b) is true with respect to the situation in question. (2c) requires only a little special attention, namely to the question of time. Of course Juliet dies by the end of the play, but it is irresistible to take sentence (2c) to mean that she was dead much earlier, say by the time she was laid in the tomb. Part of the tragedy of Romeo and Juliet was that she had only taken a potion and was not dead when she was laid in the tomb. And so sentence (2c) is false with respect to this situation. We can see the relevance of the story of Romeo and Juliet to our question whether argument (4) of §4 is strictly valid. That very story portrays the possibility of the conclusion being false despite the premises being true.

To review, we have left undefined the notion of truth in a situation, which applies to propositions, and we have only talked around the notion of truth with respect to a situation, which applies to sentences. But we actually can define the logical notion of consistency that was introduced and explained in Chapter I. A set of sentences is **consistent** if there is some possible situation with respect to which all of the sentences in it are true. That is to say, the propositions expressed by these sentences, as we are using them, with respect to the situation in question, would all be true if that possible situation were an actual one. Conversely, a set of sentences is **inconsistent** if there is no possible situation with respect to which all of the sentences, as we are currently understanding them, are true. In this case no story purporting to describe a situation and incorporating the sentences in question, as we understand them, turns out to be intelligible.

Recalling the contrasting question of whether a given sentence ("Two plus two is four") is true *in* a given situation, we should emphasize our crucial focus on the question whether the sentence is *true with respect to* a situation, in our definition of a consistent set of sentences. That ramifies into the questions what proposition is expressed by the sentence with respect to the situation and whether that proposition is true in the situation. When we ask whether the sentences are consistent, *we* are using them to describe—or misdescribe—some aspect of an actual or hypothetical situation. It is the meaning the sentence has for us that enables it to express whatever it does express.

It will clinch the point to revert to an example of inconsistency similar to one discussed in Chapter I. The sentences,

(3a)   Everyone should be punished.
(3b)   My son should not be punished.

are obviously inconsistent. There is no (possible) situation with respect to which they are both true. I can tell an intelligible story in which people mean "indeed" by the word "not." In that story sentence (3b) would mean that my son should indeed be punished, and that could well be true. But recognizing that possible situation does not show that these sentences are consistent after all. Why doesn't it? It is not a situation with respect to which these two sentences are true, though evidently the two sentences are true *in* that situation.

We have noted that it is frequently difficult to recognize when a set of sentences is inconsistent. Now we shall turn to developing techniques to aid us. These techniques will make use of our definition of consistency as truth with respect to a situation. Given a set of sentences of uncertain consistency, we will construct various sets of simpler sentences. Our hope will be to find such a set that itself is *obviously* consistent and thus describes a possible situation. The technique of construction will guarantee that the *original* sentences are true with respect to that possible situation, and thus are themselves consistent.

Exercises for Chapter II

1.   With reference to "The Night Before Christmas," which of the following words or phrases are indexicals, which are descriptive indexicals, which are anaphoric, and which are none of these? In each case, what does the word or phrase refer to? (In parentheses is given a number indicating the line in question. For example, line 8 says, "And mamma in her kerchief, and I in my cap,")

    a.   "I" (8)

    b.   "the window" (12)

    c.   "them" (21)

    d.   "Now" (25)

    e.   "St. Nicholas" (29)

    f.   "his head" (34)

    g.   "it" (44)

    h.   "then" (53)

    i.   "He" (57)

    j.   "Christmas" (60)

2.   What kinds of ambiguity occur in the following?

    a.   The black knight checked our king.

    b.   Flying planes can be dangerous.

    c.   And Satan trembles when he sees
        The weakest saint upon his knees.

d.   Jenny was out in the yard beating the rugs with her mother.

e.   Reagan accused the Russians of attacking a civilian airplane in 1983.

f.   Ludwig is a poor musician.

3.   Rewrite each example in two ways to show possible interpretations.

a.   The horse is ready to ride.

b.   I did not meet the mechanic because my car would not start.

c.   The industrious Chinese loved Chairman Mao.

d.   Every man is not an island.

4.   Explain the equivocation in the familiar bumper sticker, "When guns are outlawed, only outlaws will have guns."

5.   In each of these cases the descriptions are drawn from more or less familiar children's stories. Say whether the situation described is a possible one. Or, in the end, is the description not really intelligible? (If so, no situation that might have been has been described.)

a.   An active youth, George Washington chopped down the cherry tree on his family's property. Discovering the damage, his father asked him if he had done this. "I cannot tell a lie," young George told his father. "I chopped down the tree."

b.   "You'll see me there," said the Cat, and vanished. Alice was not much surprised at this, she was getting so well used to queer things happening. While she was still looking at the place where it had been, it suddenly appeared again.

c.   The ostrich is a silly bird
         With scarcely any mind.
      He often runs so very fast,
         He leaves himself behind,
      And when he gets there has to stand
         And hang about till night,
      Without a blessed thing to do
         Until he comes in sight. (—Mary E. Wilkins Freeman)

d. Down the chimney St. Nicholas came with a bound. . . A bundle of toys he had flung on his back. . . He was chubby and plump. . . And giving a nod—up the chimney he rose.

e. Alice replied, "I wish you wouldn't keep appearing and vanishing so suddenly: you make one quite giddy!"

"All right," said the Cat; and this time it vanished quite slowly, beginning with the end of the tail, and ending with the grin, which remained some time after the rest of it had gone.

6. Say, for each of the following sentences, whether it is true or false with respect to the situation described in "The Night Before Christmas." If you think there is any doubt, make clear what proposition you take to be expressed with respect to that situation.

a. There was no mouse stirring anywhere in the house.

b. Sleeping children were dreaming of sugar plums.

c. The narrator threw up the window sash, and St. Nicholas came in.

d. The moon itself was located on the surface of the snow.

e. Dry leaves flew St. Nicholas' coursers up to the housetop.

f. The narrator laughed when he saw him.

g. A bundle of toys he had flung on his back.

h. He was already out of sight when he yelled, "Happy Christmas to all."

7.   But immediately afterwards I noticed that whilst I thus wished to think all things false, it was absolutely essential that the 'I' who thought this should be somewhat, and remarking that this truth, 'I think, therefore I am' was so certain and so assured that all the most extravagant suppositions brought forward by the sceptics were incapable of shaking it, I came to the conclusion that I could receive it without scruple as the first principle of the Philosophy for which I was seeking.

This famous passage by Descartes occurs in Part 4 of his *Discourse on Method*. Which of the following sentences is true *in* the situation described in the passage, and which is true *with respect to* the situation? Explain why.

a. I think, therefore, I am.

b. He or she is thinking; therefore, he or she must exist.

III: Establishing Inconsistency with Tableaux

Any method for establishing inconsistency depends upon our ability—as reasoners and as speakers of a language—simply to recognize inconsistency in obvious cases. Perhaps the most obviously inconsistent are pairs of sentences directly contradicting one another. The contradiction is inescapable in the case of unproblematic assertions with no vagueness or dependence on perspective or taste.

> Today is Monday.
>
> Today is not Monday.

Even when the question is a matter of judgment, where different standards might be applied, we would find it illogical for a single person to maintain directly contradictory judgments on a single occasion.

> George is handsome.
>
> George is not handsome.

It makes no difference to add sentences to the inconsistent pair. The augmented set remains inconsistent, and pretty obviously so.

> George is tall.
>
> George is dark.
>
> George is handsome.
>
> George is not handsome.

The inconsistency is a bit less obvious when the contradictory pair are lost in a large set.   But once the offending sentences are highlighted, the inconsistency is as obvious as before.

> George is tall.
>
> **George is handsome.**
>
> George is dark.
>
> George is rich.
>
> **George is not handsome.**
>
> George is intelligent.
>
> George is not friendly.

Being obvious is a matter of degree. And so slightly less obvious are cases where the contradiction depends on the meanings of the words.

George is dark.   George is handsome.   George is handsome.

George is blond.   George is ugly.   George is ungainly.

Again when the conflicting pair are lost in a crowd, inconsistency does not jump right out. Even so, careful comparison, pair by pair, uncovers the inconsistency.

> George is tall.
>
> George is dark.
>
> George is handsome.
>
> George is intelligent.
>
> George is ungainly.

Still less obvious, but recognizable, are cases where the pairs are consistent, but not the whole set.

> George is outside.
>
> Martha is not outside.
>
> George and Martha are together.

A different kind of conflict appears in this pair.

> George is inside.
>
> No one is inside.

And a different kind again in this triple.

> George is older than Martha.
>
> Martha is older than Hilary.
>
> Hilary is older than George.

In all these cases, despite their differences, an attentive reading recognizes inconsistency without further maneuvering.

For a contrast, consider this set of six sentences, each of them fairly simple.

(1)

> George is my only uncle.
>
> I have no aunt (i.e., by biological relation).
>
> Martha is my first cousin.
>
> Hilary is my first cousin.
>
> Hilary is not Martha's sister.
>
> Hilary is not Martha's brother.

No two contradict one another. In fact not even any five are inconsistent. But the six are inconsistent. Are they obviously so? Perhaps not. Though the sentences are simple, the concepts are not.

All of the examples we have looked at, except the set (1), serve as models for obviously inconsistent sets that will be exploited in what follows. Though these inconsistencies are obvious enough, a set of sentences that are themselves complex can be difficult to judge.

What we saw in (1), where a set of sentences is inconsistent and yet eliminating any one of them produces a consistent set, can be replicated with indefinitely large sets. Such inconsistencies are rarely visible on inspection. We need a technique to apply to sets of sentences to help us judge consistency. The technique we will introduce applies where the sentences in question are complex. Where, as in the set (1), it is concepts that are complex, something more is needed.

SEMANTIC TABLEAUX: DIVIDING AND CONQUERING   §10

Our technique for assessing consistency is called the method of **semantic tableaux**. It was developed by a Dutch philosopher of mathematics named Evert Beth. As the word "tableau" suggests, the method is a graphic one, and the results are often spread out. It is a good idea when you construct tableaux to provide yourself plenty of oversize paper, so that the details of your picture remain visible.

The tableau technique exploits a strategy of dividing and conquering. Where sentences are so many or so complex that consistency is not obvious, the sentences are divided into simpler sentences. Here, as in cell division, the result is proliferation, and, again as in cell division, the offspring are not really *parts* of the parent. But though we have even more sentences to consider, and in fact more sets of sentences to assess for consistency, conquest becomes possible because after enough division we are left with sets whose consistency—or inconsistency—is obvious. In fact in most cases inconsistency ultimately can be judged pairwise, that is to say, by considering sentences, themselves fairly simple, two at a time and asking whether they contradict each other. It is worth noting that this technique depends on the ability, discussed in §9, to recognize consistency and inconsistency in the obvious cases. As with most techniques, doing something more complex depends on systematically exploiting your ability to do various simpler things, often so simple that doing them has become second nature.

It's best to learn about tableaux by way of an example. The following set of sentences is fairly large, and most of the individual sentences are complex. None of them directly contradicts any other; nevertheless it is far from obvious that they form a consistent set.

That is to say, it is far from obvious that these sentences could all be
true.

Sarah and Molly will not both go to the zoo.

Exactly one of these three—William, John, and
Kay's mother—will go.

Both Kay and Sarah will go.

Kay's mother will stay home.

If William goes, so will Molly.

Evidently these sentences express constraints, of whatever
stringency, on an upcoming outing to the zoo. In asking whether
there is a possible situation in which they are all true, we in effect
learn whether we can *make* them all come true. Is there an outcome
for our as yet indeterminate outing that will respect all of these
constraints? If the sentences are inconsistent, there is no such
outcome for the simple reason that there is no possible situation in
which all of the sentences are true.

Tableaux are sometimes called trees. Though considered as
trees they are upside down, they have a branching structure that
calls to mind several of the terms we use to describe trees. We begin
the tableau simply by writing down the sentences one on top of
another. This forms what we call the **trunk** of the tableau.

Sarah and Molly will not both go to the zoo
Exactly one of these three—William, John, and
Kay's mother—will go
Both Kay and Sarah will go
Kay's mother will stay home
If William goes, so will Molly

In asking whether these sentences form a consistent set, we are
asking whether there is any way they might all be true at once. But
considering just the first sentence, there are different ways in which
that sentence itself might be true, three in particular:

Sarah will not go	Molly will not go	Sarah will not go
Molly will go	Sarah will go	Molly will not go

In fact these are the only ways in which it can be true that Sarah and
Molly do not both go. We can construct a three-branched structure,
each **branch** representing one of these ways. When that structure is

attached to the trunk, we have three different ways in which all of the
original sentences can be true.

(1)

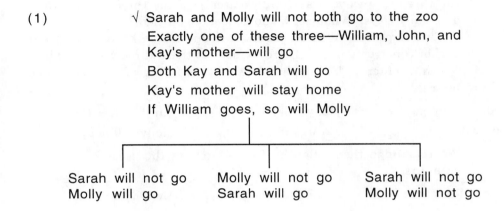

√ Sarah and Molly will not both go to the zoo
Exactly one of these three—William, John, and
Kay's mother—will go
Both Kay and Sarah will go
Kay's mother will stay home
If William goes, so will Molly

| Sarah will not go | Molly will not go | Sarah will not go |
| Molly will go | Sarah will go | Molly will not go |

Crucially, the trunk itself is a part of each of the three ways. Since
our three branches have captured the constraint expressed by the
first sentence, we have checked it off. The effect of the check is that
we no longer need concern ourselves with that sentence as such.

If we turn our attention to the second sentence, again we
recognize that there are three different ways that it could be true:

William will go	John will go	Kay's mom will go
John won't go	William won't go	William won't go
Kay's mom won't go	Kay's mom won't go	John won't go

The description of these ways is more long-winded, requiring three
simple sentences each, because the sentence in question says "exactly one." In order for it to be true, neither John nor Kay's mother can
go to the zoo, given that William goes—as envisioned on the left. We
make a point of explicitly specifying this in order that William's
going really represent a possibility for that second sentence. It's not
just William's going, but William's going *without the other two*.

A difficulty arises when we return to our developing tableau with
the idea of constructing a branching structure to represent these not
only as three ways of respecting the second sentence, but also as
different ways of respecting *all* of the sentences in the original set.
We already had three ways in which the sentences in the set could be
true—represented in tableau (1) above. And now we have given birth

to three more. But each of these three is possible together with *any one* of the three ways already represented. In order to represent all of the possibilities, we would need nine new branches, that is, each of the three new ways branching from each of the three earlier ways. Too many ways! What can we do to be more efficient?

An important efficiency can be achieved with respect to our earlier construction (1). There we set out these three ways in which the first sentence, "Sarah and Molly will not both go to the zoo," could be true.

Sarah will not go	Molly will not go	Sarah will not go
Molly will go	Sarah will go	Molly will not go

We rearrange them slightly, first switching the second and third columns,

Sarah will not go	Sarah will not go	Molly will not go
Molly will go	Molly will not go	Sarah will go

and then switching the entries in the third column.

Sarah will not go	Sarah will not go	Sarah will go
Molly will go	Molly will not go	Molly will not go

Now we can see that in fact they reduce to two.

Sarah will not go	Sarah will not go	Sarah will go
Molly will go	Molly will not go	Molly will not go

The two branches constructed below are overlapping and less fully described, but nevertheless they represent two ways in which the original sentence could be true.

Sarah doesn't go
(whether or not Molly goes)

Molly doesn't go
(whether or not Sarah goes)

And it remains that these are the only two ways we need to mention, in that if the sentence is true in neither of these ways, it is not true at all.

Taking advantage of this efficiency we have a tableau with only six branches—so far.

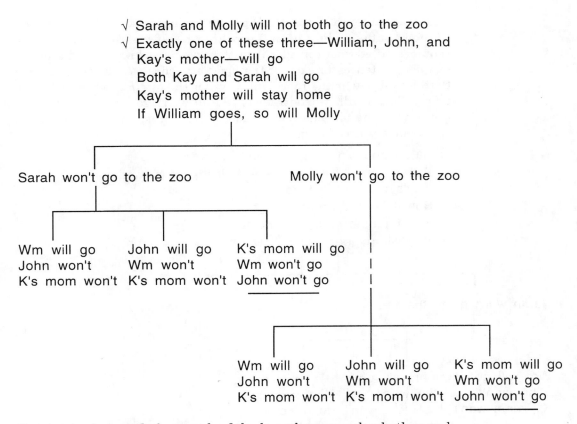

Tracing back a **path** from each of the branches, we ask whether each of the six paths really does represent a way in which the original sentences in our set might be true. Remembering that the unchecked sentences in the trunk are a part of each path, we note a difficulty with two of the paths. On them we have it that Kay's mother will go to the zoo, but also that Kay's mother will stay home. These sentences obviously contradict one another, so it is not possible for both of them to be true. We conclude that these two paths no longer represent possibilities for the original sentences to be true. We indicate that by drawing a line under the branch in question, meaning that the branch is **closed**.

Turning to the third sentence, we see that it comes in for particularly simple treatment. Clearly there is only one way for it to be true that both Kay and Sarah will go. For this to be true, both of these simpler sentences will have to be true:

Kay will go.
Sarah will go.

Since the sentence in question appears in the trunk, it lies on each of the four paths ending in an open branch. If we are to check this sentence off and not consider it further, we must first append the two simpler sentences to each of the open branches. As before, we find that not all four paths represent ways for the original sentences to be true. "Sarah will go" contradicts "Sarah won't go," and so on two of these paths lie obviously inconsistent sentences. Accordingly these two branches are closed.

(2)

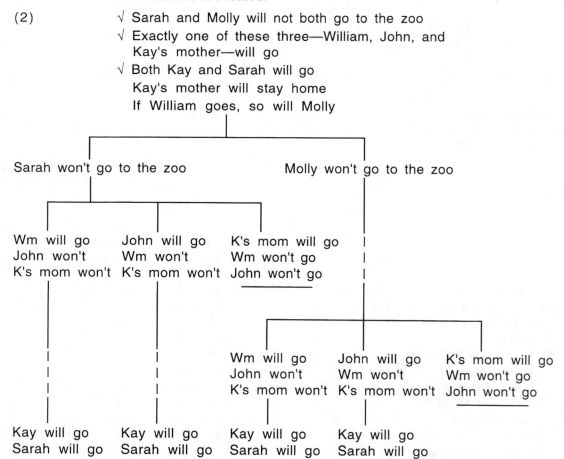

Of our original sentences, the fourth and fifth remain unchecked. "Kay's mother will stay home" is pretty simple as it stands. It may be tempting to write "Kay's mother won't go to the zoo" at each of the open branches, for indeed the only way for it to be true that she stays home is by not going. No harm would be done by

this manuever. On the other hand, we were able earlier to recognize
the relevant contradiction by simply attending to the fourth sentence
as stated. So it's not clear that anything would be gained. It is
crucial though that we leave it unchecked and continue to include it
in every path that we consider for consistency.

Finally we reach the fifth sentence, "If William goes, so will
Molly." In effect this means that William will not go without Molly—
perhaps he is a toddler and needs Molly to look after him. Three
different possibilities remain—since nothing rules out Molly going
without William:

| William will go | William will not go | Molly will go |
| Molly will go | Molly will not go | William will not go |

With three ways in which the sentence could be true the tableau
again threatens to proliferate beyond manageable bounds. We can
use the same strategy as before to reduce these ways to two. Again
we rearrange them, first moving the first column to the rightmost
position, while shifting the other two to the left.

| William will not go | Molly will go | William will go |
| Molly will not go | William will not go | Molly will go |

Then we switch the entries in the middle column.

| William will not go | William will not go | William will go |
| Molly will not go | Molly will go | Molly will go |

And again we recognize the overlaps.

| William will not go | William will not go | William will go |
| Molly will not go | Molly will go | Molly will go |

As before the two branches given below represent two ways,
overlapping and less than fully described, in which the sentence in
question—"If William goes, so will Molly"—could be true.

William doesn't go   Molly does go
(whether or not Molly goes)   (whether or not William goes)

A branching structure representing only these two ways we now
append to each of the two remaining open branches. And we check
the sentence, indicating that its force has been fully captured by these
branching structures. (We have devoted some care to this case
because sentences involving the word "if" are very important in logic.

The structure that we settled on for this example will be imitated frequently later in this and following chapters, so it is important that you understand it.)   Our various maneuvers have resulted the complicated tableau given below.   However complicated, it has the advantage that the set of complex sentences we began with has been divided into several sets of simpler sentences, ones where consistency can quite easily be judged.

(3)

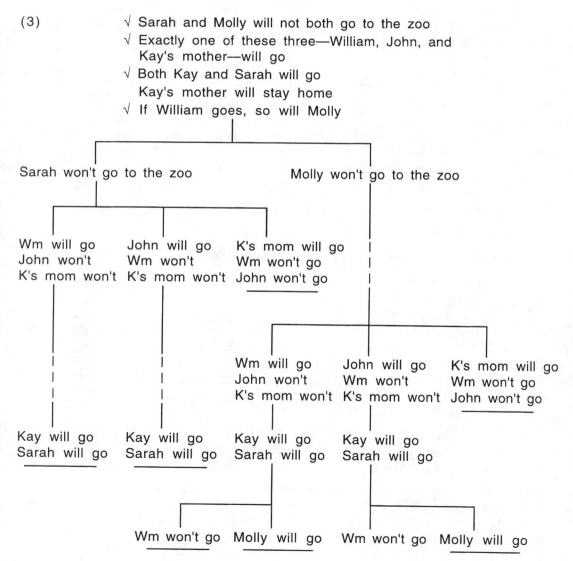

Four branches resulted from appending the branching structures to the open branches of the earlier tableau (2). Does each of
them represent a real possibility, a way in which the sentences in the
original set actually might be true? Tracing back from each of these
branches to the trunk, keeping in mind the simple sentences on the
whole path, gives the answer in each case, for in each case we are
simply recognizing whether the set of simple sentences in question is
obviously inconsistent. On the leftmost of the four, an obvious inconsistency appears in that the path includes both the sentence,
"William won't go," and the sentence, "William will go." In view of
this inconsistency, this branch is closed. Two others of the branches
are closed as well, both as a result of the inconsistency between
"Molly will go," at the tip, and "Molly won't go" back near the trunk.
But one branch remains open. And the question remains whether
this path gives us a way in which all of the original sentences could
be true at once.

To answer this question let us note first that all of the complex
sentences in the tableau have been checked. Though we will say
more about this in Chapter IV, the idea is that a checked sentence
need not be considered further. Before checking it off, we were
assured that we had fully captured its logical force, that whatever
simple sentences we wrote down, in whatever branches, specified
ways the checked sentence could be true. Thus if the *unchecked*
sentences in the remaining open path could indeed all be true at
once, together they specify a way in which all of the *original*
sentences, including the checked ones, could themselves all be true
at once. Though they are sketchy, in some cases leaving inessential
details unspecified, the unchecked sentences can be taken together as
themselves telling a story. Given their simplicity and the absence of
obvious inconsistencies among them, the story on the face of it is an
intelligible one. For that reason the situation they describe is a
possible one—at least as best we can tell. But remembering the
sentences in the original set, and using the terminology introduced
in Chapter II, the crucial point is that this is a situation with respect
to which all of the original sentences are true.

Let's make the point with reference to the tableau we have
constructed. Scanning up the open path, beginning with the tip of
the open branch, we consider the set of (simple) sentences listed on it.
(Some of them are listed more than once. Though this is a

distraction, it can simply be ignored.) These simple sentences form a set that evidently is consistent; the story that they sketch is pretty clearly intelligible. It seems evident that there *could be* an outing to the zoo in which William, Kay's mother, and Molly do not go (Kay's mother staying home) while Sarah, Kay, and John do go. Such an outing comprises a possible situation. And given the way we have constructed the open path, it is a situation with respect to which the original, much more complex sentences are true. The **verdict** then is that the original set is consistent. Comprising, as it does, several complex sentences, we could not be sure by simply inspecting them, that they could all be true together. But the tableau technique enabled us to determine that the original set is consistent by way of recognizing the evident consistency of the set of simple sentences in the remaining open path. By dividing the complex sentences into simple ones—though the paths multiply!—we are able to conquer the question of inconsistency. In the case before us, we reduced that question to multiple cases of obvious inconsistency and a remaining path where no inconsistency appeared. Since the sentences in that path are simple, we are confident that they indeed are consistent.

§11   EFFICIENCIES IN TABLEAUX

The finished tableau (3) in the previous section had the advantage of reducing questions of consistency to the point that answers were obvious. The price to be paid was that paths proliferated and several offspring sets had to be assessed. No doubt the price was worth paying in that a secure verdict was forthcoming. Still the question arises whether any less complicated route to the same verdict could be found. Practically speaking, a tableau like (3) consumes time and paper, and with a larger or more complex original set, the cost might become unbearable. In fact there are certain efficiencies that can be achieved using the same basic elements of the tableau technique that we have already learned. The key to them is very simple—the order in which the various sentences are broken down.

Proliferation of paths, and of the sentences that lie on them, results from branching. In choosing sentences for treatment in the tableau, we should follow these two rules of thumb for avoiding branching.

(1) Choose those unchecked complex sentences which do not result in branching.

(2) Choose those complex sentences some of whose branches will close because there will arise obvious inconsistencies with sentences already in the path in question.

It is best, and easiest, to avoid branching completely, so rule (1) should be followed first. With practice you will come to recognize complex sentences that can be broken down only with branching structures and others such that there is only one way for the sentence to be true. If only branching sentences remain, then follow rule (2) in choosing one of them. Recognizing which branches will close requires, in effect, that you look ahead. You can consider what simpler sentences will be written on each of the anticipated branches and whether they will conflict with sentences already in the path. You are looking for cases in which they *will* conflict because it is precisely those branches that will close. Perhaps the entire tableau will close—in fewer steps than with other choices. Or else an open path will more quickly be isolated, indicating a possible situation for the original set.

In some cases rule (2) will lead to a quicker closure. Thus the ordering of the two rules is not absolute. And in some case both rules apply at once; that is, sometimes there is a choice to be made even among nonbranching sentences, and one choice will result in closure where another choice will not. Where both rules apply, rejoice and apply them.

These rules of thumb presume that it makes no difference in what order the sentences in a tableau are treated. That presumption deserves to be examined, but first let us see the savings that result from following this strategy. There follows an alternative tableau for the sentences from §10. Instead of check marks, **small numbers** appear next to the complex sentences that have been broken down. They indicate the order in which the complex sentences were chosen, and they serve to correlate each tableau structure with the complex sentence from which it resulted. Study the tableau to see when each of the two rules of thumb was applied. And note how much less complicated is the finished tableau, how much more quickly a possible situation was isolated.

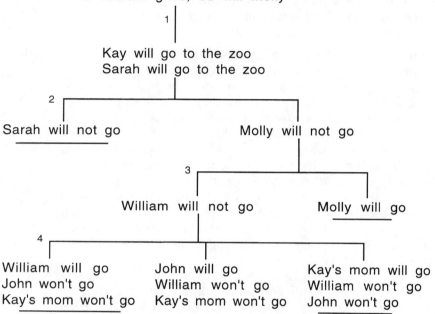

2 Sarah and Molly will not both go to the zoo
4 Exactly one of these three—William, John, and
   Kay's mother—will go
1 Both Kay and Sarah will go
   Kay's mother will stay home
3 If William goes, so will Molly

1

Kay will go to the zoo
Sarah will go to the zoo

2

Sarah will not go

Molly will not go

3

William will not go   Molly will go

4

William will go   John will go   Kay's mom will go
John won't go   William won't go   William won't go
Kay's mom won't go   Kay's mom won't go   John won't go

Considering the two tableaux on our set of complex sentences—
this one and tableau (3) of §10—we see indeed the same verdict of
consistency. Each tableau had an open path. And we see that the
same kind of situation was singled out by both tableaux: an outing to
the zoo in which John, Kay, and Sarah go, while Kay's mother,
Molly, and William do not go.

§12   A TABLEAU THAT CLOSES

In order to see a different outcome, and also to work with some other
examples of complex sentences, let's build a tableau for this set of
sentences.

(1)

> If we invite Ron to the party, we must invite Nancy too.
>
> We will invite Ron if we invite an actress.
>
> We will invite Jane, but we can't invite both Nancy and Jane.
>
> Jane is an intelligent actress.

In line with what we have learned about keeping tableaux as efficient as possible, we first try to find a sentence that will not require branching. The only way for the third sentence to be true is for both of these to be true:

> We will invite Jane.
> We won't invite both Nancy and Jane.

The fourth sentence has only one clause; even so both of these briefer sentences must be true in order for it to be true.

> Jane is intelligent.
> Jane is an actress.

The point of so dividing "Jane is an intelligent actress" is highlighted by contrasting it with sentences that are superficially similar. Situations in which "Jane is a veteran actress" would be true are not typically ones in which "Jane is a veteran" would be true. (Except in its familiar military use, the latter sentence is not even intelligible in isolation.) And "Jane is an aspiring actress" or "Jane is a wannabe actress" could be true without "Jane is an actress" being true.

To construct a tableau, we attach each of these pairs to the trunk, resulting in only one branch so far.

> If we invite Ron to the party, we must invite Nancy too
> We will invite Ron if we invite an actress
> 1 We will invite Jane, but we can't invite both Nancy and Jane
> 2 Jane is an intelligent actress
>
>   1 |
>
> We will invite Jane
> We won't invite both Nancy and Jane
>
>   2 |
>
> Jane is intelligent
> Jane is an actress

With the remaining sentences we have no choice but to branch, so we look for cases where one of the branches will close. The second sentence has the word "if" in it. Recall our treatment (in §10) of "If Molly goes, so will William." Following the pattern there established, we recognize two possibilities—(1) that we invite Ron (whether or not we invite an actress) and (2) that we don't invite an actress (whether or not we invite Ron). The appropriate branching structure is appended to the tree. Among the sentences in the path on the right are "We will invite Jane," "Jane is an actress," and "We won't invite an actress." These three cannot all be true at once, and so the right-hand branch is closed.

If we invite Ron to the party, we must invite Nancy too

3   We will invite Ron if we invite an actress

1   We will invite Jane, but we can't invite both Nancy and Jane

2   Jane is an intelligent actress

1

We will invite Jane
We won't invite both Nancy and Jane

2

Jane is intelligent
Jane is an actress

3

We will invite Ron   We won't invite an actress

To finish the tableau we introduce branching structures for two remaining complex sentences; each is similar to a sentence we have encountered before. (Note that, in the case of the sentence, "We can't invite both Nancy and Jane," the result of an earlier tableau construction is itself broken down into even simpler sentences.) Each branching structure is to be appended to every open branch that can be reached by tracing down from the complex sentence from which the branching structure originates. In the tableau below there is only one such open branch in each case.

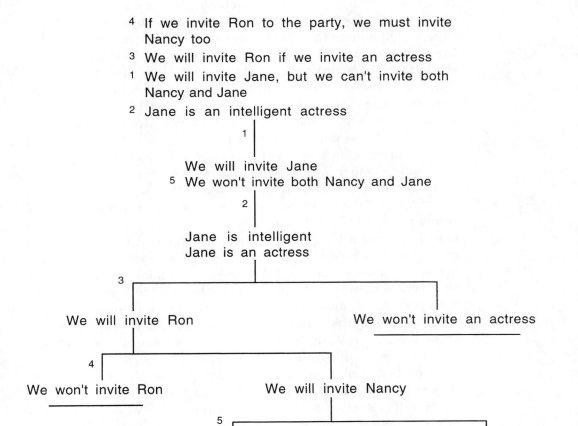

4 If we invite Ron to the party, we must invite Nancy too

3 We will invite Ron if we invite an actress

1 We will invite Jane, but we can't invite both Nancy and Jane

2 Jane is an intelligent actress

1

We will invite Jane
5 We won't invite both Nancy and Jane

2

Jane is intelligent
Jane is an actress

3

We will invite Ron

We won't invite an actress

4

We won't invite Ron

We will invite Nancy

5

We won't invite Nancy

We won't invite Jane

Multiple branching was avoidable in this tableau because various branches of the tableau were closed as we went along. (Note that this depended on the order. What if we had treated the first sentence first instead of fourth?) "We won't invite Ron" contradicted the sentence, "We will invite Ron" immediately above it. Closing that branch left only one branch to be extended. Equally, "We won't invite Nancy" couldn't possibly be true in a situation in which the sentence above it is true. And tracing up from the rightmost branch, we discover that "We won't invite Jane" is in the same path as "We will invite Jane." Obviously the set of sentences in that path is inconsistent, and so we close that branch, the only one remaining. The result is a tableau *all* of whose branches are closed. We call it a **closed tableau**. (It may happen that all branches close before some of the sentences have even been considered. No matter, the tableau is closed even so.) In a closed tableau, no way remains for the original sentences to be true. What has thereby been demonstrated in this case is that the sentences at (1) form an inconsistent set, that is to say, a set of sentences such that there is no possible situation with respect to which all of the sentences in the set are true.

In summary here is how the tableau technique can be used to determine whether a set of sentences is consistent or not. Consider each complex sentence in turn, and extend the tableau by specifying ways in which the sentence in question could be true, making use of simpler sentences. Where there are several ways, append a branching structure. Close any branch of the tableau whose simple sentences comprise an obviously inconsistent set. If all of the branches close—a closed tableau—the original set of complex sentences is inconsistent. An **open tableau** is one with at least one open branch. If, ultimately, all of the complex sentences have been considered and broken down, and yet the tableau remains open, the original set is evidently consistent. This is because the sentences in each open path tell—or at least sketch—an intelligible story. Each open path describes, at least partially, a possible situation with respect to which the original sentences are true.

Now let us return to the rules for efficiency. Can we be sure that in general our outcome will not be affected by the order in which we choose complex sentences for treatment? We must be clear about what we mean by the outcome. In the first place we are testing for consistency and inconsistency. It is a fact that if a tableau for a given set of complex sentences closes, then any other finished tableau for the same set will close as well. (By a **finished tableau** we mean one whose complex sentences have all been checked.) Rather than proving this rigorously, let us see informally why it should be so. It is relevant to notice initially that the question of consistency in a set of sentences has no reference to the order in which the sentences are listed. It is just a question of whether there is some possible situation with respect to which they are all true at once. Thinking in more detail, remember that a path in a tableau represents a way in which the original sentences can be true. If there has been multiple branching, the path represents one of several ways for each of the sentences that have produced branches. What is essential is that all possible combinations of such ways be accounted for. If a certain combination is not really possible, owing to an obvious inconsistency among some of the simple sentences describing it, it might as well be eliminated early as late.

An important feature of our method becomes visible here. As we have regarded them, the long-winded tableau (3) in §10 and the efficient tableau in §11 survey the same situations. In the open path of the more complex tableau we have "John will go" and below it, "Sarah will go." In the open path of the more efficient tableau, "Sarah will go" occurs above "John will go." Clearly we are not taking seriously the order of these sentences as they tell their story. We are not taking it, as would be more usual with ordinary narratives, that Sarah goes after John does, or the other way around. This seems fair enough inasmuch as the sentences we began with said nothing about the order of various events. In Chapter IV and later we will see sets of complex sentences involving words like "before" and "after," "while" and "since." With these sentences considerations of timing are made explicit, and inconsistencies may arise accordingly.

Besides rendering verdicts on consistency, tableaux do something else as well. An open branch in a finished tableau indicates a possible situation with respect to which the original sentences are true. By means of the simple sentences on the path ending in that branch it tells a story about how these matters might have been. So long as that story really is intelligible, the path describes a possible situation, one that may well differ from how things actually are. (Of course there may be more than one open branch and thus more than one such situation.) The order in which complex sentences are treated affects the amount of branching, though not the number of open branches. Two different open tableaux for a given set of sentences may have different numbers of closed branches. But the number of open branches will be the same, as will the various possible situations described. In summary, when the sentences in a given set are consistent with one another, a finished tableau (partially) describes—in simple sentences—each of the possible situations with respect to which the original sentences are true. It does so independently of the order in which the complex sentences have been treated.

A final note is needed on numbering tableau structures. In §11 we introduced these numbers, in place of check marks, to make evident which structures go with which complex sentences. As you are doing exercises, you may find it helpful to use numbers as well. The answers to some of the exercises include them for the same reason. But in the next chapter, we will revert to check marks. They serve an important function in tableaux that we will consider at length.

Exercises for Chapter III

Use tableaux to determine which of the following sets of sentences are consistent.

1.

> Vega is a brilliant, red planet.
>
> Mars is not a planet if Vega is.
>
> Vega is not both brilliant and white.
>
> Mars is either a planet or a star.

2.

> Gargantua is an intellectual dwarf.
>
> Gargantua is the biggest man in the country.
>
> Gargantua is neither an artist nor an intellectual; he's the king.

3.

> Either George and Mary will both go to the beach, or one of them will stay home and fix the car.
>
> George can't fix the car.
>
> If Mary stays home, she will do nothing but loaf.
>
> Mary won't go to the beach.

4.

> I will finish my core requirements next term.
>
> Of philosophy, history, and literature, I will take at least one.
>
> If I am to finish my core requirements, I must take science and speech.
>
> I won't take both philosophy and science.
>
> I won't take speech if I take literature.

5. What—in addition to the verdict on consistency—can you learn from the tableau for #4?

IV: Extending the Tableau Technique

If my argument is valid, it is inconsistent to accept the premises and yet deny the conclusion. Consider for example the most famous of all valid arguments.

| All humans are mortal. |
| Socrates is human. |
| Socrates is mortal. |

The **counter set** of an argument is the set consisting of the premises and the denial of the conclusion.

(1)

| All humans are mortal. |
| Socrates is human. |
| Socrates is immortal. |

Obviously, this set of sentences is inconsistent. Here is a place where inconsistency is a virtue. Since the counter set is inconsistent, the argument is valid, and we are entitled to infer the conclusion from the premises.

Let's try to say exactly why this is so, making use of the definition of validity given in Chapter I and also of the notions of consistency and possible situation developed in Chapters II and III. By our definition an argument is valid—not merely a reasonable inference—if it is impossible for the premises of the argument to be true while the conclusion is false. The natural way to elaborate this definition is to say that there is no possible situation with respect to which the premises are true and with respect to which the conclusion is false. In denying the conclusion we formulate a sentence which is true so long as the conclusion is false, but only so long. Again making use of the notion of a situation, any situation with respect to which the conclusion is false will be one with respect to which this denial is true, and vice versa. So, given that an argument is valid, there must not be any situation with respect to which the premises of the argument are true and with respect to which the denial of the conclusion is also true—because the conclusion would be false with respect to such a situation. Here we have spoken precisely of the counter set of the argument—the set consisting of the premises and the denial of the conclusion. We have said that there is no situation with respect to which all of the sentences in this set are true. But that is just to say that the counter set is inconsistent. Reversing the reasoning, if the counter set is inconsistent, there is no situation with respect to which the premises are true and the conclusion is false, and thus the argument is valid. We have established this general principle:

**An argument is valid if, and only if, the
counter set of the argument is inconsistent.**

Happily, in light of this generalization, we have begun to develop a system for determining whether a set of sentences is consistent. Our test for consistency can be marshalled to serve as a test for validity as well. All we need do is to construct the counter set and apply the test to it. The argument is valid exactly when its counter set turns out to be inconsistent.

For a case where the tableau test is perhaps needed to recognize the inconsistency, consider this argument.

(2)

> Either everyone will go to Florida, or everyone will go to Arizona.
> George will not go to Florida.
>
> ──
>
> Martha will go to Arizona.

We form the counter set as follows. (Remember that the conclusion of the argument is denied in the counter set.)

(3)

> Either everyone will go to Florida, or everyone will go to Arizona.
>
> George will not go to Florida.
>
> Martha will *not* go to Arizona.

In the counter set, the line—meaning "therefore"—is not included. The counter set is simply a set of sentences, perhaps consistent, perhaps not. Once the counter set is formed, there is nothing distinguished about any of the sentences in it. In particular, they can be broken down in the tableau in any order that is convenient, especially for keeping the tableau short.

Now we construct a tableau on the counter set, in order to determine whether that set of sentences is consistent.

√ Either everyone will go to Florida, or everyone
will go to Arizona
George will not go to Florida
Martha will not go to Arizona

Everyone will go to Florida   Everyone will go to Arizona

Our tableau branches because the first sentence will be true in either of the situations represented by the two branches. What's more, in a situation in which neither of these simpler sentences is true, the first sentence will not be true either. So these two branches capture all the ways in which the original sentence can be true.

Perhaps you are prepared to close each of these branches already. For surely "George will not go to Florida" contradicts "Everyone will go to Florida." And equally "Martha will not go to Arizona" contradicts "Everyone will go to Arizona." In order to make these contradictions perfectly explicit, each branch can be extended further. The branch on the left represents an attempt to make all of the original sentences true. But any way of making "Everyone will go to Florida" true must also make "George will go to Florida" true. And so it is permissible to add that sentence to the branch. Equally on the right, any way of making "Everyone will go to Arizona" true will also make "Martha will go to Arizona" true. So the right branch can be extended similarly. (These moves presume that George and Martha are among those included in the range of the word "everyone." That presumption is considered in more detail in a study of logical words—called quantifiers—like "everyone," "something," and "nobody.") With the two branches extended as indicated, there are pairs of sentences that flat-out contradict each other. So there is no doubt that the branches close as indicated.

(4)

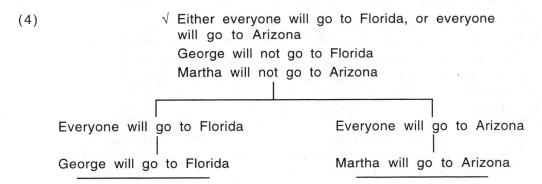

What this closed tableau shows is that the set of sentences (3) is inconsistent. But that set is the counter set for the argument (2). Since there is no situation in which all the sentences in (3) are true, there is no situation in which the premises of (2) are true while the conclusion is false. This is what it amounts to for the argument to be valid. Indeed we have marshalled the tableau technique as a technique for establishing that an argument is valid. In so using the tableau technique, it is crucial to remember two points. First, before proceeding with a tableau, construct the counter set of the argument. A tableau on the argument itself establishes nothing of interest. In fact such a tableau represents a sort of category mistake, since the notion of consistency applies not to arguments, which have premises and a conclusion, but rather to sets of sentences, such as a counter set. It is characteristic of such sets that no sentence in them has any special place and that the order of the sentences does not matter.

The second crucial point is that it is *in*consistency of the counter set that shows that the argument is valid. We are looking for all of the branches of the tableau on the counter set to close. If one of them remains open, it represents a way for the sentences in the counter set all to be true. Going back to the argument itself, the open branch represents a way for the premises to be true and the conclusion (which was denied in the counter set) to be *false*. If there is such a situation, then it is possible for the premises to be true and yet for the conclusion to be false. But then, by definition, the argument is invalid.

In order to see this strategy in action, consider this more complicated argument.

The alarm rang either because there was smoke in the room or because the batteries were low.

The batteries were four months old unless the receipt was misdated.

The charges, date, and time on the receipt were all accurate.

The batteries were fresh enough if they were less than six months old.

The alarm rang because there was smoke in the room.

In order to form the counter set we must deny the conclusion. Here the conclusion is a complex sentence. If we simply add the word "not," we get the sentence,

The alarm did not ring because there was smoke in the room.

This won't do at all. We need a construction guaranteed to express unambiguously the denial of a given sentence, whether that sentence is complex or not. To meet this need let us settle on the phrase, "It is not true that," resulting in the following.

(5) It is not true that the alarm rang because there was smoke in the room.

We will always understand (5) as simply denying that the alarm rang because there was smoke in the room, and similarly when our phrase is prefixed to other sentences. Now we are able to write down the counter set, and to proceed with the tableau test for consistency on that set.

The complete tableau appears below. Study it and see if you can tell how each structure was constructed and why each branch was closed. You will note that some of the complex sentences have been checked. The idea is that in checking a sentence we indicate that its full contribution to the logic of the original set has been captured by whatever structures we have built from it. But another of the complex sentences remains unchecked, even though a structure has resulted from it. This matter will be discussed in §16, but in the meantime see if you can recognize that there is a relevant difference in the complex sentences.

(6) √ The alarm rang either because there was smoke in the room or because the batteries were low

√ The batteries were only four months old unless the receipt was misdated

√ The charges, date, and time on the receipt were all accurate

The batteries were fresh enough if they were less than six months old

It is not true that the alarm rang because there was smoke in the room

The charges on the receipt were accurate
The date on the receipt was accurate
The time on the receipt was accurate

The alarm rang because there
was smoke in the room
———————————

The alarm rang because the batteries were low

The alarm rang
The batteries were low

The batteries were only
four months old

The receipt was misdated
———————————

The batteries
were fresh enough
———————

The batteries were *not*
less than six months old
———————————

Several aspects of the tableau are worthy of comment. The first sentence is pretty clearly true in either—or perhaps both—of two kinds of situations, and so two branches have been constructed. The left-hand branch closes because that sentence directly contradicts (5), which of course appears in the trunk of the tableau. Because that branch does close, no further treatment of the left-hand sentence is required. But in the right-hand branch, the complex sentence,

(7)   The alarm rang because the batteries were low,

does require more attention. The only way that it can be true is for both of these to be true as well.

> The alarm rang.
> The batteries were low.

Thus they have been recorded in the tableau, thereby extending the right-hand branch. But note that sentence (7) as it appears in the tableau has not been checked. Finally, branching structures were created for each of the remaining sentences in the trunk. Sentences were chosen for treatment judiciously so that branches were kept to minimum. In fact, every time branching occurred, one of the branches could be closed.

In this tableau we encountered, for the first time, a sentence involving "unless."

(8) The batteries were only four months old unless the receipt was misdated.

How was it treated in the tableau? This sentence means the same as one involving "if."

> If the receipt was *not* misdated, then the batteries were only four months old.

Note that this sentence does not rule out the batteries being only four months old even though the receipt is misdated. After all, maybe the receipt is just one day off. Quite apart from that question, we already know how to handle the "if" sentence; there are these two (overlapping) ways for it to be true.

> The receipt was *not*   The batteries were
> not misdated.   only four months old.

On the left, the two "not's" cancel each other out. And further, it is harmless to switch the two ways around, better to fit the structure of (8). This at last gives the structure that appears in the tableau.

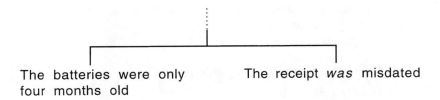

The batteries were only four months old   The receipt *was* misdated

After all of this we are ready to render a verdict. All of the branches of the tableau close. (Note the use that we made of the simple sentence, "The batteries were low," which resulted from sentence (7). It is this that conflicts with "The batteries were fresh enough," and thereby closes one of the branches.) Since all of the branches are closed, the counter set is inconsistent. But remember that here inconsistency is a virtue, for it was an argument that we began with, from which we constructed the counter set. Inconsistency here means that there is no possible situation with respect to which the premises of the argument are true and the conclusion is false. That outcome results in the verdict of "Valid," by the definition of validity that we first saw in Chapter I.

Before leaving this example it is worth reinforcing a point made in connection with (5). There we constructed a sentence denying the complex conclusion of our argument. We did so by writing down the words, "It is not true that" followed by the conclusion itself. This is a method that can be used for any sentence whatever. For example we could express the denial of "Socrates is mortal," with the sentence "It is not true that Socrates is mortal" as well as with the shorter and more natural sentence that we used in (1). We will need to write down the denial of given sentences, not only in constructing counter sets, but also in extending tableaux involving "if"-sentences and on other occasions as well. Often there are more idiomatic alternatives to be found, but when in doubt, simply put the words "It is not true that" on the front.

RESOLVING REFERENCE   §14

Soon we will consider additional tableau constructions, appropriate to other kinds of sentences, whose logic depends on other familiar expressions. Before doing so, we do well to recognize a difficulty that will arise when we break complex sentences down into simple sentences, as is characteristic of the tableau technique. The premises of this argument,

(1)

> The boss gave Mona three gifts, a ruby, a gun, and a dress.
>
> She handed at least two of them over to Liz.
>
> If the boss gave Mona a gun and Liz received it from her, the cops found it at Liz's.
>
> If the boss gave her a dress, Mona burned it rather than giving it to Liz.
>
> ---
>
> The cops found a gun.

visibly have anaphoric pronouns whose antecedents will be lost when the sentences are broken down. In other cases there will be indexical expressions, including descriptive indexicals, whose reference is understood on the basis of indications appearing earlier in the unfolding discourse comprised by the original sentences. It is essential that the reference of these anaphors, indexicals, and descriptive indexicals not be lost as the tableau is constructed. After all, recognizing inconsistencies will depend on recognizing commonalities of reference. ("Socrates is mortal" is inconsistent with "He is immortal" only if "he" is understood to refer to Socrates!) An effective method for securing the reference of these expressions is easily specified. We annotate each anaphoric pronoun with the phrase to which the anaphor reaches back (or forward), what we earlier called its antecedent. In the case of each indexical expression, something earlier in the unfolding discourse has made its reference salient, typically an earlier mention of the individual or object in question. Again we simply annotate the pronoun or descriptive indexical, this time with the name or fully descriptive expression through which the relevant object was earlier mentioned. (In the case of a lengthy full description, some standard abbreviation may be chosen, to be used in place of every expression that refers to the entity in question.)

These annotations make explicit the reference of each pronoun and descriptive indexical, enough so that the simple sentences in the tableau structure to come will have no dangling or unresolved pronominal reference. With an argument like (1) the formation of the counter set provides a good opportunity for attaching these annotations. Of course we also manipulate the premises and conclusion so as to form the appropriate set of sentences on which to build the tableau.

> The boss gave Mona three gifts, a ruby, a gun, and a dress.
>
> She (Mona) handed at least two of them (the ruby, the gun, and the dress) over to Liz.
>
> If the boss gave Mona a gun and Liz received it (the gun) from her (Mona), the cops found it (the gun) at Liz's.
>
> If the boss gave her a dress, Mona burned it (the dress) rather than giving it (the dress) to Liz.
>
> The cops didn't find a gun.

Having annotated the counter set, we construct a tableau and close appropriate branches. It is natural, as the tableau develops, simply to drop the pronouns, replacing them with the more explicit annotations.

In some cases, resolving the reference of pronouns must be done explicitly and correctly in order to reach the right verdict on validity. The following argument has numerous pronouns, most of them anaphoric.

(2)

> Mary said she reimbursed her own expenses.
>
> She said Martha cashed a check for the club by writing a check made out to herself.
>
> Martha did what Mary said she did.
>
> If she reimbursed her own expenses, Martha embezzled—because only the club treasurer is authorized to reimburse expenses.
>
> ───────────────────────────
>
> Martha is an embezzler.

Though the reference is easily enough resolved in the other sentences, the third premise has an anaphoric ambiguity that is not resolved by the context. It is not clear which of two propositions is being expressed. Thus there really are two different arguments, requiring separate tableaux. It will turn out that only one of them is valid.

As before, we use the counter set as an opportunity to annotate the pronouns, making their reference explicit. In doing so, we choose one of the alternative readings for the ambiguous premise. In the developing tableau we can drop the pronouns in favor of the names themselves.

(3)   Mary said she (Mary) reimbursed her own expenses

She (Mary) said Martha cashed a check for the club by writing a
check made out to herself

Martha did what Mary said she (Mary) did

If she (Martha) reimbursed her own expenses, Martha embezzled—
because only the club treasurer is authorized to reimburse expenses

Martha is not an embezzler

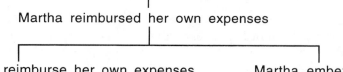

Since both branches of the tableau close, we find that the counter set
is inconsistent, and thus that argument (2), understood as annotated
in the trunk of (3), is a valid one. On this reading of the third premise
of (2), the conclusion that Martha is an embezzler indeed follows
from that and the other premises.

In addition to the novel treatment of pronouns, this tableau
introduces another novelty as well. The trunk of the tableau includes
the following two sentences.

(4)   Mary said Mary reimbursed her own expenses.
                   Martha did what Mary said Mary did.

The only way for these sentences both to be true is for the sentence,

(5)   Martha reimbursed her own expenses,

to be true as well. Thus this new sentence has been added to the
tableau, without branching. And notably neither of the orginal
sentences has been checked. (There is some similarity to the tableau
(13.4), where the sentence, "George will go to Florida," was added to
the branch that already had the sentence, "Eveyone will go to
Florida.") We have here a case in which *two* earlier sentences
together give rise to a new sentence. In more complex tableaux, the
new sentence would be added to every branch whose path included
both of the original sentences.

There is a subtlety in the two sentences at (4). In introducing sentence (5) we are taking it that what Mary said she did was to reimburse her *own* expenses. And so if Martha did that, she reimbursed *her* own expenses (not Mary's). The expression "her own" is more subtle than a simple anaphoric pronoun. Each simple anaphor can be replaced without confusion by its antecedent. But we are taking "what Mary did," to tie the reflexive expression "her own" to whoever is said to have done what Mary did. A fuller treatment of this more subtle kind of anaphora will occur in Chapter IX with our treatment of quantifier expressions. It may be that the third premise of (2) is ambiguous in another way. Perhaps it could be read as saying that Martha did what Mary said she, Mary, did, namely reimbursed *Mary*. The prospects of that reading do not seem promising, so we will not pursue them further.

What is worth pursuing is the ambiguity we first recognized in the third premise of (2). Another construal of the anaphoric "she" ties it to the antecedent "Martha." Read in that way it expresses the proposition that Martha did what Mary said she—Martha—did, namely, cashed a check for the club. Under this reading we have an entirely different argument, one whose logic needs to be assessed in its own right. Again we construct a tableau on the counter set, providing annotations that make the reference of the pronouns explicit. Again a new sentence appears in the tableau, analogous to (5) above. But in this tableau it is the sentence, "Martha cashed a check for the club by writing a check made out to herself."

(6)   Mary said she (Mary) reimbursed her own expenses

       She (Mary) said Martha cashed a check for the club by writing a check made out to herself

       Martha did what Mary said she (Martha) did

       If she (Martha) reimbursed her own expenses, Martha embezzled—because only the club treasurer is authorized to reimburse expenses

       Martha is not an embezzler

              |

         If Martha reimbursed her own expenses, Martha embezzled
         Only the club treasurer is authorized to reimburse expenses

              |

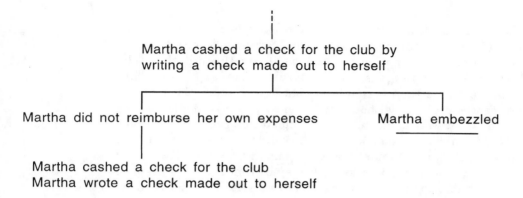

With this reading of the third premise the verdict on Martha is strikingly different. The tableau has been extended to the fullest, and yet it has an open path. Reading up this open path we have a description of a possible situation that exonerates Martha. Since the counter set is consistent, argument (2) *under this second reading* is not a valid one. There is a general lesson to be drawn about arguments with irresolvable ambiguities. In such cases, the ambiguous sentence should be annotated in two different ways, each indicating a justifiable reading of the sentence. That having been done, it becomes evident that there are two distinct arguments to be considered, with every possibility that one of them is valid and the other not. Since that makes all the difference as to the cogency of the conclusion, there is no recourse but to seek out the author of the argument and ask for resolution of the ambiguity. All that logic can do is to set out the alternatives and provide a logical assessment of each.

§15   Additional Constructions

The following set of sentences, which are concerned with the earlier topic of the outing to the zoo, includes some other kinds of complex sentences. Not only does it illustrate the general procedure of constructing a tableau, but also these other sentences serve as examples of the variety of complex sentence structures arising in English. Handling different kinds of sentences is the main challenge in applying the tableau test. Note that here we have returned to the question of consistency itself. No argument has been presented. No one is making an inference to a conclusion or trying to persuade anyone of a conclusion. We are simply asking whether these sentences might turn out—perhaps as a result of someone's planning—all to be true.

The zoo is an inexpensive treat within walking distance.
John won't go to the zoo without either Kay or his mother.
Molly is going because William is.
Sarah will go if the zoo is not expensive.
John will happily go if the zoo is nearby.
Since the zoo is for children, no one's parent will go.
Kay will not go to the zoo unless no more than four go.

Remember that even though some of the earlier sentences (from Chapter III) might seem to be relevant here, we will only deal with the sentences listed here. It is this set—no others—that we are testing for consistency now.

In line with what we have learned about keeping tableaux as simple as possible, we search first for sentences that will not require branching. The first sentence can be broken down into several simpler ones, all of which have to be true if the original is true:

> The zoo is inexpensive.
> The zoo is a treat.
> The zoo is within walking distance.

The second sentence requires branching, so we pass over it for now. But any situation in which Molly is going because William is going, surely is a situation in which both of these sentences are true:

> Molly will go to the zoo.
> William will go to the zoo.

Scanning further down the trunk for sentences that we can divide into simpler components, without creating additional branches, we see that since the zoo is for children, no one's parent will go. In any such situation these two will be true:

> The zoo is for children.
> No one's parent will go to the zoo.

Consolidating these insights, we construct a good part of our tableau without any branching whatever:

√ The zoo is an inexpensive treat within
walking distance
John won't go to the zoo without either Kay or
his mother
Molly is going because William is
Sarah will go if the zoo is not expensive
John will happily go if the zoo is nearby
Since the zoo is for children, no one's parent
will go
Kay will not go to the zoo unless no more than
four go

|

The zoo is inexpensive
The zoo is a treat
The zoo is within walking distance

|

Molly will go to the zoo
William will go to the zoo

|

The zoo is for children
No one's parent will go to the zoo

The finished tableau is on the next two pages. The first two
branching structures result from the sentences with "if "-clauses;
these have by now become familiar and are handled in the standard
way. Can you see how the rest of the sentences were treated?

Toward the bottom of the tableau, the sentence "John will happily
go" gives rise to the sentence "John will go" in the same branch. The
obvious explanation is that for John to go happily will be for him to
go, one way or another. As we saw with "because" in §13, the earlier
sentence is not checked. The explanation, to be elaborated in §16, is
that for him to go is not for him to go happily. The same treatment
would apply to any of these and similar cases.

John will certainly go.
John will go quickly.
John will go reluctantly.
Necessarily John will go.
John will go in a snit.

But it is crucial to contrast other cases. With *none* of the following sentences would it be correct to append "John will go" in the branch of a tableau.

> John will hardly go.
> John will possibly go.
> Probably John will go.
> Hopefully John will go.
> John will doubtfully go.
> John will go in your dreams.

Again the explanation is pretty obvious. Any of these could be true without it's turning out that John actually does go. Incidentally, the comparison with other sentences perhaps will set to rest the familiar complaint that there is with one of them a lapse of coherence. To say, "John will hopefully go" is no more to characterize the manner of John's going than is to say, "Possibly John will go."

Can you see why each of the branches were closed? The trickiest branch is the middle one at the bottom. In it we have—reading upward—Kay, John, Sarah, William, and Molly all going to the zoo, but no more than four going. Pretty obviously inconsistent—once someone points it out! (This judgment takes it for granted that different names mean different people—that Molly and Sarah, for example, are not one girl with two names.) And finally, again note which complex sentences have been checked and which have not. Explaining that further remains to be done in §16.

(1)
  √ The zoo is an inexpensive treat within walking distance
  √ John won't go to the zoo without either Kay or his mother
  Molly is going because William is
  Sarah will go if the zoo is not expensive
  John will happily go if the zoo is nearby
  Since the zoo is for children, no one's parent will go
  √ Kay will not go to the zoo unless no more than four go

     |

    The zoo is inexpensive
    The zoo is a treat
    The zoo is within walking distance

     |

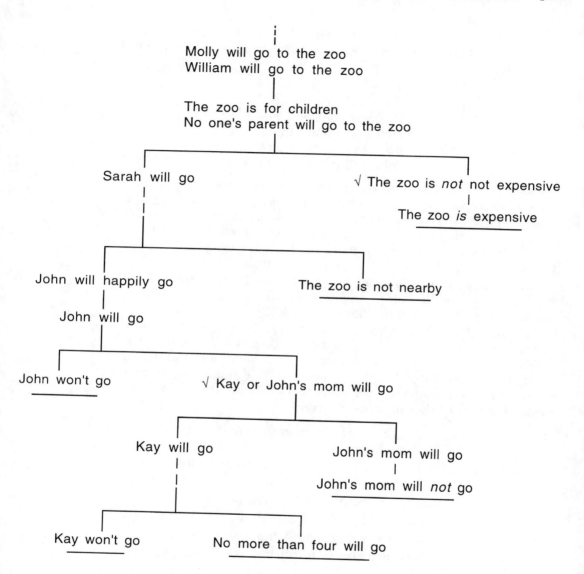

The last sentence on the right—the one that causes the right-most branch to close—has been written because in that branch there appears the sentence, "No one's parent will go to the zoo." Suppose we have a situation with respect to which that sentence is true. Surely John's mom will not go to the zoo in such a situation. So we are entitled to add the sentence, "John's mom will not go." Again note that the earlier sentence has *not* been checked.

All of the branches of the tableau have closed. So the set of sentences that we began with is inconsistent. Someone had better make some other plans, for there is no possible situation with respect to which these sentences all are true!

WHEN CAN A SENTENCE BE CHECKED?   §16

The foregoing tableaux have incorporated a variety of English sentence constructions and illustrated a variety of tableau structures. Characteristically an appropriate structure—spawned by the sentence under consideration—is placed in every open branch that can be reached by tracing down the path of the developing tableau from the sentence in question. In these a pervasive contrast has been noted. Some sentences have been checked off upon placing the appropriate structures. With other sentences, even when a structure has been placed in every lower open branch, the originating sentence has not been checked off. In this section we will explore and explain this contrast.

Before looking at cases and trying to understand the contrasting treatment, let us be clear as to the effect of checking a sentence off. Obviously the check makes it evident that in fact we have utilized the sentence in extending the tableau. If that were the purpose of the check, rather than an incidental effect, we would want to check off every sentence as we utilized it. Thus the purpose must lie elsewhere. What the check really means is that the complex sentence in question need no longer be considered as we work further with the tableau.

This intended effect of the check is made vivid by the operation of certain interactive systems that have been developed for constructing tableaux on personal computers or computer terminals. We have labored with the sprawling character of tableaux. Given the limitations of a display screen, this sprawl is particularly irksome on a computerized tableau-building system. One mitigating device that these systems employ is simply to erase checked sentences from tableaux as they develop, thereby making more room on the screen. There is a disadvantage in that you cannot look back at what you have done to be sure that it is correct, or even to keep track of your ongoing strategy. But these are merely heuristic losses. In erasing a checked sentence, the computer system signals that it plays no further role. The ultimate tableau will do as well without it.

Checking a sentence after extending the tableau with appropriate structures means that the sentence need no longer be considered. Since there are two kinds of maneuvers that involve any given sentence, it must mean that neither of these maneuvers will any longer be needed. One of these is to close a branch on whose path the sentence lies. Thus checking off a sentence means that no branch that could close when the sentence is considered would fail to close when the sentence is ignored. The other maneuver is to extend one or more branches further on the basis of the sentence in question. Thus checking off a sentence also means not only that the sentence has already been utilized in extending branches but that no further utilization will ever be required. In indicating that neither of these maneuvers will ever be needed, the check mark in effect certifies that the logical force of the sentence in question has been exhausted by the structures that it has spawned below it.

The decision whether to check off or not should be guided by this question of whether the new tableau structure fully captures the logical force of the sentence from which the new structure originates. In extending a tableau we search for a reasonably small structure which includes only sentences that are unquestionably simpler and easier to grasp (even if more numerous) than the originating sentence. Whenever we identify a structure that fully captures the originating sentence, let it be deployed. And the originating sentence should be checked. But in many cases there is no such structure to be found. The originating sentence may have content that is not exhausted by any structure of simpler sentences. Even so the addition of a structure with new, simpler sentences may result in a clearer and more explicit description of an emerging situation. In extending open branches with such structures, we gain the advantage of more easily recognizing that some of the situations are not really possible. But the originating sentence must not be checked. It must remain for further consideration.

We described two maneuvers any remaining unchecked sentence may be subject to. By focussing on these maneuvers, we can specify two tests that a tableau extension must pass in order for us to check off the originating sentence.

(1) Is there any imaginable sentence that would conflict with the originating sentence but yet would not conflict with each path in the structure spawned by the originating sentence?

(2) Is there any *further* sentence that might be spawned by the originating sentence?

If the answer to either of these questions is "Yes," then the originating sentence *cannot be checked*. Checking it would carry the risk that a tableau that would otherwise close would remain open. It would carry the risk of a false positive on the question of consistency.

In the tableaux we have constructed so far, we have seen examples that passed both of these tests. (In those cases, we *did* check the sentence in question.) And we have seen examples that failed one or the other test, that is to say where the answer to one or the other test was "Yes." (In those cases we did *not* check the sentence.) It will help make the tests more understandable to review each kind of case. Let's begin with the unchecked cases.

A paradigm of the kind of sentence that fails the first test is a sentence with the word "because." Consider the following set of sentences, and a tableau *incorrectly* constructed from them.

√ I met my mechanic because my car wouldn't start, and I met my banker because I needed a loan

√ Either I didn't meet my mechanic, or else I met him, but it was not because my car wouldn't start

|

(3)   √ I met my mechanic because my car wouldn't start
             √ I met my banker because I needed a loan

|

(4)   I met my mechanic
                 My car wouldn't start

|

                 I met my banker
                 I needed a loan

|

I didn't meet my mechanic |

                        √ I met my mechanic, but it was not because my car wouldn't start

                        |

                            I met my mechanic
(5)   It was not because my car wouldn't
                            start that I met my mechanic

The right-hand path of this tableau remains open, as it should if the unchecked sentences in the path are considered together. These remaining sentences certainly describe a possible situation. But a thoughtful reading of the original sentences should give you pause. Are they really consistent? Of course they are not, and what has gone wrong is not anything in the tableau structures that have been created. Rather, what has gone wrong is checking off the sentences at (3) in the tableau. If those sentences, which centrally involve the word "because," had not been checked, we would have seen a conflict with sentence (5). In short, without sentence (3) the right-hand path describes a possible situation even though it includes the two sentences at (4) that have been spawned by sentence (3). But when sentence (3) is included in the path, the situation that the path describes is not a possible one. Then the tableau closes, as it should.

The lesson to be learned from this incorrectly drawn tableau is a clear one: though it is worthwhile to generate simpler sentences from those involving "because," the original sentence with its "because" must be left unchecked. A similar lesson applies to sentences left unchecked in tableaux (13.4), (13.6), (14.3), and (14.6), as well as to the sentence "John will happily go" and the sentence involving "since," both in tableau (15.1).

For a case that fails the second test, consider the incorrect tableau below.

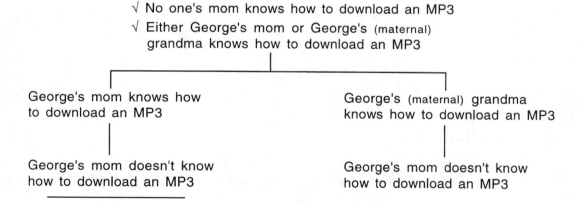

Though the left-hand branch closes, the unchecked sentences on the right clearly describe a possible situation, and so the branch has been left open. A second thought uncovers a problem. Isn't George's grandma herself someone's mom? The expression "no one" in the top sentence applies not only to George, but to George's mom as well, and in fact to many others. The top sentence should remain unchecked because further sentences might be spawned by it.

The correct tableau goes on to derive a further sentence from the first sentence, which continues to remain unchecked.

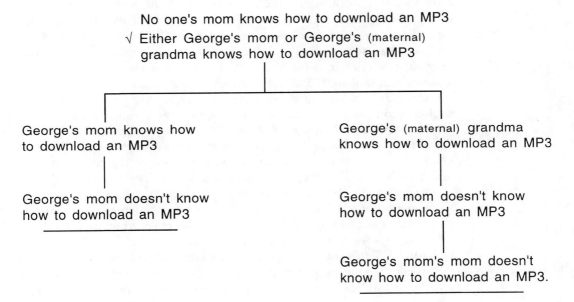

Since George's mom's mom is by definition his maternal grandma, there is a conflict. The right-hand situation is not really possible, and the tableau as a whole closes.

Going back to earlier constructions, we see a contrast. In tableau (15.1), several of the original sentences are checked. Consider the example,

(6)   John won't go without either Kay or his mother,

from which this branching structure was spawned.

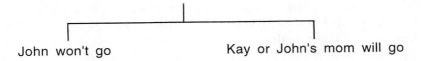

What imaginable sentence could conflict with (6)? An obvious choice is,

(7)   John *will* go without either Kay or his mother.

If (7) were to arise in a path originally including (6), it would close both of the branches spawned by (6). The same result will follow no matter what sentence you imagine in conflict with (6). That is why (6) passes the first test. As for the second test, (6) makes reference only to John, Kay, and John's mother, and only to the particular occasion in question. It will have no further offspring. In short, the logical content of (6) has been exhausted by the branching structure which it has spawned. Thus that structure can in effect *replace* the original sentence in a tableau. That is why we checked off (6) as it appeared in tableau (15.1) and ignored it thereafter.

Compared with computer-screen tableaux, our pencil-and-paper tableaux retain the advantage that we can review our constructions and survey the tableau as a whole for strategic purposes. Still we should draw a lesson from the computer systems as to checked sentences. Sentences that have been checked are typically complex and confusing. The check means that they can be ignored, and it is generally good policy to ignore them. Especially when reading up a so-far open path in order to determine whether it describes a possible situation, it is good practice to pass over the checked sentences. It is difficult to keep your attention on the situation as the description unfolds, difficult to be sure that the situation is indeed possible. Being rid of complex and confusing sentences makes that task easier and more failsafe. To be sure, in tableaux with sentences involving expressions like "everyone," "by doing such-and-such," and "predicted that," those complex sentences remain unchecked. Even so we should be grateful that other complex sentences, those involving "and," "unless," "at least so many," and many other expressions, can be checked off. Where sentences can be checked off, they should be, and the practical effect of the check should be that you pretend that the checked sentence is no longer there.

In this and the foregoing chapter we have used the tableau technique to assess both the consistency of sets of sentences and the validity of arguments. We have explained why tableaux are effective for these purposes. We have developed policies for making tableaux efficient and set out general principles about checking off sentences. Along the way we have surveyed a great many English sentences, considered their logical force, and discovered tableau structures appropriate to them. There seem to be countless sentence patterns in English and endless variety in the tableau problems that arise from them. In undertaking this general survey we hope to equip an ingenious and thoughtful reader with resources to apply to unforeseen and novel English sentences.

Even with this variety, we have had a glimpse (especially with the "if "-construction) of recurring tableau patterns. Our strategy in the second part of the book will be to identify a number of frequently occurring English constructions whose logical force is well understood by logicians. We will develop specific rules for handling a limited number of sentence constructions that are pervasive in logically sensitive discourse. In order to investigate these logically important constructions effectively, we will need a better understanding of the structure of English sentences generally. This need will be served by returning in the next chapter to the consideration of grammatical matters, which were last seen in Chapter II.

Exercises for Chapter IV

Determine whether the following arguments are valid by checking the consistency of their counter sets, using tableaux.

1.

> If the moon is a celestial object, then its surface is completely smooth.
>
> If the moon's surface is smooth, there can be no varying shadows on it.
>
> There are varying shadows on the moon's surface.
> _____
>
> The moon is not a celestial object.

2.

> The hydrogen was not ignited inside its tank if the fuel tank leaked.
>
> If there is no oxygen present, the hydrogen cannot burn in its tank.
>
> There is no oxygen present in the hydrogen tank.
> _____
>
> The fuel tank leaked.

3.

> I will take at least one science—physics, geology, or chemistry.
> If I take more than three courses, I will take music.
> I will take philosophy and either Greek or Latin.
> No one takes more than four courses.
> _____
> I will not take English.

4.

> My interview—if I am offered one—will occur before graduation.
> We will get married after I graduate if I'm not offered a job.
> I will be offered an interview, but not a job.
> _____
> Our wedding will occur after my interview.

5. Even when the following three sentences are given the most plausible readings, one of them remains anaphorically ambiguous.

Though he predicted that he would, Mussolini did not become an historically strong ruler.

If he did what Mussolini predicted he would, Hitler became his closest ally.

Hitler became what Mussolini predicted he would become.

Resolve the reference of the pronouns in two different but equally justifiable ways. Then, for each reading, use a tableau to determine whether a reader should infer that Hitler, and not Mussolini, became an historically strong ruler.

6. Given these facts, can you tell whether or not George reached the station before the police arrived? Use the tableau technique appropriately in justifying your answer.

Either George reached the station before the train left, or else the plan misfired because George was not on the train.

The train left before the police arrived, but the police found George's car in the lot.

George was on the train if his car was in the lot.

7. In each case below say whether the sentence can be checked off as a result of building below it in a tableau a structure of simpler or more specific sentences. Explain your answers.

    a. Of the next Winter and Summer Olympics, one of them will occur at least a year before the other.

    b. The reason that the nation's currency lost ten percent of its value today was that a serious trade deficit was revealed this morning.

    c. The store will be closed at least two days this week.

    d. The ministry of fisheries reduced quotas in order that the cod population on Georges Bank would recover.

    e. I reply within five minutes whenever I receive an e-mail message.

    f. From the the election of Hillary Rodham Clinton to the Presidency of the United States, it would not necessarily follow that Bill Clinton would become First Lady.

8. Use a tableau to determine whether the following set of sentences is consistent.

    > If any of Bush, McCain, or Gore is not nominated for President in 2004, surely he will not be nominated four years later.
    >
    > McCain will not be nominated in 2004 because Bush will be.
    >
    > Since Bush probably will be nominated that year, Gore won't be.
    >
    > McCain will be elected in 2008 unless Gore is.
    >
    > No one will be elected in any year unless he is nominated in that year.

V: Generative Grammar

> The following is a sentence of English. You have no doubt heard it before. But no one had heard it before 1863; surely this sentence had never been formulated before Lincoln formulated it. Even so, those listening in Gettysburg recognized it as a sentence of English, and most of them knew what it meant.

Four-score and seven years ago, our forefathers brought forth upon this continent a new nation, conceived in liberty, and dedicated to the proposition that all men are created equal.

> Though it is built up of exactly the same words, this next string of words is not a sentence of English. If Lincoln had said this, people would have looked at each other in confusion.

A ago all and are brought conceived continent created dedicated equal forefathers forth four-score in liberty men nation new our proposition seven that the this to upon years.

How do speakers of the language tell the difference? How do they know that the one is a sentence and the other is nonsense? It may be tempting to say that it is a matter of meaning. You know what the first one means, but the second doesn't mean anything. But here is a string that most readers will recognize as a sentence even though they don't know what it means.

> It is by amplitude, by frequency, or by phase that the photon
> flux can be modulated.

The words that make this sentence up are probably familiar to you, so you know they are words of English. But you probably don't know what several of the most important of them mean. So you don't know what the sentence means, but you know nonetheless that it is a sentence. In a famous example of Chomsky's, you do know what the words mean, but you still don't know what the sentence means. It seems to be nonsense.

> Colorless green ideas sleep furiously.

Even if it is nonsense, it is a different kind of nonsense from the earlier string that is not a sentence at all. That one is just word salad. Putting it that way makes it evident that we recognize a string as a sentence of English because of the way the words are put together in it.

This leads to the idea of a grammar in the sense that we will develop. There must be some ways of putting words together that make for sentences of English and other ways that do not. A **grammar**, as we will use the term, is a specification of those ways of putting words together that are grammatical, that is to say, those ways that result in genuine sentences of English. Since we are able to recognize sentences of English and distinguish them from ungrammatical strings, it follows that human beings somehow have at their command something that makes the distinction. What kind of thing is one of the great mysteries of human psychology, and one that contemporary linguistics hopes to solve. But at this stage we should be satisfied with much less. We want to be able to define the difference between sentences and word salad—between grammatical and ungrammatical—with some kind of specification, regardless of whether the specification is actually employed by human beings who speak and understand English. Such a specification, so long as it is precise enough to provide a determinate answer in every case, is what we mean by a grammar.

It is easy to specify the rather simple characteristic exemplified by the string of words given above, beginning "a ago all and are brought . . ." The words in it are in alphabetical order. We can imagine a language, call it "Alphabetese," whose words are those of English, but whose sentences are only those strings that are in alphabetical order. Its grammar is just the rules of alphabetizing. Of course the sentences of Alphabetese are nonsense, but there is an advantage here in illustrating how grammaticality can turn out not to depend on any judgment about meaning. We know when a string of words qualifies as a sentence of Alphabetese even though the string does not mean anything. The rules of alphabetizing are also very precise. Similarly we hope to find a grammar of English that does not depend on any notion of meaning and that is very precise. With a moment's thought we recognize that such a grammar will have to be much more complicated than the rules of alphabetizing, but perhaps one can be found.

The first person seriously to develop a grammar of English of this character was Noam Chomsky. Recognizing that the kind of precision desired is most readily found in mathematics, Chomsky adapted mathematical devices that had earlier been developed by such logicians as Emil Post and Rudolf Carnap and such mathematicians as Claude Shannon. The research program in linguistics that Chomsky inaugurated is called generative grammar, in reference to these devices. A **generative grammar** is an abstract device that generates strings of words. In doing so it implicitly defines a language. Any string that could be generated by the grammar in question is *ipso facto* grammatical; it is a sentence of the language so defined. Conversely, when we have already in mind a language such as English, we want a generative grammar that can generate only strings that are indeed grammatical sentences of English. If it could generate any sentence of English whatever, then it effectively distinguishes grammatical from ungrammatical. It counts as a grammar in just the sense we mean. Of course there are a great many sentences of English. As illustrated by the novelty of Lincoln's opening Gettysburg sentence, new ones are formulated and articulated every day. Thus it is only in an abstract, mathematical sense that a device could generate all of these sentences. Here is another reason that Chomsky's approach was mathematical.

To get an idea of the range of sentences that an adequate grammar of English would have to generate, we can consider the familiar nursery rhyme, "The House That Jack Built." Children of age three or four understand the rhyme, and in fact are amused by its grammatical structure. This is evidence that the knowledge of language that they have achieved at that young age includes the ability to distinguish the grammatical from the ungrammatical in the sense that we have described. It is also evidence that their knowledge ranges over grammatical sentences that are indefinitely many in number and variety. The notion that a grammar should generate the sentences rather than simply surveying them, or characterizing them in static structural terms, derives from this fact of infinite variety.

THE HOUSE THAT JACK BUILT

This is the house that Jack built.

This is the malt that lay in the house that Jack built.

This is the rat that ate the malt that lay in the house that Jack built.

This is the cat that killed the rat that ate the malt that lay in the house that Jack built.

This is the dog that worried the cat that killed the rat that ate the malt that lay in the house that Jack built.

This is the cow with the crumpled horn, that tossed the dog that worried the cat that killed the rat that ate the malt that lay in the house that Jack built.

This is the maiden all forlorn, that milked the cow with the crumpled horn, that tossed the dog that worried the cat that killed the rat that ate the malt that lay in the house that Jack built.

This is the man all tattered and torn, that kissed the maiden all forlorn, that milked the cow with the crumpled horn, that tossed the dog that worried the cat that killed the rat that ate the malt that lay in the house that Jack built.

This is the priest all shaven and shorn, that married the man all tattered and torn, that kissed the maiden all forlorn, that milked the cow with the crumpled horn, that tossed the dog that worried the cat that killed the rat that ate the malt that lay in the house that Jack built.

This is the cock that crowed in the morn, that waked the priest all shaven and shorn, that married the man all tattered and torn, that kissed the maiden all forlorn, that milked the cow with the crumpled horn, that tossed the dog that worried the cat that killed the rat that ate the malt that lay in the house that Jack built.

This is the farmer sowing the corn, that kept the cock that crowed in the morn, that waked the priest all shaven and shorn, that married the man all tattered and torn, that kissed the maiden all forlorn, that milked the cow with the crumpled horn, that tossed the dog that worried the cat that killed the rat that ate the malt that lay in the house that Jack built.

§18   PHRASE-STRUCTURE GRAMMARS; PHRASE-MARKERS

The most successful and widely used kind of generative device, for both natural and artificial languages, is what is called a phrase-structure grammar. (Some writers use the term context-free grammar. There is a technical distinction to be made here, but not one that need concern us.) A **phrase-structure grammar** consists of a set of **rewriting rules**, as illustrated by the following.

(1) A Simple Phrase-Structure Grammar

Sentence ⇒ Noun Phrase   Verb Phrase

Noun Phrase ⇒ Noun

Verb Phrase ⇒ Verb Transitive   Noun Phrase

Verb Phrase ⇒   Verb Intransitive

Verb Phrase ⇒ **are**   Adjective

Noun ⇒ **cats** | **mice** | **seeds** | **barns** | ...

Verb Transitive ⇒ **love** | **eat** | **chase** | ...

Verb Intransitive ⇒ **sleep** | **run** | **lie** | ...

Adjective ⇒ **fat** | **sleepy** | **hungry** | ...

Each rewriting rule consists of a **non-terminal symbol**, followed by "⇒", followed by a string of non-terminal and **terminal symbols**. Roughly speaking, the non-terminal symbols are the names of phrase-classes, and the terminal symbols are items of vocabulary. One of the non-terminal symbols is designated as the **initial symbol**. In this grammar, the initial symbol is "Sentence"; this names a special phrase-class in that sentences are the smallest phrases that constitute grammatical utterances in their own right. As we saw in Chapter I, in this sense, the sentence is the basic unit of language.

A phrase-structure grammar generates sentences by way of a graphical structure called a **phrase-marker**. Every phrase-marker begins with the initial symbol. Since in this simple grammar only one rewriting rule begins with "Sentence," the phrase-marker must begin as follows.

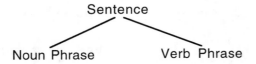

Each of the rewriting rules may be regarded as a license to extend a branch of the phrase-marker that currently ends with a non-terminal symbol, by selecting a rewriting rule for that non-terminal symbol and adding a branch for each symbol to the right of the "⇒". In fact, the "⇒" may conveniently be read as "may consist of," with the adjacent symbols to the right of the "⇒" read with the words "followed by" interposed. Thus the first and third rewriting rules say, in effect, that a sentence may consist of a noun phrase followed by a verb phrase and that a verb phase may consist of a transitive verb followed by a noun phrase. The branches of the phrase-marker are continued by successive application of the various rewriting rules until every branch ends with a terminal symbol.

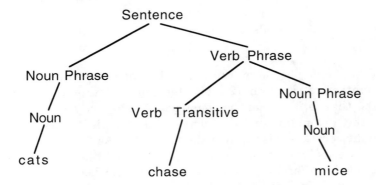

Arrayed across the bottom of the completed phrase-marker is a **terminal string**, i.e., a string of terminal symbols. The main idea of phrase-structure grammar is that such a terminal string is, by definition, a grammatical string. In effect this last phrase-marker shows that the string, "cats chase mice," is indeed a sentence of English.

   Obviously other kinds of sentence are generated by the phrase-structure grammar in (1). An even simpler phrase-marker is this one.

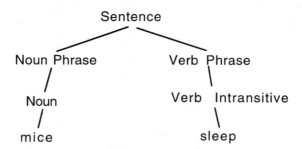

It generates the sentence, "mice sleep." Now consider the data about grammaticality listed in (2). As speakers of English we recognize that the strings on the left are grammatical, and that those on the right are not.

(2) Data About Grammaticality

Grammatical	Problematic	Ungrammatical
cats eat	seeds eat	eat cats
mice sleep		
cats chase mice	cats sleep mice	chase mice cats
mice eat seeds	barns eat seeds	
mice are hungry	seeds are sleepy	are hungry mice
seeds are brown		mice are sleep

As it happens phrase-markers can be constructed for all of the grammatical strings in (2), but for none of the ungrammatical strings, that is, they can be constructed using only rewriting rules from the grammar in (1). Thus this simple phrase-structure grammar serves to distinguish the two lists. As for the problematic cases, "seeds eat" turns out to be grammatical, as shown by substituting different terminal symbols in the last phrase-marker. ("Seeds are sleepy" does, too.) On the other hand, "cats sleep mice" is not grammatical; the rewriting rules effectively distinguish transitive from intransitive verbs, requiring a noun phrase (traditionally called the "direct object") to follow transitive verbs, but not allowing it for intransitive ones. Of course this grammar generates only a tiny fraction of the grammatical sentences of English, but for strings limited to the small number of vocabulary items mentioned in it, the range of this simple grammar is remarkably good. Our strategy will be to add to this grammar, so that more and more sentences are successively generated, all of which we recognize as grammatical strings of English. Initially we will simply adopt more rewriting rules, including rules with terminal symbols.

Let's begin this augmentation by adding the following rewriting rule to the grammar.

Noun Phrase ⇒ Adjective   Noun Phrase

With this rule, somewhat more elaborate sentences are generated, illustrated by the following.

sleepy mice sleep
cats chase brown mice
fat cats are hungry
fat sleepy cats eat

But notice that something remarkable has happened. Here we have a single rewriting rule that can be applied repeatedly in a single phrase-marker. Applying it twice results in a sentence with a string of two adjectives. In fact the single rule can be applied indefinitely many times, producing a string of indefinitely many adjectives in the sentence which is ultimately generated. We define a **recursive** rewriting rule as one in which the (non-terminal) symbol to the left of the arrow occurs again—recurs—somewhere to the right of the arrow. So here we have our first example of a recursive rule.

When we add just a few more rules, we have a grammar of surprising power, in the sense of its capacity to generate a large number and variety of sentences.

Noun Phrase ⇒ Noun **that** Verb Phrase

Noun Phrase ⇒ Noun Prepositional Phrase

Prepositional Phrase ⇒ Preposition   Noun Phrase

Preposition ⇒ **in** | **by** | **on** | **over** | ...

The following sentences are generated, as well as many more, but still no strings are generated that are clearly ungrammatical to our unspoiled ears.

cats that are hungry love mice
mice eat seeds that are brown
cats in barns chase mice
cats in corners of barns sleep

None of these new rules are recursive themselves, but they have the same explosive effect on the original simple grammar at (1). Many, many sentences are generated because structures like Noun Phrase can have additional NP's nested within them without limit. Part of the explanation for this possibility lies in the recurrence of the symbol NP in the rewriting rule for the non-terminal symbol PP, which itself occurs in the second of the new rewriting rules for NP. And so we say, more generally, that a **recursive grammar** is one in which there is some non-terminal symbol that you can reach again by successive applications of various of the rewriting rules.

Another rule involving prepositional phrases,

Verb Phrase ⇒ Verb Phrase Prepositional Phrase

licenses this phrase-marker:

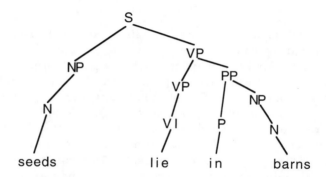

And so sentences like these are grammatical:

fat cats sleep in dark corners
mice hold seeds with tiny paws

Though we began with quite simple sentences—those generated by the rules in (1)—even the modest set of rewriting rules we have so far set out enables us to generate sentences of great complexity. In fact with these rules we can generate "House That Jack Built" sentences:

seeds lie in barns
mice eat seeds that lie in barns
cats chase mice that eat seeds that lie in barns

The phrase-marker for the third of these sentences looks like this. Scanning down the right-hand branch, notice the recurrence of NP and VP and NP and VP.

(3)

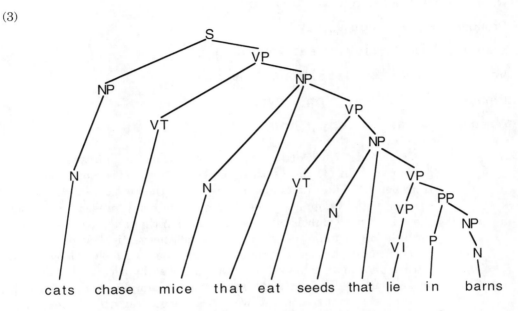

What is crucial in particular for these sentences is the occurrence of Noun Phrase in the rewriting rule for Verb Phrase that handles transitive verbs, together with the recurrence of Verb Phrase in the new rewriting rule for Noun Phrase that generates "that"-clauses. (Such clauses are traditionally called "relative clauses.")

Putting together all of the rewriting rules that we have added, we have the following rather complex grammar.

(4) A Recursive Phrase-Structure Grammar

Sentence ⇒ Noun Phrase   Verb Phrase

Noun Phrase ⇒ Adjective   Noun Phrase

      | Noun   **that**   Verb Phrase

      | Noun   Prepositional Phrase

      | Noun | Pronoun

Verb Phrase ⇒ Verb Phrase   Prepositional Phrase

      | Verb Transitive   Noun Phrase | Verb Intransitive

      | **are**   Adjective

Prepositional Phrase ⇒ Preposition   Noun Phrase

Noun ⇒ **cats | mice | seeds | barns |** ...

Pronoun ⇒ **we | you | they**

Verb Transitive ⇒ **love | eat | chase |** ...

Verb Intransitive ⇒ **sleep | run | lie |** ...

Preposition ⇒ **in | by | on | over |** ...

Adjective ⇒ **fat | sleepy | hungry |** ...

A word is in order on the notation for phrase-structure grammars. In (4) the vertical stroke ("|") appears more frequently than before. Like the double arrow ("⇒"), the vertical stroke is not a symbol of the language whose grammar is being presented. Rather these both are symbols of a special notation that we have reserved for formulating grammars. You may read the vertical stroke as "or." Thus a noun phrase may consist of an adjective followed by a noun phrase *or* a noun followed by "that" followed by a verb phrase *or* ... *or* a pronoun. The vertical-stroke notation simply abbreviates what, in a more formal treatment, would be several rewriting rules. In an unabbreviated formulation of this grammar there would be five different rewriting rules for Noun Phrase, each specifying a unique string of non-terminal and terminal symbols, namely the string to the right of the double arrow.

We can finish our introductory treatment of phrase-structure grammars by noting that many other linguistic concepts can be defined in terms of phrase-markers. Besides their utility in defining grammaticality, these grammars give us a way of portraying the structure of the sentence precisely. We can take advantage of these portrayals to define linguistic concepts that have structural content.

To **parse** a sentence is to construct a phrase-marker for it using a particular phrase-structure grammar. (We will use this term in a more general sense later in the chapter.) Parsing a sentence confirms that it is grammatical, but it also determines the structure of the sentence under the grammar. (All of these notions must be understood relative to the grammar that is used for parsing the sentence.)

We say that a non-terminal symbol **dominates** the string of terminal symbols that appears below it in the phrase-marker.

A string of terminal symbols is a **sentence** of the language if there is a phrase-marker in which it is dominated by the symbol "Sentence." The same goes for other **phrase-classes**. For example, a terminal string is a noun phrase if there is a phrase-marker in which it is dominated by the non-terminal symbol "Noun Phrase." We will generally use capital letters with these non-terminal symbols as a reminder that the phrase-class in question is supported by the rewriting rules of a plausible phrase-structure grammar.

A **constituent** of a sentence is a part of the sentence that is dominated by some non-terminal symbol or other in the phrase-marker for the sentence. Referring to the phrase-marker (3) above, we see that "seeds that lie in barns" is a constituent of the sentence,

(5)   cats chase mice that eat seeds that lie in barns.

It is dominated by the symbol "NP." On the other hand, "mice that eat seeds" is not a constituent of (5), even though it appears in that sentence. There is no symbol that dominates just this phrase, in the phrase-marker (3). (Of course it is a constituent of other sentences, e.g., of "Cats chase mice that eat seeds.") Talking about constituents is a brief way of partially indicating the structure of the sentence.

The final definition is a little harder to see through. The **scope** of a word (or of a phrase) in a particular sentence is the shortest constituent of the sentence which includes the given word (or phrase) along with something else. Again we can refer to (3), which is the phrase-marker for (5). What is the scope of "mice"? We have seen that it can't be "mice that eat seeds" because that is not a constituent. The shortest constituent phrase that includes "mice" is the noun phrase,

(6)   mice that eat seeds that lie in barns.

It certainly includes words besides "mice" so (6) is the scope of "mice" in (5). What about the following phrase? What is its scope?

(7)   eat seeds that lie in barns

The expression at (7) is dominated by "VP" in (3), so it is a constituent, but we have to include some other words along with the words in (7). In order to do so, we move up the phrase-marker from "VP." The next higher symbol in the phrase-marker is "NP," and the phrase that it dominates is (6). That will turn out to be the shortest constituent that includes (7) along with something else. So the scope of (7) is (6), just as the scope of "mice" is (6). This concept of scope may seem cumbersome, but it will turn out to be very useful in talking about ambiguity and about related logical matters.

Before giving a precise account of the transformational component of our grammar and learning how to use it in parsing sentences, let us consider an example made famous by Chomsky in early expositions of transformational grammar, namely, the sentence, "John is easy to please." At first glance it might seem that this sentence could easily be accommodated by adding slightly to our phrase-structure grammar. After all we already have sentences like "cats are hungry." But notice that we really should think of "John" as the object of the verb "to please." In fact, we might as well have used the sentence, "It is easy to please John," in which explicitly it is John to whom the pleasing is to be directed. Yet this latter sentence seems even more peculiar in the light of our phrase-structure grammar. Though indeed it can be divided into NP and VP, the main Noun Phrase turns out to be the single word "it" and the Verb Phrase everything else. The Verb Phrase seems to be doing all the work, and the Noun Phrase to be doing nothing. (What is "it" anyway?) Happily, another equivalent sentence comes to mind, "To please John is easy." Here "John" is in its rightful place, receiving the pleasing. But also, the right thing is said to be easy, namely, pleasing John, rather than John himself. And finally, not much of an addition to the phrase-structure grammar would be required to generate this third sentence, in accordance with these hunches about how it means what it does.

Whatever the force of these informal considerations, it is beyond dispute that these three sentences,

> John is easy to please.
>
> It is easy to please John.
>
> To please John is easy.

are equivalent in some strong sense. We might say that they are synonymous, that they mean the same thing. But meaning the same thing for them is not like two otherwise unrelated words—"stroll," "perambulate"—meaning the same thing. These three really seem at root to be the same sentence, with the words switched around to be sure, but switched around in a way that leaves the sentence meaning what it did before. (Of course not every way of switching them around will leave the meaning the same; compare, "It is easy for John to please," or "Please, be easy to John.") The strategy of transformational grammar is to capture this equivalence by accommodating only one of them—the last—within the phrase-structure component. That third sentence is called the **underlying string** in relation to the other two. The latter are each accounted the result of transformations operating on the phrase-marker of that underlying string. Then each of them are seen to be **transformational equivalents** of the underlying sentence.

Let's use a different example and a particularly familiar transformation to see how to handle transformations formally. The sentence,

(1) Mice are chased by cats,

exemplifies what the traditional grammar called "passive voice." Its "active voice" formulation,

(2) Cats chase mice,

is familiar to us from the phrase-structure grammar (18.4). In fact we have seen the phrase-marker for (2) before.

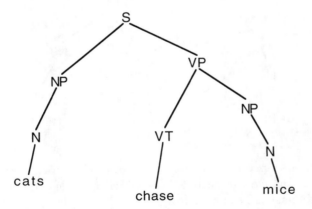

We say that (2) is the underlying string for the passive voice sentence (1). It is crucial that the underlying string be generated by the phrase-structure component of the grammar, that is, that there be a phrase-marker for the underlying string, constructed using the available rewriting rules. We call this the **underlying phrase-marker**. According to standard treatments of transformational

grammar, this underlying phrase-marker is transformed, to
generate our target sentence (1). Since phrase-markers are two-
dimensional objects, it would be difficult to actually transform them
as wholes on paper. For the sake of specifying parsing precisely, we
will represent this process somewhat differently. In order to take
this next step in parsing, we must have available a stock of
transformations. In the present case the Passive Transformation
will suffice.

(3) Passive Transformation

NP_1 VT NP_2 $\Rightarrow$

NP_2 **are**   VT   Past Participle   (**by** NP_1)

Note that the transformation has a string of non-terminal
symbols on the left and a different string, in this case including both
terminal and non-terminal symbols, on the right. When we inspect
the underlying phrase-marker, we recognize that there is a special
way of **pruning** its branches, as follows.

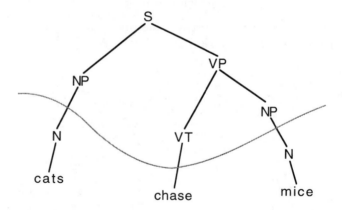

This particular pruning results in a **non-terminal string**—those
symbols just above the dotted-line—which matches the string on the
left in the Passive Transformation.

To construct the **derived phrase-marker**, we begin with that part
of the underlying phrase-marker above the pruning. Then we apply
the Passive Transformation, indicated by the large vertical arrow.
(See the next page.) The result, of course, is a transformed non-
terminal string.

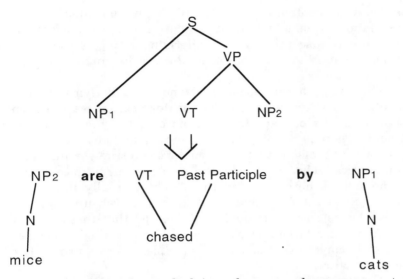

In order to complete the underlying phrase-marker, we revert to rewriting rules from the phrase-structure component. Each of the non-terminal symbols in the transformed string must be extended, in accordance with rewriting rules, until only terminal symbols remain. Notice the numerical subscripts on the transformation as it has been applied in the derived phrase-marker. Their only purpose is to provide a correlation between corresponding non-terminal symbols before and after the transformation has been effected. For each non-terminal symbol after the transformation, the phrase-marker should be extended in exactly the way it was extended, for the corresponding non-terminal symbol, in the underlying phrase-marker. The ultimate result should be a terminal string which matches, word for word, the sentence with which we began, in this case, sentence (1). Because it is this string that is actually spoken or heard, it is called the **surface string**.

Notice that the Passive Transformation itself introduces certain terminal symbols, namely, "are," "by," and even the peculiar symbol "Past Participle." If we think of the latter as a terminal symbol, we need not go beyond what is specified in the rewriting rules. We can think of the spoken form "chased" as generated by these *two* (terminal) symbols, "chase" and Past Participle, not by the phrase-structure component, but by phonological principles. The idea is that it is just a matter of how these terminal symbols are articulated vocally. More typical of our syntactic concerns is the terminal symbol "by." We see now why it is a misconception to ask, as we did early in Chapter I, what this little word means. The word "by," as used in passive-voice sentences, doesn't really have a meaning, certainly not in isolation. It simply marks the occurrence, in the surface string, of the noun phrase that in the underlying string is the main noun phrase, that is to say, the Noun Phrase dominated by the initial symbol Sentence.

The underlying phrase-marker and the underlying string that it generates constitute what is called the **deep structure** of the sentence. This term has perhaps inspired more mystery-mongering than it should. There is nothing particularly profound about deep structure. It is simply the structure that portrays the true—or fundamental— grammatical relations among the words in the surface string. For example it is here revealed that "cats" is really the main Noun Phrase of the sentence, and that "chase" is a transitive verb that has "mice" as its object. It might be expected that these fundamental grammatical relations most influence the meaning of the sentence, and so it may be that semantic principles operate primarily on the deep structure.

The parentheses in the passive transformation (3) indicate that the enclosed symbols are optional in the resulting string. We are really abbreviating a distinct transformation, called a **deletion rule**. Thus the passive transformation generates sentences like these.

>   mice with long tails are chased by cats with sharp claws
>   cats that chase mice are punished by noisy dogs

And then the deletion rule shortens them into sentences like these.

>   mice with long tails are chased
>   cats that chase mice are punished

What we have called a phrase-structure grammar remains as a part of a larger whole and thus is now called the **phrase-structure component**. In order to widen the range of available sentences, and to provide material for transformations, we will now enlarge the phrase-structure component. We will add to the grammar of (18.4) even more rewriting rules, all of which can be applied repeatedly. The first of these is itself recursive, providing for sentences with arbitrarily many subsentences. Even the rule that introduces Subordinating Conjunctions permits arbitrarily many subsentences on the left. And the new Noun Phrase goes in two steps to the rule for Finite Clauses, in which Noun Phrase recurs. These several rules result, for the first time, in whole sentences with parts that themselves are sentences, or at least clauses. We call these wholes **complex sentences**, and it will be with their analysis that we return to topics in logic, in the next chapter.

(4) Additional Rewriting Rules

Sentence ⇒ Sentence   Conjunction   Sentence

Sentence ⇒ Sentence   Subordinate Clause

Subordinate Clause ⇒ Subordinating Conj   Sentence

Noun Phrase ⇒ Clause

Clause ⇒ **that**   Finite Clause

Finite Clause ⇒ Noun Phrase   Verb Phrase

Conjunction ⇒ **and** | **or** | **but** | ...

Subordinating Conj ⇒ **because** | **if** | **unless** | **since** | ...

With these additions to the phrase-structure component of our grammar, the following complex sentences are generated, among many others. (As before we are ignoring niceties of capitalization and punctuation. But now we begin to miss these embellishments of written English; they would help us to recognize the constituent structure of complex sentences as we read along.)

mice sleep and mice eat seeds
cats chase mice and cats catch mice
cats chase mice or mice chase cats
mice eat seeds but cats eat mice
seeds lie in barns but cats chase mice and dogs chase cats
cats catch mice because barns are dark
cats are hungry if dogs chase mice
mice eat seeds but cats eat mice since seeds grow on plants
cats chase mice and cats catch mice because they are cruel

In (4) there is a new rule for Noun Phrase. In order to take advantage of it, we need to recognize some additional transitive verbs.

Verb Transitive ⇒ **know** | **fear** | **smell** | ...

With these added verbs we get sentences like these,

mice fear cats
cats smell mice

But more interesting are sentences where one of the new verbs takes as object one of the new Noun Phrases, traditionally called a "noun clause." Each of these consists of the word "that" following by a Finite Clause (which is the same as a simple NP-VP sentence).

cats know that mice are sleepy
mice fear that cats eat small animals
mice smell that seeds lie in barns

These transitive verbs that we have added are called verbs of **propositional attitude**. The noun clause that is the typical object of such a verb itself expresses a proposition. And many of these verbs have psychological import, expressing some cognitive or emotional relation—a matter of attitude—between the subject and the proposition in question. Propositional attitudes and the verbs that express them have been the focus of much philosophical inquiry, raising issues that we will not pursue.

Yet another variety of sentence comes to mind when we augment our stock of adjectives.

Adjective ⇒ **true** | **false** | **obvious** | **certain**

| **probable** | **likely** | ...

Again making use of the new kind of Noun Phrase, we get,

(5)   that cats chase mice is obvious
                        that cats eat seeds is false
                        that elephants fear mice is certain
                        that elephants remember is likely

To maintain the precision that we have insisted upon, we should acknowledge a complication that has intruded for the first time in the fragment of English that is generated by our developing grammar. The terminal symbol "**are**" was first introduced, in the grammar of (18.1), by a rewriting rule specifying that a Verb Phrase may consist of that word followed by an Adjective. Here, as with all our nouns and verbs, we have limited ourselves to the plural form. Our restraint has enabled us to avoid complications involved with grammatical **number**. (Similarly we have simplified matters of person and tense.) A complete grammar of English would treat number as a syntactic entity in its own right, perhaps as a special kind of terminal symbol. Rules would be invoked to ensure that the main NP and VP of a sentence agree in number. Just now we have had to loosen our simplifying restraint in order to accommodate the new Noun Phrases, which are inherently singular in number. For the sake of this one kind of Noun Phrase, we will write, without further comment, the singular "**is**" where it is needed.

This is a good point at which to acknowledge another complication of a really adequate grammar for English. Thoughtful readers will have noticed that we have been careful to list only favorable examples of new sentences that are generated by the additional rewriting rules that we have introduced. In fact such odd—and perhaps not really grammatical—strings as these are also generated.

> mice chase that mice are sleepy
> that cats chase mice is hungry
> that elephants remember love that cats eat seeds

These unwelcome sentences should remind you of the problematic strings of (18.2). We decided to live with sentences like "barns eat seeds" and "seeds are sleepy." To eliminate such sentences we would have to proliferate phrase-classes and rewriting rules in unacceptable profusion. Instead we admit these as grammatical and ascribe their oddity, in effect, to their uselessness. We could take the same attitude toward this new batch of odd strings. But generative grammars have another twist that quite certainly would eliminate the recent unwelcome strings, and perhaps would prevail against the earlier ones as well. What are called **selection restrictions** ensure compatibility between nouns and verbs, and even between noun phrases and adjectives, somewhat analogously to principles that ensure agreement in number. Such restrictions could be introduced to confine the new kind of Noun Phrase to verbs of propositional attitude. Similarly, only what might be called propositional adjectives—"true" and "false" rather than "fat" and "happy"—could be applied to these new Noun Phrases. (On the other hand, such strings as, "That mice are sleepy occurs to many hungry cats," or "That elephants cower amazes harmless mice," seem to be fully grammatical.) Once we have the device of selection restrictions we might well return to cases like "barns eat seeds." The distinction between agent and artifact could restrict the kind of noun that can go with action-verbs like "eat" and "chase." Again these are matters developed, with some accompanying controversy, in full-blown grammars. We do well to set them aside in order to concentrate on syntactic devices more central to our aims.

To conclude our treatment of transformations, we introduce one that is very widely applicable. Though it underlies the equivalence of "It is easy to please John," and "To please John is easy," we will introduce it in a more general form.

(6) Extraposition

Clause VP ⇒ **It** VP Clause

Our phrase-structure component, which generates but a small fraction of even basic English sentences, does include finite clauses. The grammar of English also provides for infinite clauses, but we will not add them to our small grammar. "To please John" is such an infinite, or untensed, clause. Extraposition applies to underlying phrase-markers whose main noun phrase is a clause of either kind. Four examples with finite clauses were listed at (5). The new transformation takes those underlying strings into the following surface strings.

> it is obvious that cats chase mice
> it is false that cats eat seeds
> it is certain that elephants fear mice
> it is likely that elephants remember

Perhaps it even transforms the somewhat surprising case,

> that elephants cower amazes harmless mice,

into the more familiar sentence,

> it amazes harmless mice that elephants cower.

In this section we have introduced a new kind of grammatical device, the transformation. We could have introduced a large number of new rewriting rules to account for the new sentences we have noted. Instead a transformational grammar accounts for them as transformed versions of sentences we already have in our phrase-structure component. The advantage of transformational grammar lies not only in the efficiency afforded by this means, but also in certifying an equivalence between sentences that indeed appear to be closely related. Another advantage will emerge in the next section as we develop an explanation of structural ambiguity.

§20   SYNTACTIC AMBIGUITY

In Chapter II we distinguished structural ambiguity from ambiguities arising from other determinants of the meaning of a sentence. More recently, with no greater ambition than to distinguish grammatical strings from others in a systematic way, we introduced the idea of a grammar of English. We proposed phrase-structure grammars as a generative device for effectively fulfilling that ambition, but true to their name, phrase-structure grammars also tell us something about the structure of grammatical strings. It turns out that what they tell us about structure helps us to understand ambiguity as well. Perhaps the most central kind of ambiguity due to structure is what we will call syntactic ambiguity. A string is **syntactically ambiguous** if there are two distinct phrase-markers for which it is the terminal string.

Syntactic ambiguity arises even in the relatively simple grammar of (18.4). Here is a phrase-marker, using rewriting rules from that grammar, resulting in the sentence, "Cats chase mice in dark corners."

(1)

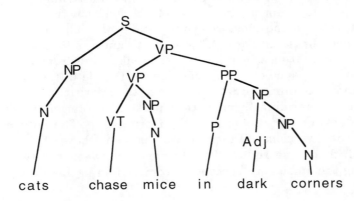

The very same sentence issues from a phrase-marker that is obviously different in its shape, and that can be seen to utilize different rewriting rules. Thus the sentence at hand is syntactically ambiguous.

(2)

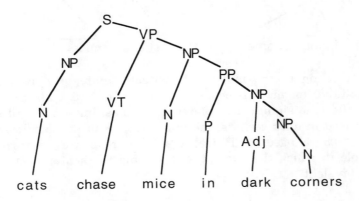

There is no question of lexical ambiguity here. Note that each of the ultimate branches uses a rewriting rule that takes us from a single non-terminal symbol to the respective item of vocabulary—e.g. "Noun ⇒ **cats.** And each of these ultimate branches appears without variation in both phrase-markers. As we reflect further, it is apparent that each of the words means the same thing in the one sentence as in the other. Thus, what we have is not a lexical ambiguity; to the extent that the sentences differ in meaning, the difference does not arise from differences in the meaning of the words, but rather from the structures in which the words are located.

Before going on to other examples of syntactic ambiguity, it will be helpful to adopt a convention of abbreviation that will help us concentrate on the most relevant details of a phrase-marker. In these two phrase-markers, all we need to know is that there is some way of generating the relevant terminal string from a particular non-terminal symbol. We can ignore the details. Thus, in an **abbreviated phrase-marker** some of the rewriting rules taking us from a non-terminal symbol to a part of the terminal string are passed over and replaced with a triangle. The following are abbreviated versions of the prior two phrase-markers, of (1) on the left and of (2) on the right. The difference between the two ways of parsing the ambiguous sentence becomes vivid in these diagrams.

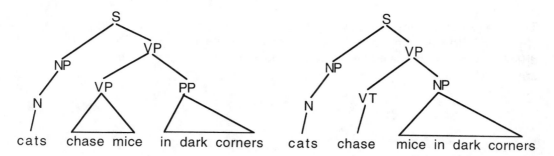

Returning to the matter of syntactic ambiguity, it might be objected that too much is being made here of different ways of parsing that reflect no significant differences in meaning. After all if mice are chased in dark corners, the mice must *be* in the dark corners in order to be chased, and vice versa. In response we turn to an example in which the two ways of parsing the sentence are clearly not equivalent.

(3)

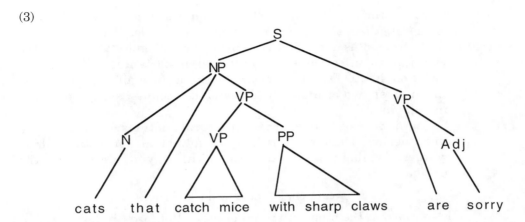

Clearly it means one thing for the mice to be caught with sharp claws, and it means another for the mice to have sharp claws.

(4)

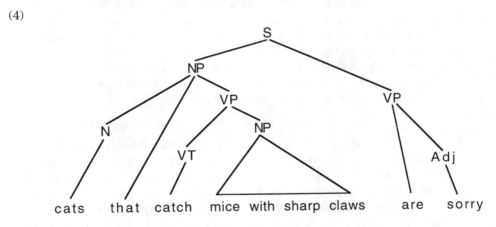

This difference reflects the difference between these two phrase-markers, even if it be granted that the meanings of all the words stay the same across the two interpretations. Here we have an illustration of how the meaning of a sentence depends not only on the meanings of the words in it, but on how the words are put together. And how the words are put together is not just a matter of the order in which they come, one after another, but also of how they are grouped together as parts of the sentence.

It is easy to imagine a situation in which cats by whom mice are caught with sharp claws would not be sorry, but yet cats by whom mice with sharp claws are caught *would* be sorry. And so the syntactic disambiguation provided by these two phrase-markers is logically crucial. We will call a sentence syntactically ambiguous whenever it has alternative phrase-markers under the grammar we have accepted as authoritative. Syntactic ambiguity always has the potential to affect matters of logical importance. Though the variation in its meaning seems subtle or insignificant, even the terminal string common to (1) and (2) counts as syntactically ambiguous.

In §18 we defined the structural notions of scope and constituency. These are especially useful notions for distinguishing syntactic ambiguities. An economical way of describing the ambiguity of

cats chase mice in dark corners

is to contrast the scope of the prepositional phrase "in dark corners" determined by the respective phrase-markers, (1) and (2). In (2), when you continue up from PP, you next come upon NP. The string that is dominated by NP is "mice in dark corners." Since that is the shortest constituent which includes "in dark corners" along with something else, the noun phrase is, by the definition of scope, the scope of the prepositional phrase. In the phrase-marker (1), the scope of the prepositional phrase is the verb phrase "catch mice in dark corners." Turning to the other example of ambiguity, we can most pointedly indicate the intended interpretation of

cats that catch mice with sharp claws are sorry

by saying that we do not intend "mice with sharp claws" to be a constituent of the sentence—that way it's not the mice that have the sharp claws! That would eliminate the phrase-marker (4), and determine that the intended parsing is the one given by (3).

An even more interesting source of ambiguity lies in the transformational component of a grammar. A single surface string like

(5)   elephants are lucky to remember

is ambiguous because two different strings may underlie it. (5) may be understood as equivalent to

(6)   that elephants remember is lucky (for them).

Or, alternatively, it may be understood as equivalent to

(7)   (for anyone) to remember elephants is lucky.

We will not spell out the underlying phrase-markers because, among other things, we would need further to augment both our phrase-structure and transformational components. But the rough idea is that (6) is transformed by Extraposition into

(8)   it is lucky that elephants remember,

and (8) is further transformed into (5) by a ubiquitous transformation called Raising. By contrast (7) is transformed, again by Extraposition, into

(9)   it is lucky to remember elephants,

and (9) is further transformed into (5) by a quite special transformation called "Tough"-Movement. Only a limited class of adjectives, including "tough" and "lucky," are subject to this transformation, which raises the *object* of the transitive verb "to remember." ("Elephants are unprecedented to remember" is not grammatical, though "Elephants are novel to remember" seems to be.)

The ambiguity of (5) is rather hard to discriminate. Hearing its different interpretations is rather like switching from one reading to the other of the famous gestalt drawing of an old crone in profile versus a standing ingénue viewed from the back. In order to easily move from one way of parsing of (5) to the other, remember the parallel contrast between "Elephants are likely to remember" and "Elephants are tough to remember."

A final caution is in order. For the sake of brevity, we have lately been speaking of one terminal string being transformed into another. But of course transformations really operate on phrase-markers, or perhaps on non-terminal strings, as in our formal notations for the Passive Transformation and for Exposition. In order fully to portray the operation of these transformations and the resulting ambiguity— of (5), for example—two complete parsings would have to be given. In each parsing, there would first be given the underlying phrase-marker, which terminates in the underlying string. Then there would be given the derived phrase-marker. In each complete parsing of (5), two different transformations would each be portrayed in the derived phrase-marker.

This account of syntactic ambiguity is the most visible fruit of our structural theory of grammaticality. Within a phrase-structure grammar, a single string can issue from two different phrase-markers. Because of such ambiguity, a great many sentences turn out, in the terminology of Chapters I and II, potentially to express two or more distinct propositions. With the addition of transformations, with their powers of rearranging and deleting various segments of the underlying sentence, many more syntactic ambiguities emerge, presumably including many of those surveyed in §6.

Also remember, as we return to logical analysis, that our account of grammar can contribute much more. As we dissect and manipulate sentences, we have a basis for recognizing their true constituents—even underlying constituents, which appear only in underlying phrase-markers. And transformations carry with them a precise notion of equivalence between two sentences, one of which might yield to logical analysis more readily than the other. All of this is achieved without recourse to claims about meaning, a notion that appeals to ordinary sensibilities, but that does not enter into theorizing so fruitfully as does the notion of structure.

Exercises for Chapter V

1. Construct phrase-markers to show that the phrase-structure grammar of (18.4) generates each of the following strings.

    a.   cats on corners sleep

    b.   seeds love hungry cats in fields

    c.   mice that eat fat seeds chase cats that are sleepy

2. Explain why the phrase-structure grammar of (18.4) does *not* generate these strings:

    a.   cats that mice lie by are sleepy

    b.   mice love seeds that mice are hungry

3. Extend the grammar of (18.4) to generate the following sentence. Then list its constituents.

    Greedy cats gleefully chase frightened mice.

4.   Construct a phrase-marker for each of the following sentences. The rewriting rules of (19.4) will be needed, in addition to those of (18.4).

    a.   Cows are contented if forlorn maidens milk them by full mangers.

    b.   Elephants fear mice since they know that mice scamper over toes.

    c.   That leprechauns wear green hats is obvious on holidays.

5.   Using both the phrase-structure and transformational components of the grammar in §§18-19, supply complete parsings for each of these sentences. (As before, the vocabulary will have to be extended.) Proceed as follows: (i) Write down the underlying sentence, which of course must be generated by the phrase-structure rules alone. (ii) Construct the underlying phrase-marker, i.e., the phrase-marker for that underlying sentence. (iii) Construct the derived phrase-marker, using one or more appropriate transformations.

    a.   Banks are robbed by desperate men in black masks.

    b.   Families that are homeless are helped by people that care.

    c.   It is amazing that daredevils traverse high wires.

    d.   That stars are distant was known by ancient Greeks.

6.   Using the rules of (18.4) and (19.4), with obvious extensions of vocabulary, supply two distinct phrase-markers for each of these syntactically ambiguous sentences.

    a.   Lazy widows crochet lacy fringes on soft pillows.

    b.   Children blow whistles that glow in dark rooms. (Hint: Compare, "Children blow whistles that glow in your ears.")

    c.   Elephants remember and donkeys forget unless they are asleep.

7.   Again using both the phrase-structure and transformational components of the grammar in §§18-19, supply *two different* complete parsings for this sentence. (Since the sentence is syntactically ambiguous, the first task is to find *two* underlying sentences, with clearly different meanings.)

                    Gullible customers are swindled by banks.

    For a precise solution, a more complex version of the passive transformation is needed, as follows.

    NP$_1$ VT   NP$_2$ PP $\Rightarrow$

                    NP$_2$ **are**   VT   Past Participle   (**by**   NP$_1$)   PP

8.   Add plausible transformations to the grammar in §§18-19, to account for the
     following sentences.

     a.   Camels, which live in deserts, store water in ugly humps.

     b.   Vegetarians prefer hard, red wheats, which have valuable nutrients.

9.   Add a rewriting rule to the grammar of (18.4) so that it generates these
     sentences.

          seeds that mice eat lie in barns
          mice that cats chase eat seeds
          cats that dogs worry chase mice
          dogs that cows toss worry cats

     Does your new grammar generate these strings as well? Do you think that
     they are sentences of English?

          seeds that mice that cats chase eat lie in barns
          mice that cats that dogs worry chase eat seeds
          mice   eat seeds
               that cats   chase
                    that dogs   worry
                         that cows   toss

VI: Logical Analysis of Complex Sentences

In Chapter V we recognized complex sentences of English that were generated by applying one or two of these three rewriting rules.

Sentence ⇒ Sentence   Conjunction   Sentence

Sentence ⇒ Sentence   Subordinate Clause

Subordinate Clause ⇒ Subordinating Conj   Sentence

In (1), on the next page, we have a list of all of the conjunctions of English. The left-hand column contains what we have called simply Conjunctions. (Sometimes they are called coordinating conjunctions.) The other three columns list Subordinating Conjunctions. In this chapter we will systematically analyze sentences formed with these conjunctions from a logical point of view. So far our primary logical technique has been the construction of tableaux, something we conducted in a more or less *ad hoc* way, tackling sentences as they confronted us, figuring out on the spot what tableau structure was appropriate. Now our aim will be to reduce the treatment of many conjunctions to a small number of simple patterns and thereby be justified in replacing them with what we will call rule-governed connectives.

(1) Conjunctions of English

and	if	because	while
but	though	lest	since
or	although		till
yet	unless		until
for			as
so			when
			before
			after

It will turn out that all of the conjunctions in the two left-hand lists will submit to such systematic treatment. We will also consider such phrases as "only if" and "provided that," phrases that are not conjunctions grammatically speaking, but whose logical force is like that of rule-governed connectives.

In Chapter IV we built tableaux involving "because." We noted that sentences whose conjunction was "because" could not be checked off after the appropriate tableau structure was built. That fact is a symptom of a deeper difficulty with words like "because"–and "lest"–that resist this systematic treatment.

As for the conjunctions in the right-hand column of (1), they all have implications with respect to time and temporal order. Certainly there are valid inferences that make essential use of these conjunctions, inferences that turn on considerations of the sequence and coincidence of events and processes in time. Here is an example.

The prime minister will not criticize the opposition candidates until a front-runner emerges.

A front-runner will not emerge until their party congress meets.

___

The prime minister will not criticize the opposition candidates until their party congress meets.

And here is another.

The voters will not rest easy while the current vice-president is in office.

The current vice-president will still be in office after the party convention is held in the summer.

When the party convention is held in the summer, the voters will not be resting easy.

The conjunctions in these examples also resist the systematic treatment we will develop below, at least in their primary, temporal meaning. (We will note a secondary meaning in several cases, e.g., "while.")

Of course we are not helpless when confronted with arguments that make use of the conjunctions in the right-hand two columns. We can continue to build tableaux, treating these sentences in the *ad hoc* way characteristic of Chapters III and IV. Later in this chapter we will see conjunctions like "because" and "before" combine with rule-governed connectives in single tableaux, sometimes with strikingly powerful results.

Before we go forward with our logical treatment of conjunctions, let's take note of a transformation in English that will be useful in what follows. Note that it requires a grammatical distinction between Conjunctions like "and," "or," and "but," and Subordinating Conjunctions like "if" and "because."

(2) Clause-Switching

$$S_1 \ \text{Sub Conj} \ S_2 \ \Rightarrow \ \text{Sub Conj} \ S_2 \ , \ S_1$$

The result of this transformation is what was traditionally called an introductory dependent (or subordinate) clause. A similar transformation with the stock of Conjunctions in the left-hand column of (1) would transform the sentence, "cats chase mice and cats eat mice," into the ungrammatical string, "and cats eat mice, cats chase mice." Here we have a syntactic basis for distinguishing two categories of conjunction, which up until now might have seemed alike.

For the first time, in this transformation, we have specified a mark of punctuation, namely the comma, between the two clauses. Every exacting school teacher insists upon such a comma because without it the compound sentence is nearly unintelligible.

> because barns are dark, cats catch mice
> if dogs chase mice, cats are hungry

These are sentences that are generated, by means of Clause-Switching from the underlying sentences given below. Remember that the underlying sentences are generated by the phrase-structure component, working by itself.

> cats chase mice because barns are dark
> cats are hungry if dogs chase mice

In the next section it will be particularly important to remember that this transformation has no effect on meaning. As is usual with the transformations we have seen so far, the derived string and the underlying string are completely equivalent to one another.

§22　　　　　　　RULE-GOVERNED SENTENCE CONNECTIVES IN TABLEAUX

The following tableau is one that we can construct using the methods of chapter III. Having done so, we will reflect back on some of the patterns used in it and in similar examples to reduce the construction of many tableaux to a matter of following rules.

> If Georges was born in the US and has not given up his citizenship, then Georges is a citizen of the US.
>
> Georges has not given up his citizenship.
>
> Georges is not a citizen of the US.
>
> ---
>
> Georges was not born in the US.

(1)

```
      2  If Georges was born in the US and has not given up his
         citizenship, then Georges is a citizen of the US
         Georges has not given up his citizenship
         Georges is not a citizen of the US
      1  It is not true that Georges was not born in the US
                     1 |
              Georges was born in the US
                       |
      2 ┌──────────────┴──────────────────┐
        |                                  |
        |                    Georges is a citizen of the US
        |                    ───────────────────────────────
        ┊
```

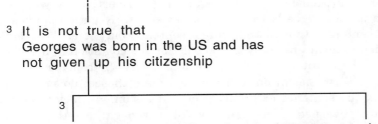

3 It is not true that
Georges was born in the US and has
not given up his citizenship

3

Georges was not born in the US   George has *not* not given up his citizenship

The maneuver that we developed most systematically in chapter III is marked by the "2" in this tableau. For sentences with the Subordinating Conjunction "if," we routinely constructed a branching structure in which we placed the main clause in one branch and the denial of the "if"-clause in the other branch. In order to encode that practice in a manageable rule, let's consider the general case of a sentence,

$$\text{if } S_1, \ S_2$$

to which Clause-Switching has already been applied. We introduce a symbolic connective "→," which we think of as always governed by the rule,

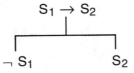

$$S_1 \rightarrow S_2$$

$$\neg S_1 \qquad S_2$$

For that reason we call "→" a **rule-governed connective**. We call this particular connective the **conditional**; it is only the first of several that we will introduce. In the rule we have introduced a second symbol "¬." This symbol is called **negation** and simply means "it is not true that." The latter phrase, a cumbersome one, was often used in earlier tableaux. It will be a relief to have a brief way to indicate the denial of any sentence; you simply prefix the negation symbol to the sentence, first enclosing the sentence in parentheses if it is already complex. Note that the rule for conditionals specifies that the negation always be on the left branch, the branch corresponding to the upstream side of the arrow. The upstream side of the arrow is the "if"-clause (remember Clause-Switching); thus we have insured that it is the "if"-clause that is denied in the branching structure, just as shown in Chapter III.

For convenience we call negation a connective as well, even though it doesn't really connect two sentences. Negation applies to a single sentence, though that single sentence may itself be complex. Negation is useful not only in the rule for the conditional, but also in forming the counter set. There we must deny the conclusion, which we can do with negation and perhaps parentheses, no matter how complex the sentence expressing the conclusion. In fact negation is also rule-governed. The primary rule for negation—there will be several more—has been applied at "1" in tableau (1). It captures the grammar teacher's admonition that a double negative amounts to an affirmation.

It may be tempting to short-cut this step in the case of tableau (1), for example, by eliminating the occurrence of "not" in the conclusion, as a way of constructing the counter set. Though harmless in practice, this policy would frustrate the aim of the current chapter, the aim of making the construction of certain tableaux entirely a matter of following rules. The rules we are stating are simple and, for an important class of tableaux, will turn out to handle all cases that will ever arise. For these systematic purposes, short cuts are not worth the trouble.

A more basic rule-governed connective suggests itself when we consider the following sentences.

Grace was born in the US, but she has given up her citizenship.

Grace was born in the US, yet she has given up her citizenship.

Though she was born in the US, Grace has given up her citizenship.

Grace was born in the US although she has given up her citizenship.

Another case uses "while" in its secondary, non-temporal sense, signalled by a difference of stress,

While she was *born* in the US, Grace has given up her citizenship.

Though these sentences differ from one another in their rhetorical effects and in the contrasts they highlight, it is quite clear what is to be done with any of them when constructing a tableau. In each of these cases, there is only one way for the sentence to be true, namely for both of the constituent sentences themselves to be true. Thus we can introduce a rule-governed connective and use it to rewrite any of them as,

> Grace was born in the US & Grace has given up her citizenship.

We see that, to break down a complex sentence whose main connective is "&," we invariably apply the following rule.

$$\sqrt{}\ S_1\ \&\ S_2$$
$$|$$
$$S_1$$
$$S_2$$

This is the rule that is dictated by our use of "&." As the ampersand symbol suggests, another conjunction that is to be rewritten using this rule-governed connective is the rhetorically neutral word "and."

At this point you might be reminded of the move marked "3" in tableau (1) above. Using rule-governed connectives, what we had there could be rewritten,

> ¬ (Georges was born in the US & Georges has not given up his citizenship).

And what we did in the tableau was in accordance with the following rule.

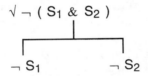

$$\sqrt{}\ \neg\ (\ S_1\ \&\ S_2\ )$$

¬ S₁   ¬ S₂

In fact this is exactly the treatment given—in Chapter III—to "Sarah and Molly will not both go." What we have discovered is that this most basic connective—"&"—is governed by *two* rules, one for its occurrence in an affirmative sentence, and another for its occurrence under the scope of the negation sign. The latter is in effect another rule for negation, that is, for negation when it governs "&."

By now we have mentioned many of the conjunctions in the two columns on the left side of (21.1). But there is an obvious one yet to be considered. It appears in a proposition that is supported by history and constitutional law. There is a clause of the Constitution of the United States that says, "No person except a natural-born citizen, or a citizen of the United States at the time of the adoption of this Constitution, shall be eligible to the office of President." Since, as school children of that country know, George Washington was

President of the United States, in fact the first President under the Constitution, this sentence expresses a truth.

George was a natural-born citizen or a citizen at the time of the adoption of the Constitution.

We symbolize the English conjunction "or," which is sometimes accompanied by the word "either," using the symbol "∨."

George was a natural-born citizen ∨ George was a citizen at the time of the adoption of the Constitution.

This is perhaps the easiest of all rule-governed connectives to satisfy. All that is required is that either one of the constituent sentences be true.

As was emphasized in Chapter III, two branches of a tableau may overlap in the sense that a single situation may be (partially) described by the sentences in both branches. Rather than adopting a more complex rule for "∨," the rule we have given provides that one way for the complex sentence $S_1 \vee S_2$ to be true is for S_1 to be true, whether or not S_2 is, and another way is for S_2 to be true, whether or not S_1 is.

Have we successfully captured the meaning of the English "or"? Well, consider the expression at hand. Perhaps it is not clear whether George Washington *was* a natural-born citizen. Though he certainly was born in Virginia, the United States had then not yet been founded, so it might be argued that he was not a natural-born citizen. Must this argument succeed in order for George Washington to have been eligible to be President? What if he were *both* a natural-born citizen *and* a citizen at the time of the adoption? Would this exclude him from eligibility for the Presidency? Of course it wouldn't. The English "or" in the eligibility clause is not intended to exclude the case where someone meets both qualifications, nor is any other comparable clause. (Though it is not so well known, during the years from 1783 till 1789, the United States subsisted under the Articles of Confederation and had citizens "natural-born" during that period. One of them, Zachary Taylor, was born in Virginia in 1784 and thus was a citizen at the time of adoption.

Fulfilling both qualifications was no barrier to his becoming President in 1840.) Even when the word "either" appears as a companion to the "or," it would be unreasonable to construe the "or" as exclusive. "Having fulfilled the Mathematical Reasoning requirement, George has taken either a math course or a logic course." Have we denied that George has taken both? Of course not.

In the interest of avoiding litigation, lawyers have adopted the clumsy expression "and/or" to mean, with no question of ambiguity, what was meant in the Constitution of the United States by the simple "or." It seems obvious enough that no serious threat of ambiguity arises there, and even less does it arise in ordinary speech and writing. Much ordinary writing, and even ordinary speech, has pedantically adopted the lawyer's "and/or." We have seen that the pedantry is unnecessary. And we have seen that the non-exclusive, "at least one," sense of "or" is safely assigned to typical uses of the English "or," even when accompanied by "either." Thus these typical uses are safely symbolized with the rule-governed connective "∨."

Revolutionary patriots in the United States rested assured that their nemesis, George III of England, was not eligible to be elected President under their new constitution. The grounds of that assurance can be expressed in the following words.

> George III was neither a natural-born citizen nor a citizen at the time of the adoption of the Constitution.

The sentence is to be symbolized as follows.

> ¬ (George III was a natural-born citizen ∨ George III was a citizen at the time of the adoption of the Constitution)

That is to say, the negation of an "either . . or" sentence is fluently expressed in English with "neither . . nor." But then, what is the second rule for "∨," that is, the rule for negation when it governs "∨"?

$$\checkmark \neg\, (\, S_1 \vee S_2\,)$$
$$|$$
$$\neg\, S_1$$
$$\neg\, S_2$$

The only way for "neither S_1 nor S_2" to hold true, is for neither of them to hold true! That is to say, the only way is for both of them to be denied, and our negation sign serves handsomely for the purpose.

Before leaving "∨" behind, let us remember the treatment of "unless" in Chapter IV. The tableau structure that we settled on for sentence (8) of §13 is exactly the one given by the rule for "∨." What that tells us is that this rule-governed sentence connective can go in place of the subordinating conjunction "unless," as well as the (coordinating) conjunction "or." As we have seen in earlier cases, the difference in meaning between the two conjunctions is purely rhetorical.

Having introduced four rule-governed connectives (namely, "¬," "&," "∨," and "→"), it is time to consider some other English expressions that can be reduced to them. In the tableau (1), we had the sentence,

> If Georges was born in the US and has not given up his citizenship, then Georges is a citizen of the US,

referring, perhaps, to Georges Laraque, up-and-coming winger of the National Hockey League's Edmonton Oilers. With someone who lives in the United States, we would typically accept the simpler formulation.

(2)   George is a citizen if he was born in the US.

Now notice the difference the little word "only" makes,

(3)   George is a citizen only if he was born in the US.

Unlike (2), sentence (3) is false.   For an example of a *true* sentence with "only" before the "if" consider the case of George Romney. Some years ago he ran for President. He had been born very close to, or perhaps just across the Mexican border, to parents who were US citizens. There is no doubt that he was a citizen, but there was some question whether he qualified legally to be President. Sentence (4) sums up what was at issue. (By the 20th century there was no longer any worry about those who were citizens at the time the Constitution was adopted!)

(4) George is constitutionally eligible to be President only if he was born in the US.

A little thought makes it evident that this sentence is equivalent to,

> If George is constitutionally eligible to be President, he must have been born in the US,

and we recognize this as the transformational equivalent—through Clause-Switching—of,

> George was born in the US if he is constitutionally eligible to be President.

Sometimes the word "then" is used, perhaps to emphasize the sequence of thoughts, if not the sequence of events,

If George is constitutionally eligible to be President, *then* he must have been born in the US.

Thus we have the equivalence of four different forms. (Pay close attention to the subscripts.)

if S_1, then S_2
S_2 if S_1
if S_1, S_2
S_1 only if S_2

It is easy to confuse these, which are equivalent, with another, which is not equivalent to them. Carefully compare the first of them, with the following, which is called the **converse**.

if S_2, then S_1.

Note what would appear if this converse were expressed with the symbolic connective. We would have the arrow running in the opposite direction, from S_2 to S_1, instead of from S_1 to S_2. Logicians have deliberately chosen the arrow, an asymmetric symbol, because it makes a crucial difference which constituent sentence is at the tail of the arrow and which is at its head. The example (5) makes it vivid that the converse is not equivalent to the others.

(5) If George was born in the US, he is constitutionally eligible to be President.

It will be helpful to shift the example to George Prescott Bush, the nephew of George W. Bush, known in the celebrity press as "P." If read as referring to him, (4) and its three equivalents remain true, while (5) is false. George Prescott Bush is *not* eligible to be President because he is under thirty-five.

To have a sufficient condition for eligibility, both qualifications must be fulfilled.

(6) George is eligible to be President if he was born in the US and is at least 35.

Since no one survives from the days of the founding of the republic, these are necessary conditions as well, and thus

(7) George is eligible to be President only if he was born in the US and is at least 35.

When sentences (6) and (7) are joined by "and," we get,

George is eligible if he was born in the US and is at least 35,
and
George is eligible only if he was born in the US and is at least 35.

An obvious transformation, which eliminates the repetition of the clauses, results in the following equivalent.

(8)   George is eligible to be President
                                          if, and only if,
                        he was born in the US and is at least 35.

Sentence (8) has the ring of a mathematical definition. Compare it with a statement that might be illustrated in a geometry text.

                              Figure 1 is a square
                                  if, and only if,
                    it has right angles and four equal sides.

Both are examples of what philosophers call "necessary and sufficient conditions." The complex phrase, "if, and only if," itself acts like a grammatical conjunction in that any two sentences can flank it, resulting in a complex sentence that is itself grammatical. The expression is so common in mathematical, philosophical, and legal settings that it deserves its own symbol. (6) and (7) illustrate that it is the combination of both arrows, and so the symbolic version is "$S_1 \leftrightarrow S_2$." Logicians call this connective the **biconditional**.

"If, and only if" is very commonly confused with the simpler "only if." This would be to confuse (8) with (7), which is only the half of it. Or consider (4) yet again. Though it is true that George Prescott Bush is eligible only if he was native born, it is not true that he is eligible *if*, and only if, he was native born. More is required; he must be old enough.

We can discover an additional tableau rule by taking seriously the definition implicit in the double arrow and applying tableau rules we already have. Consider the following fragment of a tableau, which would be good no matter what sentences went in for "S_1" and "S_2."

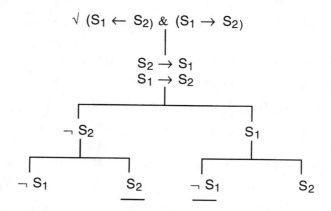

For the first time we can see in operation a rule for closing a branch in a rule-governed tableau. Suppose you have a path containing a sentence and the negation of that very same sentence. The two obviously conflict, and so the situation that has been described in the path is not a possible one. Thus the branch automatically closes. In the tableau we have built, two branches have been closed in accordance with the rule,

**Close any branch whose path contains a sentence
and the negation of that very sentence.**

Since only two branches remain open in our detailed tableau, we can boil down the result to the following.

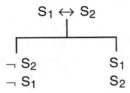

A harmless rearrangement yields the conventional tableau rule for "$S_1 \leftrightarrow S_2$," which we will use hereafter.

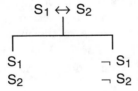

To conclude our treatment of the conditional and the biconditional, let's take note of several additional English expressions—none of them simple conjunctions—that can be replaced by one or the other of these rule-governed connectives. With its logical intricacy, the expression "if, and only if" typically appears only in quite technical or exacting discourse. Alternative expressions to be replaced by the double arrow are occasionally used, including "just in case," "just if," "precisely if," and "exactly if." Awkward as they are, they pretty obviously betray their exacting character.

Expressions which should be replaced by the single arrow are employed more frequently, but the challenge always lies in having the arrow point the right way. Think of what I am committed to if I say, "I'll buy you a new car provided that I get a raise." Suppose that

I get the raise but don't buy you the car. You have a complaint. But I haven't ruled out buying you one with my inheritance. So the sentence is equivalent to "I'll buy you a car if I get a raise," and should be rewritten as,

I will get a raise $\rightarrow$ I will buy you a car.

Once we have settled on using the single arrow, this kind of analysis will be effective in determining its direction. Besides "provided that," the single arrow (that is, the conditional) can be introduced in place of "given that," "assuming that," "on the supposition that," and "supposing that." Oddly enough, the expression "even if" cannot be replaced with the arrow. To say I will buy you a car *even if* I can't afford it is to say that I will buy you a car *period*!

§23   TRANSFORMATIONS IN LOGICAL ANALYSIS; GROUPING

We first introduced rule-governed connectives in order to capture the patterns that emerged in tableau (22.1). Rereading the sentences in the trunk of (22.1), we encounter an anomaly. Among the constituent sentences is "Georges was born in the US and has not given up his citizenship." In it occurs the conjunction "and," but that conjunction does not conjoin two sentences in the manner required by the rule-governed connective "&." The explanation perhaps is obvious. (In fact we took it for granted when we introduced "&.") Even so, it deserves to be made explicit.

Switching to examples more nearly falling under our laboratory grammar of Chapter V, we note that, to our ears, the following are grammatical sentences.

(1)   Bowser chased both Felix and Robin
                 Both Bowser and Felix chased Robin
                 Bowser both barked and whined
                 Felix both scratched and worried Bowser

Unfortunately, the only source of the conjunction "and" in our rewriting rules is the rule,

Sentence $\Rightarrow$ Sentence   Conjunction   Sentence.

But in the sentences at (1), "and" occurs between two Nouns and between two Verbs. To accommodate these sentences, we could introduce additional rewriting rules, but doing so would ignore their respective equivalence to the lengthier–and more explicit–sentences that are generated by the rewriting rules that we already have.

(2)   Bowser chased Felix and Bowser chased Robin
            Bowser chased Robin and Felix chased Robin
            Bowser barked and Bowser whined
            Felix scratched Bowser and Felix worried Bowser

It is evident that these can safely be treated as underlying the corresponding surface sentences at (1). All that is needed are appropriate transformations; those that follow will do the trick.

$$NP_1 \quad VT_1 \quad NP_2 \quad \textbf{and} \quad NP_1 \quad VT_1 \quad NP_3 \Rightarrow$$
$$NP_1 \quad VT_1 \quad \textbf{both} \quad NP_2 \quad \textbf{and} \quad NP_3$$

$$NP_1 \quad VT_1 \quad NP_2 \quad \textbf{and} \quad NP_3 \quad VT_1 \quad NP_2 \Rightarrow$$
$$\textbf{both} \quad NP_1 \quad \textbf{and} \quad NP_3 \quad VT_1 \quad NP_2$$

$$NP_1 \quad VP_1 \quad \textbf{and} \quad NP_1 \quad VP_2 \Rightarrow$$
$$NP_1 \quad \textbf{both} \quad VP_1 \quad \textbf{and} \quad VP_2$$

$$NP_1 \quad VT_1 \quad NP_2 \quad \textbf{and} \quad NP_1 \quad VT_2 \quad NP_2 \Rightarrow$$
$$NP_1 \quad \textbf{both} \quad VT_1 \quad \textbf{and} \quad VT_2 \quad NP_2$$

Having unearthed the underlying sentences at (2), we readily introduce the connective "&," which is limited in its application to connecting only complete sentences.

Bowser chased Felix & Bowser chased Robin

Bowser chased Robin & Felix chased Robin

Bowser barked & Bowser whined

Felix scratched Bowser & Felix worried Bowser

It must be something like this that carries us from,

Georges was born in the US and has not given up his citizenship,

to,

Georges was born in the US & Georges has not given up his citizenship.

The following "or"-transformation is analogous to the first of the "and"-transformations given above.

$$NP_1 \quad VT_1 \quad NP_2 \quad \textbf{or} \quad NP_1 \quad VT_1 \quad NP_3 \quad \Rightarrow$$

$$NP_1 \quad VT_1 \quad \textbf{either} \quad NP_2 \quad \textbf{or} \quad NP_3$$

It will provide for the rule-governed "∨." By applying it, we can derive the surface sentence,

(3)   Bowser chased either Felix or Robin,

from the underlying sentence,

Bowser chased Felix or Bowser chased Robin.

Thus when confronted with (3), we are justified in introducing,

Bowser chased Felix ∨ Bowser chased Robin,

and using the tableau rules for "∨." Similarly "**either . . or**" can replace "**both . . and**" in the other transformations, providing for "∨" to connect complete sentences wherever we introduce it.

Stepping back from these particular transformations, we take note of the surface sentence, "Bowser barked at both George and Martha," which is derived from the underlying sentence, "Bowser barked at George and Bowser barked at Martha." Also the surface sentence, "George gave either Felix or Bowser the biscuits," is plausibly derived from the underlying sentence, "George gave Felix the biscuits or George gave Bowser the biscuits." Rather than introducing a large number of specialized transformations to handle all these varied cases, we postulate a **generalized transformation.**

(4) And/Or Transformation

$$X_1 . . X_m \quad Y_1 \quad Z_1 . . Z_n \quad \textbf{and} \,|\, \textbf{or} \quad X_1 . . X_m \quad Y_2 \quad Z_1 . . Z_n \quad \Rightarrow$$

$$X_1 . . X_m \quad (\textbf{both} \,|\, \textbf{either}) \quad Y_1 \quad \textbf{and} \,|\, \textbf{or} \quad Y_2 \quad Z_1 . . Z_n$$

Here the "X's," "Y's," and "Z's" stand in for whatever non-terminal or terminal syntactic symbols you please, so long as the phrase-structure grammar provides for a phrase marker that can be pruned to yield the string in question. Using only transformation (4), together with the rewriting rules of Chapters V and VI, a complete parsing of this elaborate sentence can be given.

I buy both peaches and apples at roadside stands on equestrian trails after autumn games.

Our motivation in postulating the generalized And/Or Transformation has been to justify introducing the rule-governed

connectives "&" and "∨" in cases where, on the surface, the
conjunctions "**and**" and "**or**" conjoin not whole sentences, but lesser
constituents, be they Noun Phrases, Verb Phrases, Verb Transitives,
or perhaps even Adjectives or Prepositions.   If these surface
sentences are derived from underlying sentences in which it is whole
sentences that are conjoined, we are safe to introduce the appropriate
rule-governed connectives, remembering that they are permitted to
"connect" only complete sentences.

The unexpected appearance of "both" and "either" in these
transformations raises the question of what the function of these odd
little words is. (As we have already seen with respect to other words,
they certainly have no meaning in isolation.) Pursuing this question
with respect to "both" leads us to recognize that a full grammar of
English does permit "and" to conjoin constituents of less than
sentence length with one another, whether they be Nouns, Verbs, or
even Adjectives.   In such cases it would be a mistake to seek
underlying sentence-length constituents and equally a mistake to
introduce "&." And in fact the little word "both" helps to make the
contrast.

> I prepared peaches and cream for dessert.
>
> I bought both peaches and cream at the farmers' market.
>
> George and Martha are married.
>
> George and Martha are both married.

In each of the sentences with "both," there *are* two constituent
sentences in the underlying (complex) sentence, and it is correct to
introduce "&."

> I bought peaches at the farmers' market &
>
> > I bought cream at the farmers' market

(5)   George is married & Martha is married

Where the "both" does not occur, this analysis would not be correct.
Peaches and cream is a sumptuous dish combining the two
ingredients, perhaps with sugar as well, and "peaches and cream"
is a complex Noun that denotes that dessert.   Similar complex
phrases include "black and blue," "advice and consent," "rolled and
tucked," "duck and cover," and "scotch and soda."

The "George and Martha" case is a little different.   It's not that
the complex noun denotes them as a combination; it's rather that
each is married *to* the other.   What is really being expressed is a

relation between them, a symmetric relation at that. We will study such relations further in Chapter VII, but for now we should make a few observations relevant to the rule-governed "&." Supposing that George is married to Martha–and *vice versa*–(5) indeed is true, that is to say, each of them is married to *someone*. The failing rather is in a loss of information, that it is Martha to whom George is married, and that it is George to whom Martha is married. That information may be crucial to closing the tableau, so the rule-governed "&" should not be introduced. There are a large number of analogous cases: "George and Martha are friends,"   ". . are neighbors," ". . are holding hands," and so on. Without the "both" and with no other indicator, do not supplant the "and" with "&" connecting whole sentences.

In the generalized And/Or Transformation, "both" was enclosed in parentheses, indicating that the word can be deleted. Sometimes speakers are lazy, saying, "Bowser and Felix chased Robin," meaning that they both did so, not that they chased Robin in tandem. So it is correct sometimes to introduce "&" even though "both" does not appear. Before introducing the rule-governed connective, subject the case to the "both" test by making explicit what perhaps has been deleted.   Only where "both" can be inserted without change in meaning in the position provided by the And/Or Transformation are there indeed underlying constituent sentences which can correctly be connected by "&."

We welcome the brevity facilitated by the And/Or Transformation and welcome the occurrence of "both" and "either" as indicators that "&" and "∨" may properly be introduced, yet these little words serve an additional function that is even more important. Drawing on Chapter II, we recognize that the sentence,

We will invite Ron, and we will invite Nancy, or we will invite Jane,

is hopelessly ambiguous. To discern its structure we need a phrase-marker or a constituent analysis. In ordinary speech, the little words "both" and "either" serve to disambiguate the surface sentences that result from their corresponding transformations.

We will invite either Ron and Nancy or Jane,

leads to a different dinner party than,

(6)   We will invite Ron and either Nancy or Jane,

Again,

Both Jane or Nancy and Ron will attend,

contemplates a social dynamic different from that projected by,

(7)   Either Jane or both Nancy and Ron will attend.

Despite the "either," the sentence,

(8)   Either Jane or Nancy and Ron will attend,

remains ambiguous. We see that in many but not all cases, "both" and "either" effectively indicate the scope of "and" and "or" respectively. Selective application of the And/Or Transformation often serves the same purpose, and the little words can be left out.

(9)   We will invite Ron, and we will invite Nancy or Jane,

serves as well as (6). And each of the following disambiguates (8) in its own way.

          Jane or Nancy will attend, and so will Ron.

(10)   Jane will attend or Nancy and Ron will.

When we introduce rule-governed connectives, these graceful and efficient devices of English grammar are lost. In fact any resulting complex sentence with more than one connective is threatened with syntactic ambiguity. The palliative we adopt is borrowed from algebraic notation: parentheses to indicate grouping. Thus, when faced with (6) or (9), we introduce the "&" and "∨" as follows,

          We will invite Ron & (we will invite Nancy ∨ we will invite Jane),

and we say that "&" has **wide scope**, "∨" has **narrow scope**. (Refer back to §18 for the definition of scope, the general notion on which these depend.) When faced with (7) or (10), we write,

          Jane will attend ∨ (Nancy will attend & Ron will attend),

and we say that "∨" has wide scope, and "&," narrow.

Again drawing from Chapter II, we recall ambiguous sentences that have not been—perhaps cannot be—resolved by any idiomatic device of English diction.

(11) Partridge will be nominated and Quayle will be his running mate only if Rooster withdraws.

Standing alone, this sentence carries no indication as to whether it is "and" that has wide scope, or rather it is "only if." In the context of a tableau, a choice must be made between two alternative paraphrases.

> Partridge will be nominated & (Quayle will be Partridge's running mate →
> Rooster will withdraw)

> (Partridge will be nominated & Quayle will be Partridge's running mate) →
> Rooster will withdraw

And perhaps the choice will determine whether the tableau closes or not. That very fact—or sometimes features of other sentences in the tableau—should guide us, but a choice cannot be avoided.

It is in the nature of our tableau rules that the scope of each connective in a sentence must be made explicit. The animating idea behind rule-governed connectives is that the construction of the tableau is dictated by the rules. What this requires in practice is that, for any given complex sentence, it be completely determined which rule to apply. This requires that there be a rule-governed connective with widest scope. The appropriate rule is picked to match that connective. Where "¬" is followed by a left parenthesis, the negation is to apply to the entire complex sentence between that parenthesis and its corresponding right parenthesis. The question of scope applies also to that subsidiary complex sentence; whatever connective has wide scope within the subsidiary sentence leads us to the appropriate negation rule.

This niggling requirement serves us well in the case of (11) because the logical force of that sentence depends crucially on its structure. We want to apply only that tableau rule appropriate to the intended structure. But here, as in life, important formalities sometimes intrude uselessly. Suppose we are faced with,

> We will invite either Jane or Nancy or Martha.

In order to apply the "∨" rule effectively, we must choose between one of these two.

> We will invite Jane ∨ (we will invite Nancy ∨ we will invite Martha)

> (We will invite Jane ∨ we will invite Nancy) ∨ we will invite Martha

In this degenerate case it does not matter which one we choose, but we have to choose one. Whichever we choose, after two applications of the "∨" rule, we will have three different branches, exactly as we would have constructed them without the aid of the rule or the rule-governed connectives.

In emphasizing the scope of "¬" and the choice of the appropriate negation rule, we have been brought to the theoretical questions of how many rule-governed connectives there are and why certain conjunctions among those in table (21.1) have been chosen for this systematic treatment and others have not. It turns out that the crucial consideration is the existence of a negation rule, a matter that is closely related to the issue of whether or not a sentence can be checked. The central case to illuminate these issues is "because."

Remember in Chapter IV we considered a tableau with the simple example,

I met my mechanic because my car would not start.

The question to address now concerns the negation of that sentence as a whole, which might be expressed with the ambiguous sentence,

I did not meet my mechanic because my car would not start,

but is more clearly expressed by,

(1) It is not true that I met my mechanic because my car would not start.

In extending a tableau we wish to describe kinds of situation with respect to which the sentence in question is true. It is clear that there are at least two for sentence (1). Suppose I did not meet my mechanic at all. In that case, sentence (1) holds. And suppose that it is not true that my car wouldn't start. Again sentence (1) clearly holds. Since neither of these requires the other—though we might have both—a branching structure suggests itself.

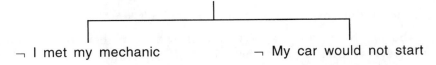

On second thought, are these the only kinds of situation that bear out (1)? Something has been left out.

Suppose that, though I did indeed meet my mechanic and though my car indeed wouldn't start, that was not why I met him. (Perhaps I met him in order to pay him for my prior roadside rescue.) The two branches we have are not sufficient. There might very well be a situation that fits sentence (1) even though it fits neither of the suggested branches. In order to treat sentence (1) with a tableau structure we would need another branch, one perhaps saying,

It was not because my car wouldn't start that I met my mechanic.

The result would be a branching structure like this:

(2)

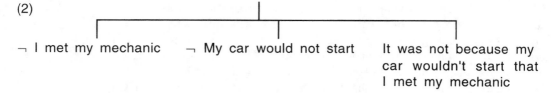

¬ I met my mechanic   ¬ My car would not start   It was not because my car wouldn't start that I met my mechanic

There would be no harm in constructing such a structure in a tableau. If (1) is inconsistent with other sentences, it is because one way or another those other sentences rule out all of the three possibilities displayed in the branching structure. But will anything be gained?

The strategy of the tableau method is to simplify our descriptions of a situation by breaking down the sentences we begin with. We accept branching with its attendant increase in the number of paths and thus in the number of sets of sentences to be considered for inconsistency because those sentences are simpler and inconsistency is more obvious. Is that strategy furthered by the three-branched structure (2)? The left and middle branches indeed have sentences simpler than (1), the originating sentence. But how about the right-hand sentence? We want to tease out inconsistencies, so what other sentence conceivably would conflict with the right-hand branch in particular? The most obvious case would be,

It was because my car wouldn't start that I met my mechanic,

or in other words,

I met my mechanic because my car wouldn't start.

Either of these sentence, occurring elsewhere in the tableau, would obviously contradict sentence (1) itself. Nothing will have been gained in proliferating paths by constructing (2).

Thus it is that no rule for,

$$\neg\,(\,S_1 \text{ because } S_2\,),$$

is worthwhile. It is not that no rule could be stated, but rather that the rule would be useless. It would not make either consistency or inconsistency more obvious. What is peculiar to "because" is the relationship thereby attributed (in the example) to my meeting my mechanic and my car not starting. To deny a "because"-statement is perhaps to deny that such a relationship holds, but no simpler or clearer expression of that denial is available than the negation of the "because"-statement itself.

It is no accident that the "because"-sentence cannot be checked off. Though there is a pattern to be followed with "S_1 because S_2," illustrated at (3) of §16, we found that we shouldn't check off the originating sentence itself. We had to provide for its not being true that I met my mechanic because my car wouldn't start even though it wouldn't start and I did meet him. Sentence (1) is exactly the kind of prospective sentence that we were providing for by leaving the "because"-sentence unchecked. Conversely if sentence (1) arises in a tableau, we can't reduce what it says to a set of more simply described possibilities.

In effect we have arrived at a standard for introducing a rule-governed sentence connective: there must be two rules, one to apply when simpler sentences are joined by the connective, the second to apply to negations of the first kind of case. And we have found that whether the affirmation can be checked is an indication of whether a worthwhile negation rule can be devised. So far we have introduced four proper connectives—"&," "∨," "→," and "↔"—each with a rule for the affirmative case. And we have devised negation rules for "&" and "∨." What remains is the question whether we can devise negation rules for "→" and "↔," the conditional and the biconditional. If we settle the issue for the conditional, it is likely that the case of the biconditional will be a corollary.

Let us begin with the related question, which we have so far avoided. Can conditional sentences be checked off when the rule we devised for their affirmations has been executed? To use an example from §22,

(3)   If George was born in the US, he is eligible,

suppose the rule from that section has been applied, giving the following structure.

(4)
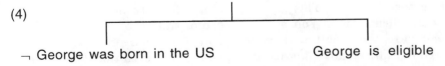

Let's apply the first of the tests set out in §16. It is easy to specify a sentence that conflicts with (3) but yet does not conflict with each of the two paths in the branching structure.

(5) Just because George was born in the US, that doesn't mean he is eligible.

> Sentences (3) and (5) are inconsistent with one another, but if (3) is
> *replaced* by the branching structure (4)—the effect of checking off
> (3)—at least the right-hand path will remain open. Thus sentence (3)
> should not be checked off, nor in general should the "→"-rule have
> us check off the originating conditional sentence.
>
> Conversely if (5) itself appears in a tableau, it seems that there is
> no way of breaking it down into alternative possibilities that can be
> described in any simpler terms than (5) itself. But that means that
> no rule will be worthwhile for the negation of "→" because (5) is the
> idiomatic way of denying (3). It is very nearly synonymous with,
>
>   It is not true that if George was born in the US he is eligible.

Though the issue has been controversial among philosophers and
logicians, this seems to be where we must leave the general case.
Though there is a useful rule for the affirmed conditionals, there
seems to be none for negations.

One consideration keeps us from leaving it at that. We have
noted that conditionals are pervasive in reasoned discourse. Not only
do conditional sentences frequently appear as premises of deductive
inferences, they frequently appear as conclusions. Applying the
tableau technique to such arguments requires us to construct the
counter set, and so to deal with negated conditionals in tableaux. Is
there no help for us? It turns out that for this particular case of a
negated conditional, which in fact is by far the most frequent, we can
devise a rule. We will see what the rule is by considering a familiar
strategy for arguing for conditional conclusions, a strategy in fact
called **conditionalization**, or sometimes, hypothetical reasoning.

Think how you reason about what will happen if tuition increases
next year by 25%. Perhaps your conclusion is expressed as follows.

(6)   If tuition increases by 25%, my shortfall will be $3,000.

In order to explain your reasoning, or perhaps to convince your rich
uncle of your conclusion, you do just as you did in your own
reasoning. You assume for the sake of argument that tuition will
increase by 25%. This gives you a specific percentage to enter into
your calculations. You multiply current tuition by 125%. Then you
compare the result with your resources, which perhaps include a
scholarship grant that itself depends on the tuition level and so
depends on the assumed increase. All of this reasoning, which
obviously includes arithmetical reasoning, issues in the conclusion
that your shortfall will be $3,000. But that is not your real conclusion.
You do not ask your uncle to write you a check for that amount right

now. Your reasoning has been hypothetical, based on the dire assumption that tuition will increase by 25%, something you fervently hope will not be true, even though it has been rumored. You are just asking your uncle to be prepared. To help him see why, you have asked him to assume that it will be true and thereby reasoned that you will be $3,000 short. What this justifies is your real conclusion—a conditional—namely (6).

How can we adapt this familiar strategy to the tableau technique? Ordinarily we form the counter set, which consists of the premises of the argument and the negation of the conclusion. (Since we have not tried to spell out your entire reasoning with your uncle, we have not made the premises explicit. They would be facts about current tuition, your current scholarship grant, your summer earnings, what remains of your savings, and so on. Many of these premises would be in terms of dollars and cents, which is appropriate to the arithmetical character of the reasoning.) A closed tableau on the counter set shows that it is impossible for the premises to be true while the conclusion is false. Conclusions like (6) are awkward for the counter set procedure because we have no systematic way of handling negated conditionals. But what if we added the "if"-clause to the set of premises, in effect assuming it for the sake of argument? Then we could treat the main clause as if it were the conclusion. That is to say, we could take the negation of the main clause and see if it is consistent with the premises augmented by the "if"-clause.

What if this set of sentences turns out to be inconsistent? This will show that it is impossible for the "if"-clause to be true while the main clause is false, so long as the premises are true. That is to say, so long as the premises are true, then if the "if"-clause is true, so is the main clause. That is to say—in application to our example—so long as the premises are true, if tuition increases by 25%, your shortfall will indeed be $3,000. Your reasoning is valid.

On the other hand, this new set—consisting of the premises, the "if"-clause, and the negation of the main clause—may turn out to be consistent. That would show that there is a possible situation in which the premises are true and tuition does increase by 25% and yet you don't have a $3,000 shortfall. It would show that in some possible situation, even though the premises are true, just because tuition will increase by 25% that doesn't mean you will be $3,000 short.

Rather than dwelling further on this analysis, let's gather what we have said into a rule for handling negated conditionals *as they arise in forming counter sets.* You have a set consisting of the premises and a negated conditional conclusion. You form a new set consisting of the premises, the "if"-clause of the conclusion, and the negation of the main clause. In effect you have applied the following rule to the negated conditional conclusion.

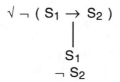

$$\sqrt{\neg} \ (\ S_1 \rightarrow S_2\ )$$
$$S_1$$
$$\neg S_2$$

Without saying more, we will settle on this rule for the rather special case of conditional conclusions that have been negated in counter sets. How far it can be extended to other contexts of discourse or tableau construction in which negated conditionals arise is a problem that we will leave for the consideration of specialists.

Even so confining the rule carries us farther than might first appear. Many conclusions have the form of iterated conditionals, as exemplified here, where the main clause is itself an (embedded) conditional.

If tuition increases by 25%, then if my grant increases by only 25%, my shortfall will be $3,000.

Where this iterated conditional is the conclusion of an argument, as usual the counter set will include its negation. (We introduce the rule-governed "→" and the needed parentheses.)

$\neg$ (Tuition increases by 25% →
(my grant increases by 25% →   my shortfall will be $3,000))

When we apply the rule, we get two sentences,

Tuition will increase by 25%

$\neg$ (My grant increases by 25% →   my shortfall will be $3,000)

the second of which is itself a negated conditional. Remember what this second negated conditional represents. In effect the embedded conditional is the conclusion of the argument that used the extra premise, which had been assumed for the sake of argument. So this negated conditional itself can be considered a conditional conclusion that has been negated to form a counter set. The upshot is that the rule for negated conditionals does apply again, and so ultimately we have three sentences in the developing tableau:

Tuition will increase by 25%

My grant will increase by 25%

$\neg$ My shortfall will be $3,000

Though our rule is confined to negated conditionals that arise in counter sets from the conclusions of arguments, the rule applies to as many such negated conditionals as might arise from repeated applications of the rule itself.

Despite being restricted to conditional conclusions of arguments, the rule carries with it another bonus. What if the conclusion is a *bi*conditional? We have explained the biconditional simply as two conditionals joined by "&." An argument to a biconditional conclusion is the condensation of two arguments, each with a conditional conclusion. Of course the rule for negated conditionals should apply in each case. Without detailing the justification, we can record the upshot here, namely a rule for negated biconditionals.

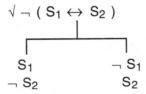

This rule completes our set of rule-governed connectives. For each of the four proper connectives we have introduced two rules, one for the sentence itself and one for its negation.

TABLEAUX CONSTRUCTED BY RULES   §25

The table on the next page summarizes the work of this chapter so far. It displays all of the rule-governed connectives we have introduced, including a negation rule for each of them. It also indicates whether the originating complex sentence can be checked after the rule is applied. Notably the entries in the tableau structures are simpler than the complex sentences which spawn them. Though there are more of them, and even more branches, the number of connectives within the spawned sentences has always been reduced. This is a very important theoretical generalization, one that we preserved by resisting a negation rule for "because." Logical theorists have concentrated on a special class of arguments whose tableaux can be completely developed by proceeding in accordance with these rules.

(1) Tableau Rules for Sentence Connectives

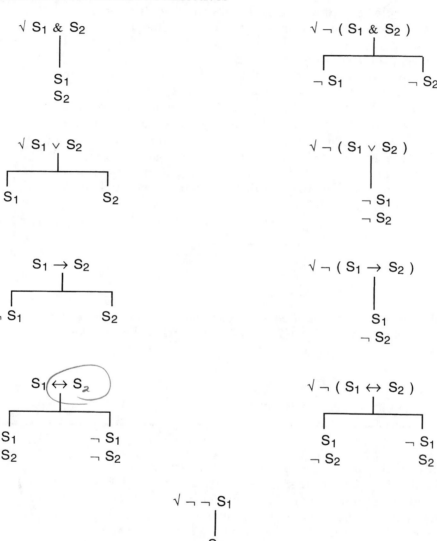

Without dwelling on the theoretical result concerning rule-governed tableaux, it is worth our examining an instance of the special class of rule-governed arguments. The following example employs a variety of English conjunctions all of which can be captured from a logical point of view by using rule-governed sentence connectives.

George is eligible to be President if, and only if, he was born in the US and is over thirty-five.

George is a citizen, but was not naturalized.

George is a citizen only if he was born in the US, was born of US citizens, or was naturalized.

George is not eligible to be President.

If he was not born of US citizens, then George is not over thirty-five.

When we recover all of the underlying sentences and introduce parentheses as needed, the argument appears as follows. Notably its conclusion is a conditional, so we should be prepared to think of the tableau to come as an application of the reasoning in the previous section about negated conditionals as they arise in forming counter sets.

George is eligible to be President ↔ (George was born in the US & George is over thirty-five)

George is a citizen & ¬ George was naturalized

George is a citizen → ((George was born in the US ∨ George was born of US citizens) ∨ George was naturalized)

¬ George is eligible to be President

¬ George was born of US citizens → ¬ George is over thirty-five

Of course the negation sign comes in handy for forming the counter set. (See the next page.) Since the conclusion is a conditional sentence, we surround it with parentheses to insure that we have denied the conclusion as a whole, not just the first part of it. They give the negation sign wide scope, with the result that the special negation rule for conditionals is invoked, rather than the rule for double negation.

Having constructed the counter set, we are ready to apply the tableau method to assess its consistency. But now that method has become mechanical, a matter of calculation. By successively applying the appropriate rule for the connective that presents itself, we construct the tableau as displayed below, entirely in accordance with rules. Even though we haven't checked off the conditional and biconditional sentences, there is no point in applying the rules for them repeatedly. What we have saved them for is the possibility of an unexpected conflict with another complex sentence. In a completely rule-governed tableau, such a conflict will never arise. Because each application of a rule results in eliminating at least one—and sometimes two—connectives, we inevitably run out of connectives to which to apply the rules. At that point we are finished with the tableau, whether or not branches remain open.

George is eligible to be President ↔ (George was born in the US & George is over thirty-five)

√ George is a citizen & ¬ George was naturalized

George is a citizen → ((George was born in the US ∨ George was born of US citizens) ∨ George was naturalized)

¬ George is eligible to be President

√ ¬ (¬ George was born of US citizens → ¬ George is over thirty-five)

George is a citizen
¬ George was naturalized

¬ George was born of US citizens
√ ¬ (¬ George is over thirty-five)

George is over thirty-five

¬ George is a citizen

√ ((George was born in the US ∨ George was born of US citizens) ∨ George was naturalized)

√ (George was born in the US ∨ George was born of US citizens)

George was naturalized

George was born in the U.S

George was born of US citizens

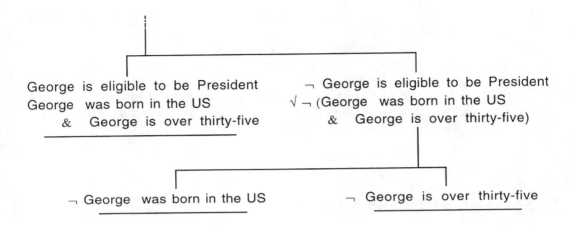

Just as each stage of construction is guided by a rule, so is the closure of branches. In each case where we have closed a branch, the path includes a tell-tale pair, namely both a sentence and the very same sentence preceded by the negation sign. Since these are obviously inconsistent with one another, we are justified in closing the branch. From the point of view of the rule, we simply look for the tell-tale pair. Where such a pair appears, the path can be closed. In the end, all of the paths in our example have closed. Of course this establishes that the counter set is inconsistent. And that means the original argument is valid.

In this chapter we have concentrated on tableaux that can be constructed by following rules which apply to a special set of conjunctions of English. In order to signal their rule-governed character, we have assigned symbolic connectives to these conjunctions, even extending the use of these connectives to certain other grammatical constructions that result in complex sentences. In treating the sentences covered by this chapter we are relieved of the repeated burden of figuring out how to act on each new sentence as we build the tableau. We systematically accrue the advantage of experience. The prior tableau illustrated the reach of these rules in a complicated yet realistic inference that is completely explained and vindicated by them. Nevertheless there are other arguments, perhaps even more representative of ordinary inference, in which the rule-governed connectives are intermingled with other grammatical constructions, perhaps including "because" or temporal conjunctions. When constructing a tableau for such an argument, it is effective to use rule-governed connectives where possible and to handle other sentences in an *ad hoc* manner. We call the result a **mixed tableau**.

Having seen the advantage of rules operating in tableaux, we now are ready to expand our stock of rules. Doing so will take us inside the boundaries of sentences that are grammatically simple, that is to say, sentences consisting of a Noun Phrase followed by a Verb Phrase, sentences of the sort we treated with our first simple phrase-structure grammars.

Exercises for Chapter VI

1. Paraphrase each of the sentences in the following set, using rule-governed connectives. Then construct a tableau using only the tableau rules.

    > Although all Democratic Senators will support it, the tax proposal will lose.
    >
    > The majority leader will support the tax proposal provided that the Democratic Senator from Texas supports it.
    >
    > The tax proposal will be passed unless the majority leader does not support it.

2. Paraphrase the sentences in the following argument using rule-governed connectives.

    > If Holmes does not arrive, Moriarty will escape unless we contact Watson.
    > We will contact Watson only if Holmes arrives.
    > _____
    > Moriarty will escape if neither Holmes nor Watson arrives.

    Does it matter which of the connectives has the widest scope in the first premise? (Hints: Compare the tableau structures that result from the two choices. Or try applying Clause-Switching to see whether your ear detects a difference.)

3. Find the conventional form of the following argument. Then paraphrase using rule-governed connectives. Finally, determine whether the argument is valid with a tableau that uses only tableau rules.

> I should think you will have a cold unless you were taking vitamin C. "Why?" you ask. Because you will have a cold if, and only if, you were exposed to one and your resistance was down. Your resistance was down only if you were not taking vitamin C. And you were exposed to a cold, even though not for very long.

4. Considering both the phrase-structure and transformational components of the grammar introduced in Chapter V and extended in this chapter, find the underlying sentence for each of these examples. Construct the underlying phrase-marker and prune it to be able to apply the generalized And/Or Transformation. Show how to match the non-terminal string to the generalized And/Or Transformation. (As before, the vocabulary will have to be extended.)

   a. Daredevils train both lions and tigers.

   b. Plumed ladies both execute somersaults and ride on fine horses.

   c. They wore shoes with either swoshes or stripes on them.

   d. Mt. Rainier erupted either before or while we hiked toward it. *No solution?*

   e. If Cal beats either UW or UCLA, Michigan will play Cal.

   f. Mary enrolled in logic both because she loves logic and because logic fulfills two requirements.

5. Again using both the phrase-structure and transformational components of the grammar developed in Chapters V and VI, find *two different* complete parsings for this sentence. (Since the sentence is syntactically ambiguous, the first task is to write two underlying sentences, with clearly different meanings.) Then write out only the two derived phrase-markers.

> Little John both ducked and thumped Robin Hood.

6. None of the following sentences are generated by the phrase-structure grammar that we have developed. It is tempting to add appropriate transformations that operate to generate them. Without worrying about the specifics of such transformations, find an underlying sentence for each of the following; that is, find an equivalent sentence that *is* generated by the phrase-structure grammar.

   a. George was supervised by Mary because it was Mary that knew X-bar theory.

    b.   It was because Gonzaga was small that UConn beat Gonzaga.

    c.   There were two small colleges that UConn played.

    d.   It was Duke that was beaten by UConn.

    e.   UConn played Duke because Duke beat Temple, which beat Gonzaga, or because Duke beat both Temple and St. Johns.

7.   Rewrite the sentences in the following argument using rule-governed connectives wherever possible. Then construct a tableau to determine whether the argument is valid. (Be sure to say what your tableau shows.)

> George is required to file a return if his total income was over $5,000 and if his investment income was over $800.
>
> George was unemployed all last year, but his investment income was over $800.
>
> George will file a return if, and only if, he is required to.
>
> ――――――――――――――――――――――――――――――――――
>
> George will file a return even though he was unemployed all last year.

8.   When confronted with a situation described by the following sentence, we would quickly make an unsettling inference. State the depressing conclusion that follows from this premise, and construct a mixed tableau showing that the inference is a valid one. (Hint, use "before" as well as "→.")

Each of Oceania and Eastasia will disarm only if the other
disarms first.

VII: Identity and Other Relations

In Chapter VI we considered grammatically complex sentences in which two or more simpler sentences were joined together, usually by grammatical Conjunctions like "and" and "or." Many arguments owed their validity to the appearance and reappearance of such simple sentences together with the logical behavior of the Conjunctions in question. In order to understand validity—and consistency—in connection with other cases it is now time to consider the simple sentences themselves. We have already seen a *grammatical* analysis of these sentences; what we call parsing is a matter of dividing the sentence first into the main Noun Phrase and the main Verb Phrase. Further analysis comes as the details of the phrase marker are worked out. Though the phrase marker will be helpful, we will find that the analysis of such sentences from a logical point of view takes a rather different route. One potential source of confusion is that in giving the analysis we will make use of a term drawn from traditional grammar. Traditionally the main Verb Phrase of a sentence was called the predicate. Even though our use of the term "predicate" descends historically from that traditional use, you will do best to start afresh with the notion of a predicate. For our purposes a predicate will be defined on the basis of another notion, that of a **designator**. We will turn to that first.

Designators form a subset of the Noun Phrases, but not all noun phrases are designators. Noun Phrases of the following sorts all qualify.

(1) Proper names

(2) Singular pronouns in the nominative or objective case and singular demonstratives

(3) Numerals and number words

(4) Common nouns that do not take the plural

(5) What philosophers since Bertrand Russell have called definite descriptions

When we speak of Noun Phrases, Pronouns, Conjunctions, and so on, we are speaking of phrase-classes. A phrase-structure grammar makes explicit what the expressions in a phrase-class have in common, and what distinguishes them from other expressions, with respect to the variety of ways in which such expressions can be put together to form grammatical sentences. It is easy to see that Noun Phrases of the five kinds listed are interchangeable with other Noun Phrases in forming grammatical sentences. Thus designators do not form a phrase-class in that they do not behave syntactically in a way common and peculiar to them. Understanding what the varied Noun Phrases we have categorized as designators have in common, and how they differ from Noun Phrases that are not designators, will be a major aim of this chapter, as it has been a major achievement of twentieth-century studies of language. It will turn out that designators are a category of logic rather than of grammar.

Without trying to be very precise, it is worth elaborating categories (1) through (5) briefly. **Proper names** are epitomized by the names people have, whether considered as their given names alone, or their full legal names. Dog, cats, cars, and boats also have their names, as do cities, nations, months, holidays, and lots of other things. Titles of books, songs, and other works of human art also seem to fit this category. As for **singular pronouns**, in English those in the nominative case are "I," "you," "he," "she," and "it." In the objective case are "me," "you," "him," "her," and "it" again. Those in the possessive case—"my," "mine," "your," "yours," "his," "her," "hers," and "its"—have been excluded here because special problems

arise with them.   The singular demonstratives are the pure
indexicals, "this" and "that." **Numerals** are the symbolic "0," "1,"
"2," and so on, up to "9." They have their corresponding words,
"zero," "one," "two," "nine," but also "ten," "eleven."   More
complicated expressions—"seventeen," "fifty-nine," "one trillion and
one"—no doubt should be included in this category of designator.
Just how far this category goes is a matter for mathematical inquiry,
but note that here as in arithmetic we are talking about pure
numbers—*seven* rather than seven days.

To move on, **common nouns that do not take the plural** are
typified by "water" and "sugar," in contrast with so-called **count
nouns**, like "drop." (To make the contrast, note that we speak of
seven *drops* and of numerous *grains*, indicating with the plural the
propriety of counting.)   All to be included among the designators,
non-count nouns range over a surprisingly wide variety, among
them the following.

salt	oxygen	courage	green
gold	sulfur	justice	broccoli
earth	vitriol	selfishness	humankind
fire	venison	vice	carpentry
pottery	:	independence	tuberculosis
:		:	triangularity
			:

In many sentences, such a noun constitutes an entire Noun Phrase,
as in,

> Sugar is sweet.

But also the noun can take adjectives or other modifiers, to form a
larger Noun Phrase, as in,

> Brown sugar is made with molasses,

and,

> Sugar grown in Cuba is like sugar grown in Hawaii.

What is essential here is that there are no articles or counting
expressions in these Noun Phrases. In such cases the Noun Phrase
as a whole qualifies as a designator.

To be sure there are contrasting uses of these words, where the
plural does appear:

> Two different sugars, fructose and sucrose, are found in
> some soft drinks,

and,

> She chose one of the greens from the palate of color samples.

As the examples make clear, these plural forms mean *kinds* of sugar and *shades* of green, and thus use "sugar" and "green" in a different sense. Such a noun is lexically ambiguous, taking the plural in one sense, but qualifying as a designator in the sense that is intended in the examples on the previous page.

Lest we leave them out altogether, even though count nouns standing alone do not qualify as designators, we regain them as constituents of **definite descriptions**. By definition these are *singular* Noun Phrases beginning with any of the following:

(6)   the   my   George's
        this   your   Martha's
        that   :   :
                           i.e., any   i.e., the possessive
                           possessive   form of any noun or
                           pronoun   Noun Phrase

A count noun standing alone is not a definite description, nor is any expression whose count noun is in plural form, nor is a count noun introduced by other words like "a" or "every." Instead there must be a multi-word phrase beginning with a word like those listed in (6) and including a noun, which may or may not take a plural form, but in either case must have its singular form here. The great majority of Noun Phrases we end up with—"the woman in the BMW," "her BMW," "George's sister's car," "the gas in its tank"—are pretty clearly examples of descriptive indexicals, which we discussed in Chapter II. There our emphasis was on relating sentences to the propositions they expressed in various contexts. Here our emphasis will be on the logic of these expressions and what they have in common with proper names and the other kinds of designator we have canvassed. It is the effect of the initial word, taken from the lists in (6), that led Russell to call them "definite."

The survey that we have just now conducted does not exhaust the designators. There is an even greater variety of them than we have yet noticed. But since the ones listed are already so varied, and the expressions that do not qualify seem to be so similar to them, we do better to study these designators in action before looking further. As already noted, it is the logic of these expressions that sets them apart from other Noun Phrases, in particular the logic of the identity relation, which we will take up in §28. First though we should return to the logical analysis of simple sentences.

What we have seen so far is that, under logical analysis, many of the Noun Phrases to be found in simple sentences turn out to be designators. The companion notion to that of a designator is a predicate. That is to say, from a logical point of view, a great many (though not all) of the grammatically simple sentences can be analyzed into designators and predicates. The definition of a predicate naturally follows from this observation. Thus, a **predicate** is an expression that results from removing one or more designators from a sentence, leaving an unfilled position—a blank—in its place.

PROPERTIES AND RELATIONS; TYPES OF RELATIONS §27

In the prior section we saw a procedure for analyzing a simple sentence into logical components. Beginning with a sentence,

Hamlet was indecisive,

we identify in it a designator, "Hamlet." When we remove that designator from the sentence, leaving a blank, what remains is a predicate:

(1) __ was indecisive

Another case fits the same definition:

There was an air of mystery about Hamlet.

What remains when "Hamlet" is removed is another predicate:

(2) There was an air of mystery about __

(The grammatical heritage of the technical term "predicate" is obvious, for "was indecisive" is the main Verb Phrase of the sentence, what traditionally was called a predicate. But the predicate found in the second example doesn't fit that heritage.)

In both of these cases, one designator has been removed, leaving one blank. Thus these are called **one-place** predicates and are said to express **properties**. A property is something like a proposition in that it is expressed by a certain kind of linguistic expression, namely a one-place predicate. But it is distinct from the expression because, as we will see, different predicates can express the same property. In fact there may be properties that have no linguistic expression at all.

That is a philosophical claim as yet unsettled. To revert to our example, some people—like Hamlet—have the property of being indecisive, and some people—also like Hamlet—have the property of having an air of mystery about them. When the name of a person with the first of those properties is put into the blank in (1), the result is a sentence that expresses a true proposition:

Neville Chamberlain was indecisive.

Similarly, when the name of a person with the second of those properties is put into the blank in (2), as here,

There was an air of mystery about Greta Garbo,

the result again expresses a truth.

When we have a sentence with two designators,

Hamlet killed Polonius,

a one-place predicate may result from dropping only one of them:

(3)   Hamlet killed __

Here the property of having been killed by Hamlet is shared by Polonius and Claudius, and even Laertes. In these cases the blank can be maneuvered into subject position using a grammatical transformation. Thus the predicate (3) expresses the same property as this one.

__ was killed by Hamlet

It may be that a designator reappears in a sentence, or more smoothly, that an anaphoric pronoun reaches back, as in,

After Hamlet killed Ophelia's father, Ophelia killed herself.

The predicate that results from dropping all three of the designators for Ophelia is,

(4)   After Hamlet killed __'s father, __ killed __

It expresses the property of killing yourself after Hamlet has killed your father. As it happens, no one but Ophelia has this property.

As you will have anticipated, we have not only one-place predicates, but **two-place** predicates as well. A two-place predicate arises from removing two designators from a sentence,

Polonius was the father of Ophelia,

leaving two blanks:

__ was the father of __

The King was related to Hamlet in just the way Polonius was related to Ophelia. This fact is propounded by the sentence that results in putting their respective names in the blanks:

The King was the father of Hamlet.

We say that a two-place predicate expresses a **relation**. People stand in lots of different relations with those we ordinarily call their *relatives*—being the father of, being a cousin of, being a brother of, even being betrothed to and being an in-law of. For logical purposes we want to work with other relations as well, including the one that Hamlet stands in with Polonius, expressed as follows.

__ killed __

But something is lacking here. It is Hamlet that bears the relationship to Polonius, not vice versa, because Polonius did not kill Hamlet. To mark this distinction in the predicate, we need to distinguish the two places.

(5)   _1_ killed _2_

Through the transformation we can express the same relation with this predicate,

_2_ was killed by _1_

or, making use of another transformation, by this one.

It was _1_ who killed _2_

Thus relations are distinct from 2-place predicates, but they are expressed by 2-place predicates.

Seeing this discrimination of blanks takes us back to (4). There it was a property of Ophelia's that we had in mind, not a relation. We can secure our intention that it be a one-place predicate by cleverly using the same numbering device.

After Hamlet killed _1_'s father, _1_ killed _1_

An alternative numbering of the blanks will give us a two-place predicate, which does express a relation:

After Hamlet killed _1_'s father, _1_ killed _2_

Since the sentence,

After Hamlet killed Laertes' father, Laertes killed Hamlet,

expresses a truth, Laertes bears that unusual relation to Hamlet. But also Ophelia bears it to herself, as she does in the relation expressed by (5).

Logicians find it convenient to speak of properties, and even more convenient to speak of relations. Even so it is quite certain, for reasons that we won't go into (they concern Russell's Paradox) that not every one-place predicate expresses a property. And there are reasons to doubt (they concern what is called a "Bradley regress") that every two-place predicate expresses a relation. Nevertheless, we will indulge the convenience and speak freely of relations.

If you have the patience, there is no reason not to go on to a three-place predicate like this one,

> After Hamlet killed _3_'s father, _1_ killed _2_

or even to a four-place predicate like this.

> After _4_ killed _3_'s father, _1_ killed _2_

There is nothing sacred about the order of the numbers, inasmuch as this three-place predicate amounts to the same thing as the earlier one.

> _1_ killed _2_ after Hamlet killed _3_'s father

And the following predicate gets all the blanks in the more usual numerical order, but comes to the same as the earlier four-place example.

> _1_ killed _2_ after the father of _3_ was killed by _4_

Complications can continue to multiply, and logicians include predicates of arbitrarily many places in their theoretical treatments, but properties and relations are what ordinarily capture our attention in logically sensitive contexts. In fact certain relations are special in ways that we can exploit to great advantage in tableaux. These special characteristics of some relations will occupy the remainder of this chapter. In fact the machinery of predicates that we have developed so far in this section will not be exercised much in what follows. But it will help you connect material in our subsequent chapters—on quantifiers—to the treatment in books on formal logic, where predicates play a prominent role.

We saw that Polonius didn't kill Hamlet, but rather Hamlet killed him. By contrast, in other examples we said that not only did Hamlet kill Laertes, but Laertes killed Hamlet. (Perhaps we have been taking these notions too loosely to please some readers of the play.) Switching to a family relation, we have it that Laertes was the brother of Ophelia, though Ophelia was not the brother of Laertes. But again by contrast, not only was Claudius the brother of the King, but the King was also the brother of Claudius. On the other hand, there is no case where one is the father of another, and the other is also the father of the first.   Concentrating on the relations themselves—killing, being a brother of, being the father of—rather than the details of who is related to whom, we see that they differ from one another in fundamental ways.

When we loosen brotherhood up a bit, we get the relation of being a sibling of—these days kids speak of their "sibs." Ophelia is the sibling of Laertes, as he is of her.   And also with the pair Claudius and the King.   These are not peculiar cases, as with Hamlet and Laertes killing each other.   Whenever one is the sibling of another, the other is the sibling of the first.   That's just the way it is with being a sibling.   The relation is special in that it is **symmetric**.   Because this is a powerful tool of inference, we specify by way of definition that a relation is symmetric if whenever one is related to the other, the other is related to the first by that same relation.   Symmetric relations are "hand-holding" relations.   You can't hold hands with someone without that person holding hands with you.   There are lots of other relations with this character.   Other family relationships that are symmetric are cousinhood and marriage, and being an in-law, as well as the very general family relation of "being related," that is, of having an ancestor in common.

We already noted (in Chapter VI) that our ordinary ways of speaking give notice of mutual relations.   We typically say, "George and Martha are married," meaning each is related to the other.   We say that Romeo and Juliet are kissing, meaning that each is kissing the other.   This manner of speaking is much more common with symmetric relations than with others.   But take care: we say that the King and Claudius were brothers, meaning that each was the brother of the other, even though brotherhood is not a symmetric relation.   In short this manner of speaking is a very strong signal that a mutual relation is intended, rather than the logically weaker conjoining of "Romeo is kissing (someone or other)" with "Juliet is kissing (someone or other)." And it is also a signal, though a weaker one, that the relation is a symmetric one.   It is quite unusual for some relationships to be mutual, so we have to say that Hamlet and Laertes killed *each other*.   There is no idiom of mutuality.

Another peculiar manner of speaking comes to our attention when we consider these relations—or perhaps just a sloppy manner of speaking.   We say, "Claudius is the brother of the King," or "the King's brother." The Noun Phrases qualify as designators under our lists in §26.   But who is to say that the King didn't have other brothers?   Is it that only Claudius is a character in the play and so only he could be salient as a brother of the King, a case of a descriptive indexical? Evidently not, for we equally say in one breath that Lisa is Bart's sister and Maggie is also Bart's sister, so Bart has two sisters. It seems that speaking strictly we should say, "Maggie is a sister of Bart," and "Lisa is a sister of Bart." From now on, we will speak strictly in this way.

Symmetric relations are worthy of notice in logical contexts because when the symmetry is violated the result is an inconsistency. These are fairly obvious inconsistencies, but the pattern is worthy of note because this kind of inconsistency occurs so frequently in counter sets. That is simply to say that the symmetric character of a relation is very frequently the basis of an inference. Hearing that the Senator is married to the President, we infer almost without notice that the President is married to the Senator. The search for possibilities made vivid by the tableau method should serve as a warning when we hastily infer, perhaps in reading a novel, that since the Governor is a brother to the President, the President must be a brother to the Governor.

Another special type of relation is a **transitive** relation. These are usually easy to spot, but the explicit definition is cumbersome to state. It is obvious that if the King was older than Claudius and Claudius was older than Gertrude, then the King must have been older than Gertrude. Being older than is transitive. Anyone who is older than someone who is older than another is himself older than the other. That is what it takes for being older than to be transitive. Transitivity is characteristic of ordering relations; when we say that someone is taller than, or heavier than, or faster than, or more ambitious than, another, we are attributing a transitive relation. But there are other transitive relations, some of them even more interesting. It seems to be universally true that anything that is a part of something that is a part of another thing is itself part of the other. And so the relation expressed by this predicate,

_1_ is a part of _2_

is a transitive relation.

Again the special character of a relation, here transitivity, can help us recognize inconsistencies. If in a single path of a tableau we have the following three sentences, we have a pretty obvious inconsistency, and so we can close the branch.

Alex is older than Bo
Bo is older than Cam
¬ Alex is older than Cam,

Unfortunately the numbers can multiply and the sentences fall in another order, and the inconsistency becomes less obvious.

> Dee is older than Bo
> Alex is older than Flo
> Bo is older than Eddie
> ¬ Dee is older than Flo
> Eddie is older than Alex,

An expedient, though an imperfect one, is repeatedly to take sentences pairwise and spawn a new sentence based on the transitive character of the relation.

> Dee is older than Bo
> Alex is older than Flo
> Bo is older than Eddie
> ¬ Dee is older than Flo
> Eddie is older than Alex
> |
> Dee is older than Eddie
> |
> Dee is older than Alex
> |
> Dee is older than Flo
> ———————————

When the flat-out contradiction emerges, we can close the branch.

Perhaps the most interesting relations of all, from a logical point of view, are relations that are made to be transitive. The paradigm case is expressed by this predicate.

> _1_ is an ancestor of _2_

In a fairly obvious sense, parenthood is the most basic of all biological relations. But it obviously is not transitive. Your parent's parents are not your parents. They are your grandparents. On the other hand, an ancestor of an ancestor of yours is also an ancestor of yours. And ancestry can be defined in terms of parenthood. A logical device that was discovered by Frege provides for similarly defining a transitive relation on the basis of any asymmetric relation; as with ancestry a kind of chaining is involved. Unlike ancestry and descent, most of these are not expressible with ready-made predicates of English.

Some relations are both symmetric and transitive. In the context of a tableau, one step can be taken at a time, at each step using one characteristic or the other, to bring out a hidden inconsistency. We will see the method at work with the musical relation expressed by this predicate,

$$\_1\_ \text{ is in tune with } \_2\_$$

which relates one musical instrument, under a certain adjustment of slides or pegs, with another. In a simple argument, the conclusion pretty obviously follows. But let's work through some steps so as to be able to use the method when we need it.

> The oboe is in tune with the violin.
>
> The clarinet is in tune with the trumpet.
>
> The clarinet is in tune with the violin.
> _____
> The trumpet is in tune with the oboe.

We build from the counter set though in this tableau that familiar method may seem inefficient. As further examples will show, the inefficiency is unusual. Be sure that you can see how each step has been derived from one or two of the prior sentences in the single path, by way of symmetry or transitivity.

The oboe is in tune with the violin

The clarinet is in tune with the trumpet

The clarinet is in tune with the violin

¬ The trumpet is in tune with the oboe
|
The violin is in tune with the clarinet
|
The oboe is in tune with the clarinet
|
The oboe is in tune with the trumpet
|
The trumpet is in tune with the oboe
_____

The overall justification in terms of possible situations is that at each stage, the only situations with respect to which the originating sentences are true are those with respect to which the newly spawned sentence is also true. This is guaranteed by either the symmetry or the transitivity of the relation.

In fact this method can be short-circuited with another powerful idea. You may be quick to conclude that all of the instruments mentioned in the premises above are in tune with each other. What you are recognizing is the idea of an **equivalence class**, which is determined by an **equivalence relation**. With symmetry and transitivity, you are well on the way to that essentially mathematical idea.

Before moving on to an even more powerful relation, let's put the notions of transitivity and symmetry to work on a complex argument.

If Darnley and Mary Queen of Scots were cousins, James I was doubly descended from Henry VII, unless of course they didn't conceive him together.
James II was descended from James I.
Queen Anne was descended from James II if she was a sister of Mary II.
Mary Queen of Scots married her cousin Darnley and conceived James I with him after she returned from France.
Mary II and Queen Anne were sisters.

Queen Anne was descended from Henry VII.

The monster tableau below begins with the counter set, in which pronouns have been annotated and rule-governed connectives have been introduced. In particular, for the premise asserting that the two queens were sisters, we introduce separate sentences joined by the "&." Also in calling him her cousin, the fourth premise licenses a conjoined sentence stating that Darnley was a cousin of Mary Queen of Scots. Most of the early steps in the tableau are applications of rules for connectives, though the conjunction "after" comes into it as well.

(Darnley and Mary Queen of Scots were cousins →
    James I was doubly descended from Henry VII) ∨
      ¬ they (Darnley and Mary Queen of Scots) conceived him (James I) together
James II was descended from James I
She (Queen Anne) was a sister of Mary II →
    Queen Anne was descended from James II
√ Darnley was a cousin of Mary Queen of Scots &
    ((Mary Queen of Scots married Darnley &
    Mary Queen of Scots conceived James I with him (Darnley))
    after she (Mary Queen of Scots) returned from France)
√ Mary II was a sister of Queen Anne &
    Queen Anne was a sister of Mary II
    ¬ Queen Anne was descended from Henry VII

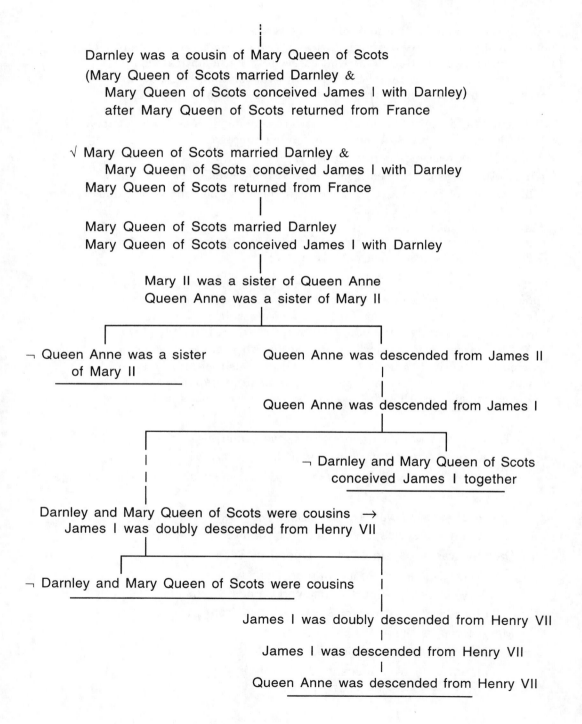

Darnley was a cousin of Mary Queen of Scots

(Mary Queen of Scots married Darnley &
    Mary Queen of Scots conceived James I with Darnley)
    after Mary Queen of Scots returned from France

√ Mary Queen of Scots married Darnley &
    Mary Queen of Scots conceived James I with Darnley
Mary Queen of Scots returned from France

Mary Queen of Scots married Darnley
Mary Queen of Scots conceived James I with Darnley

Mary II was a sister of Queen Anne
Queen Anne was a sister of Mary II

¬ Queen Anne was a sister
    of Mary II

Queen Anne was descended from James II

Queen Anne was descended from James I

¬ Darnley and Mary Queen of Scots
    conceived James I together

Darnley and Mary Queen of Scots were cousins →
James I was doubly descended from Henry VII

¬ Darnley and Mary Queen of Scots were cousins

James I was doubly descended from Henry VII

James I was descended from Henry VII

Queen Anne was descended from Henry VII

Farther on in the tableau the relations do their work. At the top right of this page we derive that Queen Anne was descended from James I by way of the transitivity of that relation. Then the right-hand branch closes because earlier in the path it says that Mary conceived James I with Darnley. Similarly, the left branch at the end closes because earlier it says that Darnley was a cousin of Mary. Some more transitivity of descent finishes off the right branch at the end.

THE PECULIAR RELATION OF IDENTITY   §28

Of all relations that play a powerful role in logic, the most important is the relation of identity. It is a peculiar relation, and one that has generated philosophical perplexity, because it is a relation that everyone bears to him or herself. We call such relations **reflexive**, which reminds us of seeing our reflection in the mirror. But unlike other reflexive relations—you can often see others in the mirror as well—no one bears the identity relation to anyone else. It is a wonder that any relation so commonplace could be powerful logically. Its power derives from a principle named after the seventeenth-century genius, Gottfried Wilhelm Leibniz.

Leibniz's Law: If (1) D and E are designators, and (2) the identity sentence,

$$D = E,$$

is true with respect to a situation, and (3) sentence S_2 is exactly like sentence S_1 except for having (one or more) occurrences of E where S_1 has occurrences of D, then S_2 is true with respect to that same situation if, and only if, S_1 is.

It seems that it is Leibniz's Law that underlies much of our reasoning involving identity. Thus since Putin, a former officer of the KGB, has become the President of Russia, we unhesitatingly conclude that the President of Russia is a former officer of the KGB. We barely even notice the transition. The reasoning that in fact we carry out can be represented by this argument.

Putin is a former officer of the KGB.

Putin is now the President of Russia.

The President of Russia is a former officer of the KGB.

Where D is the designator "Putin"—a proper name—and E is the designator "the President of Russia"—a definite description—the argument has its justification in Leibniz's Law as it is stated above. The given labeling shows how the Law applies to these sentences.

S_1	(Putin) is a former officer of the KGB.
$D = E$	(Putin) = (the President of Russia).

S_2	(The President of Russia) is a former officer of the KGB.

Obviously S_2 is the result of replacing the occurrence of D in S_1 with E. According to Leibniz's Law, if the identity sentence, D = E, is true with respect to a situation, then S_2 is true with respect to that situation if S_1 is. But that means that there is no situation with respect to which these premises are true while this conclusion is false, and thus by definition we have a valid argument.

We might speak of E being **substituted** for D in S_1, producing S_2. In this manner of speaking, Leibniz's Law is called the **Principle of Substitutivity**. It has its most familiar application in mathematics, where, as they say, "equals can be substituted for equals." Constantly in algebraic derivations we make such substitutions, as for example, when we have $v = v_0 + at$, and the equation,

$$K.E. = (mv^2)/2$$

we derive,

$$K.E. = (m(v_0 + at)^2)/2$$

As this example shows, S_1 and S_2 might themselves be identity sentences, but in the more general case they are not. In fact there is nothing peculiarly mathematical about the reasoning we have applied to these equations and the substitutions we have made. From the logical point of view, they are simply applications of Leibniz's Law, which applies to sentences in whatever domain of interest, so long as the relation of identity is in place.

As we have formulated it, Leibniz's Law also validates an argument where, relative to the other premise, the identity statement is the other way around. Thus learning that Putin has become the President of Russia and knowing that the President of Russia commands the world's second-largest nuclear force, we correctly infer that Putin commands the world's second-largest nuclear force. It is the following argument that represents the inference this time.

(1)

> The President of Russia commands the world's second-largest nuclear force.
>
> Putin is now the President of Russia.
> _____
>
> Putin commands the world's second-largest nuclear force.

The labeling has to be different for us to see how Leibniz's Law applies to this new argument. (Note that, in effect, D has been substituted for E this time.)

> S_1 (the President of Russia) commands the world's second-largest nuclear force.
>
> $D = E$ (Putin) = (the President of Russia).
> _____
>
> S_2 (Putin) commands the world's second-largest nuclear force.

Given that $D = E$ is true with respect to a situation, S_2 is true with respect to that situation *only* if S_1 is true as well. Thus as before, there is no situation with respect to which the premises are true and the conclusion is false, and so again the argument is a valid one. For the purposes of applying Leibniz's Law, simply remember that it doesn't matter which way the identity sentence goes, so long as the conclusion is the result of substituting one of the designators for the other—in the appropriate premise.

Having Leibniz's Law in hand, we can return to the contrast between designators and the other Noun Phrases. The application of Leibniz's Law to a Noun Phrase that is not a designator is fallacious. In the following argument, the Noun Phrase "a former officer of the KGB," occurs in the first premise.

> A former officer of the KGB commands the world's second-largest nuclear force.
>
> Primakov is a former officer of the KGB.
> _____
>
> Primakov commands the world's second-largest nuclear force.

That Noun Phrase has been treated like a designator in that the proper name, "Primakov"—which indeed is a designator—has been substituted for it to form the conclusion. Since the premises are actually true and the conclusion is actually false, the argument certainly is not valid. The fault does not lie with Leibniz's Law. Rather it lies in misapplying it. The crucial difference between this argument and (1) above is the seemingly minor difference between the words "the" and "a." It may have seemed arbitrary to focus on singular Noun

Phrases beginning with just the words listed in (6) of §26, but the choice there yields a class of designators right for the purposes of Leibniz's Law. Designators can be inter-substituted on the basis of statements of identity; it is this that best characterizes them. Calling them designators suggests that in each case there is some individual thing that is designated; however suggestive this idea is, what it is that is designated will often elude us. Yet in each case the Noun Phrase will turn out to be workable under Leibniz's Law.

Some accounts emphasize another aspect of the sentence,

(2)   Primakov is a former officer of the KGB.

Perhaps the word "is" in that sentence does not even express the identity relation. This example reminds us of cases where the word "is" appears as the main Verb of a sentence though the identity relation certainly is not involved. The clearest cases are those generated by the following rewriting rule—the singular version of a rule given in Chapter V.

Verb Phrase   ⇒   **is**   Adjective

One such sentence is,

(3)   Primakov is human.

Clearly no relation has been expressed; rather, the simple property of being human has been attributed to Primakov. It is a peculiarity of English—and similarly of many other languages—that this attribution requires not just the adjective, but the word "is," called here the **copula**. (Sometimes, the copula is called the "is" of predication—since "human" has been predicated of Primakov.) Arguably another sentence closely paralleling (2) expresses the same proposition.

(4)   Primakov is a human being.

If the identity relation does not enter into (3), so this account goes, then it equally does not enter into (4). Whatever the merits of this argument, there is no denying that the identity relation is not expressed in (3), and this makes the essential point that identity is not just a matter of the word "is."

The most vexing case shares with (3) its derivation from the adjectival rewriting rule.

(5)   Mary-Kate is identical to Ashley.

Despite the employment of the word "identical," this sentence does not predicate the identity relation of Mary-Kate and Ashley. The proof is again in the failure of Leibniz's Law. Clearly "Mary-Kate" and "Ashley" are both designators, yet equally clearly this argument is fallacious.

> I saw Mary-Kate on *Full House* today.
> Mary-Kate is identical to Ashley.
> ___
> I saw Ashley on *Full House* today.

The substitution has been made correctly, so we are left with denying that (5) is a case of "D = E." Despite appearances, this predicate

_1_ is identical to _2_

does not express the identity relation, but rather expresses a relation of similarity, to a greater or lesser degree. Even when we say that two things are *exactly* similar, we still leave it open that they are two—as with identical twins, with photocopies, or with products of an assembly line. When we predicate the identity relation of two things, we really assert that they are not two, but one. This becomes explicit in what is perhaps the least equivocal predicate for expressing the identity relation:

_1_ is *one* and the same as _2_

When another argument is proffered, one which makes use of this formulation, we see that the conclusion indeed follows. (Of course another designator has been chosen, one for which the identity statement will be true.) And once again Leibniz's Law has been vindicated.

> I saw Mary-Kate on *Full House* today.
> Mary-Kate is (one and the same as) the first-born Olsen twin.
> ___
> I saw the first-born Olsen twin on *Full House* today.

For practical purposes it is worth setting out some pointers as to how to recognize formulations of the identity relation. The relation is symmetrical, so when we have a genuine identity sentence,

The President of Russia is Putin,

the two designators can be switched around,

Putin is the President of Russia,

resulting in something that sounds all right, and in fact means pretty much the same thing as the original. Contrast the case where "is" does not express identity, but merely functions as the copula.

> The President of Russia is unfamiliar,

When the expressions are switched around,

> Unfamiliar is the President of Russia,

we get a sentence that is perhaps grammatical, but certainly archaic in its feel. It sounds like the Biblical phrasing,

> Strait is the gate, and narrow is the way,

which is now usable only poetically. This indicates that we do not have a case of the identity relation. Applying this test to our earlier case (2) gives a similarly stilted result.

> A former officer of the KGB is Primakov.

So again (2) is not an identity sentence.

We have already seen that besides the brief formulation,

> The President of Russia is Putin,

we have the unequivocal,

> The President of Russia is one and the same as Putin,

and the more informative,

> The President of Russia is one and the same *man* as Putin.

Other common formulations of the identity relation include,

> The President of Russia is the same as Putin,

> The President of Russia is none other than Putin,

> The President of Russia and Putin are one,

and even the mathematical version,

> The President of Russia equals Putin,

but *not*,

> The President of Russia is identical to Putin.

Except for the last one, any of these formulations can be recognized as the identity relation, and all of them can be symbolized as,

> The President of Russia = Putin,

in preparation for handling the identity relation in a tableau. Since identity sentences occur in arguments, and since Leibniz's Law undergirds the validity of many such arguments, it is time to develop more systematic means of assessing arguments in which the identity symbol occurs. That is the topic of the next section.

We want to adapt Leibniz's Law for the purposes of building tableau and thereby discovering whether a set of sentences variously involving the identity relation is or is not consistent. This rule is just a permission. You would make a mess by applying it wantonly, at every opportunity. The trick is to recognize which applications of the rule will make the various branches of a tableau close.

> **Leibniz's Rule for Tableaux:** If in any path of a tableau there occurs both S(D) and D = E (or E = D), you may append S(E) to any branch *below* those occurrences. *Do not* check off any of the sentences.

This formulation makes the substitution vivid. Obviously what is meant is that S(E) is just like S(D) except for having an occurrence of E where S(D) has an occurrence of D.

We illustrate Leibniz's Rule first with an argument that involves identity, but no other logical considerations.

> The eldest son of the Queen is the heir to the throne.
>
> Elizabeth is the Queen.
>
> Charles is the eldest son of Elizabeth.
> ───
> Charles is the heir to the throne.

We rewrite the several sentences, symbolizing the identity relation with "=," and construct the counter set. Then we proceed to apply the rule.

> The eldest son of the Queen = the heir to the throne
> Elizabeth = the Queen
> Charles = the eldest son of Elizabeth
> ¬ (Charles = the heir to the throne)
> |
> Charles = the eldest son of the Queen
> |
> Charles = the heir to the throne
> ─────────────────────────────────────

Since there are no other logical constructions, there is no branching in the tableau. In the first application of Leibniz's Rule, "the Queen" has been substituted for "Elizabeth." In the second, "Charles" has been substituted for "the eldest son of the Queen." The resulting sentence conflicts with the negated conclusion, and so the tableau closes.

A more complex argument again involves not only identity, but grammatically complex sentences and anaphoric pronouns.

Juliet is forbidden to see the Montague heir.

Even if the Montague heir is the boy on the balcony, Juliet is forbidden to see him.

Unless he was Mercutio, the boy at the dance was Romeo.

The boy at the dance wore blue, but Mercutio did not.

If Romeo wore blue, then he is the boy on the balcony.

Juliet is forbidden both to see the boy at the dance and to see the boy on the balcony.

Thus, as we construct the counter set, we not only symbolize the identity relation, but we introduce rule-governed sentence connectives and annotate pronouns as well.

Juliet is forbidden to see the Montague heir

Even if the Montague heir = the boy on the balcony,
     Juliet is forbidden to see him (the Montague heir)

The boy at the dance = Romeo $\lor$ he (the boy at the dance) = Mercutio

The boy at the dance wore blue   & $\neg$ Mercutio wore blue

Romeo wore blue $\rightarrow$ he (Romeo) = the boy on the balcony

$\neg$ (Juliet is forbidden to see the boy at the dance &
     Juliet is forbidden to see the boy on the balcony)

In arguments involving identity, the treatment of anaphoric pronouns is especially delicate. After all, the whole point of such pronouns is to share a reference with their antecedents, which is to say that whatever the pronoun refers to is one and the same as whatever the antecedent refers to. If the antecedent is not correctly chosen, the work to be done by Leibniz's Rule may be short-circuited. For that reason you must take care to annotate each anaphoric pronouns with the right antecedent. (Note especially the anaphor in the second premise.) As the sentences are broken down in later stages of the tableau, the antecedent expression can take the place of the pronoun that it annotates.

The tableau is on the next page. Notice in particular that some of the identity sentences occur not in the trunk of the tableau, but in one branch or another. It is very important to observe the qualification in Leibniz's Rule: you may append S(E) only to branches *below the occurrence of the relevant identity sentence*. These branches describe ways of making the original sentences true in which the identity sentence itself is true; there are other ways of making the original sentence true in which that identity does not hold.

Juliet is forbidden to see the Montague heir

Even if the Montague heir = the boy on the balcony,
   Juliet is forbidden to see the Montague heir

√ The boy at the dance = Romeo   ∨   the boy at the dance = Mercutio

√ The boy at the dance wore blue   &   ¬ Mercutio wore blue

Romeo wore blue   →   Romeo = the boy on the balcony

√ ¬ (Juliet is forbidden to see the boy at the dance &
   Juliet is forbidden to see the boy on the balcony)

The boy at the dance wore blue

¬ Mercutio wore blue

The boy at the dance = Romeo

The boy at the dance = Mercutio

Mercutio wore blue
_____

¬ Romeo wore blue

Romeo = the boy on the balcony

¬ The boy at the dance wore blue
_____

¬ Juliet is forbidden to
see the boy at the dance

¬ Juliet is forbidden to
see the boy on the balcony

¬ Juliet is forbidden
to see Romeo

¬ Juliet is forbidden
to see Romeo

Perhaps it surprises you that the tableau does not close. Are you taking it for granted that Romeo *is* the Montague heir? Adding a premise to that effect, and applying Leibniz's Rule, will cause both open branches to close, for they both include these two sentences.

Juliet is forbidden to see the Montague heir

¬ Juliet is forbidden to see Romeo

But what about the argument in the absence of that premise? The branches should stay open because there is a possible situation with respect to which both of those sentences are true. It would be easy to tell a story of the right sort. It would have *two* characters, Romeo and the Montague heir. It doesn't matter whether it is impossible by some other standard for Romeo not to have been a son of old Montague. What matters is whether we can tell an intelligible story in which Romeo is not the son of Montague.

Before leaving the tableau, do notice the effect of wrongly assigning "the boy on the balcony" as the antecedent of the anaphoric pronoun "him" in the second premise. We would have the sentence,

Even if the Montague heir = the boy on the balcony,

Juliet is forbidden to see him (the boy on the balcony)

in the trunk of the tableau. And from that we could spawn the simpler sentence,

Juliet is forbidden to see the boy on the balcony,

in the main path. The branch on the bottom right would close directly. The branch on the bottom left would close with one more application of Leibniz's Rule. And so we would arrive at the fallacious verdict that the argument is valid. This brings out the pivotal and subtle character of anaphoric reference.

Having analyzed sentences into designators and predicates, and having seen in particular the logical role of two-place predicates that express special relations like identity, we are ready to consider another kind of Noun Phrase that can fill the blank in a predicate. That will be the subject of the next two chapters.

1. Find all of the designators which occur *as constituents* of the following sentences; say which of the five types each designator belongs to.

> Not everyone believes that God created the world in seven days. Whoever does must answer the question why He created not only sugar to please the palates of the people He created, but ants to eat the sugar and ruin picnics. This is a puzzle. And why is the number of ants greater than one billion? Perhaps that question is not so puzzling.

2. In each case below, write down a conclusion that follows from the premises listed by either the symmetry or the transitivity of the relation in question. (Say which. And be aware that it might involve both.) In those cases where no conclusion follows *by these considerations*, say so.

a. Sir John was Prime Minister before Sir Wilfrid.
    Sir Wilfrid was Prime Minister before Pierre Elliott.

b. Teddy Roosevelt was a cousin of Franklin Roosevelt.

c. Brussels sprouts belong to the same species as cabbage.
    Cabbage belongs to the same species as cauliflower.

d. John Locke was smarter than Benjamin Franklin.
    Benjamin Franklin was smarter than Leonardo da Vinci.

e. Sybil was married to someone that Elizabeth was married to.
    Elizabeth was married to someone that Debbie was married to.

f. My Red Sox pennant coincides with your Maple Leafs pennant.
    Your Maple Leafs pennant coincides with her Princeton pennant.

g. The new drummer was introduced to Sarah McLachlan.
    Sarah McLachlan was introduced to the Queen.

h. Yellowknife is north of Edmonton.
    Edmonton is north of Calgary.

i. Lisa is a sister of Bart.
    Maggie is a sister of Bart.

j. The highway is parallel to the railroad track.
    The highway is parallel to the telephone wires.

3.   In each case, write down a conclusion that follows by Leibniz's Law from the
        two premises listed. In those cases where no conclusion follows *by this law*,
        say so.

   a.   Water is transparent.
            Water is the world's most common liquid.

   b.   The Morning Star rises in the East.
            The Morning Star is one and the same thing as the Evening Star.

   c.   A dog bit my youngest daughter.
            Kathleen is my youngest daughter.

   d.   God is love.
            God is the creator of the universe.

   e.   My daughters paid for the party together.
            Kathleen is my daughter.

   f.   My Jaguar is in the shop for repairs.
            Your Jaguar is identical to my Jaguar.

   g.   George W. Bush was governor of Texas.
            The President of the United States is none other than George W. Bush.

   h.   The eldest son of George H. W. Bush became President of the US in 2001.
            The 41st President of the US was George H.W. Bush.

   i.   A dog bit my daughter.
            Bowser is a dog.

   j.   My bank balance is the sum of my former balance and my deposit.
            The sum of my former balance and my deposit is enough to cover the
            rent.

For each of the following arguments, reformulate using rule-governed sentence
connectives and the identity sign. (Put into the conventional style if necessary.) Then
show that the argument is valid by constructing a tableau.

4.   Baffin Island is a part of either Nunavut or Labrador. And Labrador is a part
        of Newfoundland. But both Nunavut and Newfoundland are part of Canada.
        So in any case Baffin Island is a part of Canada.

5.

   | The bank is next to the cleaners and between the grocery and the avenue.
   | The cleaners is between the bank and the avenue.

   | The cleaners is next to the bank and between the grocery and the avenue.

(Hint: In addition to this 2-place predicate,

_1_ is next to _2_

make use of another 2-place predicate:

_1_ is between _2_ and the avenue

Which predicate expresses a symmetric relation? Which, a transitive relation?)

6.

> Either the cellist or the violist is the President's daughter.
>
> The cellist has blue eyes, though the President's daughter has brown eyes.
> _____
>
> The violist has brown eyes.

To close one of the branches you will have to add a suppressed premise; the one that works best is simple, weak, and obviously true.

7.

> If Percy was not in bed at midnight, then Percy is the murderer.
>
> If Percy was in bed at midnight, then Percy heard her scream.
>
> The murderer heard her scream.
> _____
>
> Percy heard her scream.

8.

> If the lady in the black Mercedes visited him, then Ortcutt is the Soviet spy.
>
> Ortcutt knows the NATO defense strategy.
>
> The lady in the black Mercedes drove down Ortcutt's lane and visited him.
> _____
>
> The Soviet spy knows the NATO defense strategy.

9.

> The Vice-President who replaced the running-mate of the President who resigned was never elected to national office.
>
> Ford was the Vice-President who replaced Agnew.
>
> Agnew was the running-mate of Nixon.
>
> The President who resigned was Nixon.
> _____
>
> Ford was never elected to national office.

10.   The essential characteristic of a designator is that it be usable under Leibniz's
       Law. On that basis identify at least six designators in what follows, none of
       which falls into the five categories listed in §26.

              "Euclid" is the name of a Greek geometer. Even before 300 B.C.E.
              he proved that √2 is irrational. The Pythagorean Theorem entails
              that √2 is the diagonal of a unit square. The question I would ask
              is why the Greeks were so surprised. That Euclid proved it first is
              not true. Learning about diagonals was not the only thing the
              Pythagoreans did with numbers. They also studied the ratio of
              middle C to the note an octave higher. What I also wonder is
              whether Sunday was in their week.

VIII: One-Word Quantifiers

In one of the most influential passages of modern philosophy, René Descartes wrote about being and nothingness.

On looking for the cause of [my] errors, I find that I possess not only a real and positive idea of God, or a being who is supremely perfect, but also what may be described as a negative idea of nothingness, or of that which is farthest removed from all perfections. I realize that I am, as it were, something intermediate between God and nothingness, or between supreme being and non-being.

It is not our purpose glibly to criticize great philosophers, yet it must be said that many logicians have thought that these remarks invite confusion of a peculiarly noxious sort. (What is it that participates in this idea of nothingness? Nothing?) Similar confusions and ambiguities underlie the appeal of the anarchist bumper sticker,

> No government is better than no government.

The slogan would have us understand that it is as good to have no government at all as it is to have a government of any variety. Unfortunately, if it can be so understood, the slogan equally can be taken to express the absurdity that not having any government at all is better than not having any government at all. And, even as the (seemingly) contrary doctrine that not having any government at all is *not* better than having a government of whatever variety you choose. Taken literally and carefully, what the sentence means is that there is no worst government (that is, none better than no other), a proposition that perhaps is true even by anarchist lights. But you are not likely to get this message as a car bearing it races by.

These perplexities all arise from a failure to appreciate the logic of quantifier expressions. In Chapter VII we recognized that for logical purposes the syntactic category of Noun Phrase had to be subdivided. Eligible substitutions under Leibniz's Law were there confined to designators, which were to be distinguished from other Noun Phrases. However difficult designators were to delimit, the need to distinguish them from quantifier expressions is illustrated by the following travesty.

(No number) is greater than every other number.	True
(No number) = (every number).	True
(Every number) is greater than every other number.	False

As in Chapter VII the relevant expressions have been bracketed and the identity symbol introduced in order to make visible the purported application of Leibniz's Law. To make the difficulty unmistakable we should ask ourselves whether indeed no number is greater than every other number and indeed no number is identical with every number. Even as we assent to these arithmetical propositions, we yet will deny that every number is greater than every other. And there will lie the difficulty for Leibniz's Law—unless, as in our formulation of it, that law is restricted to apply only to designators.

What we are beginning to recognize is a category of Noun Phrase whose logic is at odds with the traditional definition of a noun as the name of a person, place, thing, or idea. The passage from Descartes tempts us to misunderstand the noun "nothing" as indeed the name of a thing, but not of any ordinary thing. As a name, "nothing" seems to refer to a particularly mysterious thing, *alluring* to some among us, a ghost or a shadow of a thing. In the sections to come we will learn why this is a serious logical misunderstanding. More constructively we will begin to learn how to handle the logic of a very wide and very fascinating class of linguistic expressions.

The following are grammatical sentences of English, each with its own Noun Phrase followed by the Verb Phrase "loved Maria." (As it happens the sentences are all true with respect to the situation of the musical *West Side Story*.)

Two guys loved Maria.

Not many Jets loved Maria.

Some Polish guy loved Maria.

None but young people loved Maria.

Most of those fighting loved Maria.

No Jet other than Tony loved Maria.

A handsome, serious one loved Maria.

None of the Jets' girlfriends loved Maria.

Only Tony and the Puerto Ricans loved Maria.

Some members of the two gangs loved Maria.

All of the girls working in the dress shop loved Maria.

Fewer guys than you might expect to love her loved Maria.

Some guys that didn't know each other very well loved Maria.

None of these main Noun Phrases are designators. All of them turn out to be **quantifier expressions**, a term that seems appropriate to "two guys," but less so to "no Jet other than Tony" or "all of the girls." The term is traditional among logicians, and indeed there are ever so many numerically definite quantifier expressions—"three guys," "fifty-nine members of a gang," "a trillion and one grains of sand," and so on. As we understand them better we will see that in fact all quantifier expressions have implications as to quantity or number, though in many cases—"Nobody shot Maria"—the number in question is zero.

Without explicitly defining quantifier expressions, we can say a few things to help get a feel for them. They are all Noun Phrases. **One-word quantifiers**, among them "everyone," "something," "nobody," "ever," and "somewhere," consist of just one word. (In §31 we will begin investigating the logic of quantifiers by focussing on the simplest of these.) With the exception of one-word quantifiers, quantifier expressions characteristically incorporate one or more general terms. Common nouns like "guy" and "Jet," adjectives like "handsome" and "serious," and verbs in adjectival form like "fighting," are general in that they apply to more than one thing. Characteristically the common nouns in question are count nouns;

the nouns "guy," "member," and "Jet"—unlike "sugar," "courage," or "five"—have a plural form. Occasionally such count nouns stand alone as Noun Phrases, as in the sentence, "Roses are red." But more frequently there are words that go with the count noun to form a Noun Phrase, words like "a," "some," "no," "fifty-nine," "none but," "most," "all," and "each." In the more long-winded cases there seem to be clauses incorporated into the quantifiers, taking advantage of recursive rules of English grammar that let the expression grow without bound. These are some of the Noun Phrases that qualify as quantifiers. It would be no simple matter to specify the syntax of quantifier expressions in more detail, and we will not attempt to do so. More important is to recognize that the quantifier expression as a whole does not designate a specific person or thing. In fact the logical function of quantifier expressions is not to refer or designate at all. Their function is more subtle and is best understood by considering inferences that involve quantifier expressions as we will do before long.

This last point applies in particular to quantifier expressions involving the indefinite article "a" (or "an") and the closely related word "some." When Maria sings, *"FOR I'M LOVED BY A PRETTY WONDERFUL BOY!"* of course she has Tony in mind. But her friends, using the same expression, are thinking of Chino. The quantifier expression may well apply to both Tony and Chino in that each of them may be a pretty wonderful boy. But unlike a designator ("the wonderful boy that sang to Maria on the fire-escape"), the quantifier expression "a pretty wonderful boy" does not designate either of them. This can be seen by again considering Maria's friends. Suppose Chino had been killed, or that he had realized that Maria was in love with Tony. In either case, she might well not have been loved by Chino at the time her friends were singing. But her friends' sentence, "She is loved by a pretty wonderful boy," would have remained true, and not because it is ambiguous. Even if what her friends had in mind was that Chino loved her, even if *they* in some sense were referring to Chino, the sentence they were using simply meant that some wonderful boy or other loved her as they sang. Since Maria felt—and was—so pretty, it wouldn't be surprising if lots of them did!

There is a familiar convention of narrative that complicates this point. In introducing a particular person or thing into a narrative, it is conventional to initially use the indefinite article, and thereby provide a context that secures a reference for descriptive indexicals using the *definite* article.

(1)

A pretty, young girl moved from Puerto Rico to join her family in New York. The young girl had a daring brother who belonged to a gang of street kids. Her brother was the leader of the gang.

In this passage the expressions "a pretty, young girl," "a daring brother," and "a gang of street kids" are used to indicate that the narrator has in mind a specific girl, brother, and gang. These are subsequently referred to by the descriptive indexicals, "the young girl," "her brother," and "the gang." Those indexicals are indeed designators, referring respectively to Maria, Bernardo, and the Sharks. Even so, "a pretty, young girl" remains perfectly general, whoever the narrator means to introduce. The point is clinched by remembering the stricture on Leibniz's Law. Knowing that Bernardo was her brother, we are entitled by Leibniz's Law to infer from the sentences in (1) that Bernardo was the leader of the gang. But knowing that Anita was (also) a pretty, young girl does *not* entitle us to infer that Anita moved from Puerto Rico to join her family in New York. The difference between "a" and "the," which at first seems minuscule, turns out to be all the difference between designators and quantifiers.

THE SIMPLEST QUANTIFIERS: "EVERYONE," "SOMEONE," AND "NO ONE" §31

Arguments whose validity depends essentially on quantifier expressions are numerous and varied. That their logic can be complex is illustrated in the following valid argument.

> Most of the Sharks know Maria.
> Most of the Jets know Bernardo.
> Any who do not know Maria do not know Bernardo.
> All of the gang members are either Jets or Sharks.
>
> Most of the gang members know Maria.

When it is changed slightly, the result is an argument that is not valid.

> Most of the Sharks know Maria.
>
> Most of the Jets know Bernardo.
>
> Any who do not know Maria do not know Bernardo.
>
> *Most* of the gang members are either Jets or Sharks.
> _____
> Most of the gang members know Maria.

It is easy to describe a possible situation with respect to which all of the premises of the latter argument, including the revised fourth one, are true but yet the conclusion is false. Doing so involves specifying how many there are of various sorts, and so the logic of the argument pretty clearly verges on arithmetic.

To establish a beachhead with quantifier logic, while avoiding numerical calculation, logicians have focussed first on the simplest quantifiers, here represented in these grammatically simple sentences, each with a one-word main Noun Phrase, each true with respect to the situation in *West Side Story*.

(1a)   Everyone knew Maria.

(1b)   Someone loved Maria.

(1c)   No one killed Maria.

A glimpse of the logic of these sentences will enable us to become clearer about their meaning. Since—by the time of the last scene, which centers on her—**everyone** knew Maria, both Tony and Bernardo did (obviously) and so did Officer Krupke (less obviously). But what about Vladimir Putin? Since everyone knew Maria, must Putin have known her? No. When we say "everyone," the force of the quantifier is relative to a **universe of discourse**. Here the discourse is a musical play, so it is natural to take the cast of characters to comprise the universe over which the quantifier ranges. In other cases the boundaries of the universe of discourse might not be so clear, and perhaps there are assertions ("God loves everyone") whose universe of discourse is meant to be all-encompassing. It is not only in cases where the individuals are fictional that the universe of discourse is restricted. If a teacher says, "Everyone passed," she is not including Putin. Presumably the universe of discourse for her "everyone" is the class of students she is teaching.

Let's go on with our survey of these simplest quantifiers. Since Tony loved Maria, **someone** did. But Chino did also, so in saying that someone did we don't mean exactly one. Note that even if everyone loved Maria, it would still be true that Tony loved her, and thus that someone did. So the sentence (1b) "Someone loved Maria," does not conflict with the sentence "Everyone loved Maria," that is, it does not mean that someone, but not everyone, loved Maria, though it is sometimes used with that implication. Finally, if Chino had killed Maria, or she had killed herself, it wouldn't be true that **no one** killed her. And thus since it is true, Chino must *not* have, and Maria herself must *not* have. Equally Krupke must not have. Again the generalization is relative to the universe of discourse. When the teacher says, "No one may leave the room," her prohibition does not extend to the principal.

As we mentioned from the outset, each of the sentences in (1) is very simple grammatically, as simple as,

(2)   Tony killed Bernardo,

whose phrase-marker would be exactly the same, short of the terminal symbols. Even so, their implications are much wider. For each of these one-word quantifiers, we will formulate two logical rules for use in tableaux, one for the sentence itself, and one for its negation, as it might arise in a rule-governed tableau.

As for negations, these occur in ordinary discourse as well as in the constructions of tableaux. A survey of some sentences expressing them and their syntactic derivations calls our attention to new grammatical complications. The negation of (1a) is pretty smoothly formulated as

(3)   Not everyone knew Maria,

whereas the negation of (2) would be

(4)   Tony did not kill Bernardo.

When that modification is applied to (1a) we are in for a surprise.

(5)   Everyone did not know Maria.

Sentence (5) is ambiguous. It might be meant as equivalent to (3), the negation of (1a). But equally it might be meant as denying that anyone knew Maria, i.e., as saying of each of them that he or she did not know Maria. What we have here is an ambiguity of *scope*, similar to syntactic scope ambiguities that we explored in Chapter VI, but not as simply explained. Still it's worth a try.

In Chapter V we explained syntactic ambiguities by providing distinct phrase-markers for a single terminal string. A phrase-marker for (3) is pretty easy to put forward, even without benefit of appropriate rewriting rules.

(6)

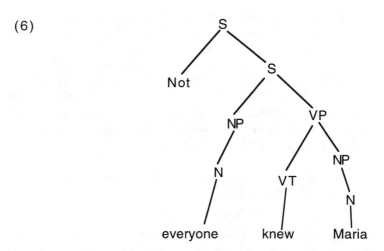

Here the negating word "not" applies syntactically to the sentence within. That same phrase-marker with different terminal symbols gives the terminal string,

> Not Tony killed Bernardo,

which is not grammatical. But it is easy to suppose that an obligatory transformation,

Not NP VP ⇒ NP **do not** VP

applies to the phrase-marker, yielding the derived string (4). And, on the understanding of (5) as equivalent to (3), the same transformation would seem to be at work.

Another parsing of (5), to make manifest the syntactic ambiguity, would look like this.

(7)

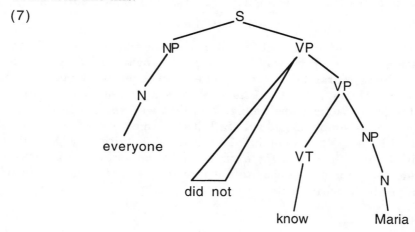

Whether or not further linguistic inquiry would provide support for a grammar with the requisite rewriting rules and transformations, these phrase-markers make the essential point that in one way of understanding (5), the (underlying) phrase-marker (6) has "everyone knew Maria" within the scope of "not," while in the other way of understanding (5), the phrase-marker (7) has "did not know Maria" within the scope of "everyone." Like the cases we studied in connection with grouping in Chapter VI, the syntactic ambiguity is an ambiguity of scope as we defined that notion in §18.

Let's see what happens when we try to extend this explanation to similar cases with other one-word quantifiers. How is the negation of a "someone"-sentence smoothly expressed? In analogy with (4), we might expect,

Not someone wanted to fight,

to become acceptable to our ears by being transformed into,

(8)   Someone did not want to fight.

If so, we are on thin ice, because in saying (8), which is unambiguous, we do not deny,

(9)   Someone wanted to fight.

To deny (9), we should say,

(10)   No one wanted to fight.

Focussing on (10) in its own right, we formulate,

(11)   No one did not want to fight.

This latter, unlike (5), is also unambiguous. But it does not exactly negate (10); it might be that neither (10) nor (11) is true.

The difficulties and curious behavior of (8) through (11) can be sorted out only by considering their logical relations with instances and rules for them in tableaux, something we will get to in §32. However that turns out, the general worry about quantifiers and the scope of "not" illustrated in the contrasting phrase-markers (6) and (7) seems to be present in sentences (8) through (11) as well. It turns out that the Conjunctions "and" and "or" give rise to similar worries about scope. To address these worries adequately, we must challenge a grammatical principle that was implicit in the allusion to transformations in the previous paragraphs and that underlay the deployment of transformations in logical analysis in Chapter VI.

According to the methods of §23 we are to analyze the sentence,

Riff supported either the Jets or the Sharks,

as the transformational equivalent of the underlying sentence,

Either Riff supported the Jets or Riff supported the Sharks,

and introduce the rule-governed connective "∨" between the simple sentences. In calling it an equivalent, we presume that the two sentences are synonymous. Here we implicitly rely on what has been known to linguists as the **Katz-Postal Hypothesis**, which is the supposition that grammatical transformations always preserve meaning. According to this hypothesis the underlying string is synonymous with the derived string whenever a transformation operates. Linguists have long known of cases that apparently disprove this hypothesis in its full generality. And we are on the verge of recognizing a case that itself counts as an exception. Since the quantifier "everyone" is a Noun Phrase, the same account that we saw above with the Noun Phrase "Riff" applies to the sentence,

(12)   Everyone supported either the Jets or the Sharks.

On this account, it derives transformationally from the underlying sentence,

(13)   Either everyone supported the Jets, or
                        everyone supported the Sharks.

This violates the Katz-Postal principle—because (12) and (13) clearly differ in meaning. In fact, with respect to the situation in *West Side Story*, (13) is obviously false, while (12) is arguably true.

Our thin ice has broken, and we find ourselves in the deep water of linguistic theory. Let's stick with the explanations we developed in Chapters V and VI for whatever guide they give us as to the syntactic structures, including underlying structures, of sentences like (12). But let's recognize that the Katz-Postal Hypothesis is not true in full generality and that the use we made of it in Chapter VI is confined to a class of cases. We want to draw a contrast between (12) and (13), one that is pretty clearly a matter of scope. Since we are sticking with the transformational account of the syntax of (12), we cannot appeal to distinct parsings to support the contrast we want. So we will begin speaking of **logical scope**. In (12) the logical scope of "or" is narrow, within the scope of "everyone." What this means is that, in a tableau, the rule for "or" cannot be applied to (12). By contrast, in (13) the logical scope of "or" is wide, and within that scope are two occurrences of "everyone."

With the notion of logical scope we can contrast,

(14)   Somebody loved Tony, and somebody killed Tony,

which is true with respect to *West Side Story*, with,

(15)   Somebody loved Tony and killed Tony,

which is not true. In (14) the Conjunction "and" has wide logical scope vis-à-vis the quantifiers. The sentence can be paraphrased using the rule-governed "&," and in a tableau the rule for "&" can be applied directly. But in (15), the logical scope of "and" is narrow, within the scope of "someone," and so the sentence cannot be paraphrased using "&," which after all is a *sentence* connective. Similarly,

(16)   No one belongs to both the Jets and the Sharks,

is true with respect to *West Side Story*, while,

(17) No one belongs to the Jets, and no one belongs to the Sharks,

is not true, and so the distinction of logical scope must be made for them. The Conjunction "and" has narrow logical scope in (16), within the scope of "no one," while in (17) "and" has wide logical scope.

As is already evident, this notion of logical scope relates to the kinds of situations with respect to which the sentence in question is true. Thus it rightly influences the construction of tableaux. We will make substantial use of it in the next two sections as we introduce tableau rules for quantifiers and bring them into play with rules for connectives. As for the Katz-Postal Hypothesis and the mysteries of what is the grammatical basis of logical scope, let's linger over another contrast, this one implicating the passive transformation. In the sentence,

(18)   Either Riff or Tony restrained everyone,

the Conjunction "or" has wide logical scope. Here the sentence is synonymous with the underlying sentence,

    Either Riff restrained everyone, or Tony restrained everyone,

or at the very least it *can* be understood that way. Surprisingly, the passive voice version of (18),

(19)   Everyone was restrained by either Tony or Riff,

is not synonymous with them. In (19) "everyone" has wide scope. Unlike the favored reading of (18), sentence (19) is true with respect to a situation in which Tony restrained some, Riff restrained others, but neither restrained everyone, though everyone was restrained by one or the other of them. Figuring out why we leave to theoretical linguistics.

Summing up what we have learned, one-word quantifiers indeed qualify as a kind of Noun Phrase, and syntactic explanations of what is grammatical and what is not carry over from Chapters V and VI without ramification. (The explanations make use of phrase-markers and transformations of the sort developed in those chapters.) When we consider the logic of these quantifiers, on the other hand, we recognize that this unramified syntax is deceptive. For logical purposes, we must make distinctions of scope that are not explained by it. To appreciate the force of those distinctions, we will consider inferences involving quantifiers. To apply the method of tableaux to such inferences, we will need to develop rules for quantifiers in tableaux. It is to these tasks that we now turn.

§32   TABLEAU RULES FOR THE SIMPLEST QUANTIFIERS

Having glimpsed the logic of the simplest quantifiers, we are ready to codify what we have noted, in rules that will serve to handle these quantifiers where they arise in tableaux. To fall under these rules a sentence must be grammatically simple—no Conjunctions or Subordinating Conjunctions—and in it there must occur a single one-word quantifier. That is to say, among its Noun Phrases there must occur exactly one quantifier expression and it must consist of a one-word quantifier. We also will give rules for the negations of sentences meeting these restrictions. As we will see, these rules will serve arguments with complex premises and conclusions so long as the quantifiers do not participate in the complexity. In particular, these rules will accommodate tableaux in which rule-governed connectives also occur, so long as all of the quantifiers have narrow scope relative to those connectives, narrow scope under the familiar syntactic definition of §18. In each case in what follows, we will see first a precise formulation of the rule in question, followed by an explanation.

Simple Rule for "Everyone": If in any path of a tableau there occurs a simple sentence with the single one-word quantifier "everyone," you may append to any branch below that occurrence the result of replacing "everyone" with any designator that already appears in the tableau. Do not check off the sentence with "everyone."

We begin with a rule that is particularly easy to justify. It is an application of this rule that takes us from "Everyone knew Maria" to "Tony knew Maria." Since "everyone" means everyone, any name or other designator can replace it in a simple sentence, so long as the bounds of the universe of discourse are not breached. Thinking in terms of the rationale for tableaux generally, any open path of the tableau in which an "everyone"-sentence occurs represents a way for that sentence and the others in the path to be true. Anyone who is mentioned in the path is *ipso facto* in the universe over which the "everyone" ranges. And whatever is true of everyone in that emerging situation is of course true of the particular individual just mentioned. Thus any way of the "everyone"-sentence being true is also a way of the new sentence being true as well.

The developing tableau reflects the discourse comprised by the argument or set of sentences under consideration. Thus any designator already occurring is fair game. But the rule gives license for no other designator (not "Putin"!). Not only does this restriction keep us in bounds, it also keeps us from profligacy in application of the rule. With a cast of even a dozen characters the logic of "everyone" would yield a dozen instances. Not all of them are relevant to the aim of the tableau, which is to make inconsistencies explicit. If a quantifier sentence conflicts with other sentences in a set, the conflict will become explicit by means of designators that already do or will occur in the tableau. Even with the restriction to designators in the tableau, many potential applications of the rule will not be fruitful, so the rule permits us to append instances without requiring it. Of course the "everyone"-sentence should not be checked off since further instances may become relevant later in the tableau.

Simple Rule for "Someone": If in any path of a tableau there occurs a simple sentence with the single one-word quantifier "someone," append to each branch below that occurrence the result of replacing "someone" with a proper name that *does not* already occur in the tableau. (Conventionally we choose the alphabetically next neutral proper name.) Check off the sentence with "someone."

Unlike the one for "everyone," the rule for "someone" can be executed once and for all. Only one sentence is appended, and the "someone"-sentence is checked off. Yet despite its simplicity of execution, the "someone"-rule is harder to explain and justify. It will help us to see the rule in action. Let us begin with a consistent

set of two sentences and see that applying our rules will be harmless
in that no inconsistency will be introduced.

> Someone was a gang member.
>
> Someone was not a gang member.

First notice that both of these sentences are true with respect to the
situation of *West Side Story*, bearing out our conviction that they are
consistent. Even so, the result of replacing "someone," in the first
sentence, with "Maria" or "Krupke" would not be true. Equally, the
result of replacing "someone" with "Bernardo" or "Riff " in the
second sentence would not be true. And if we replaced both cases of
"someone" with "Tony," our tableau would close even though the
original sentences are perfectly consistent. We need a better-
conceived strategy for introducing a designator in place of
"someone."

Your impulse might be to pick a designator—for example, "Riff
"—that results in a sentence—"Riff was a gang member"—that is
true with respect to the situation you have in mind. There are two
serious drawbacks to this prospect. First, as in the example,

Someone called the police,

the "someone"-sentence might be true with respect to your favored
situation though you do not know who the someone was. Second, and
more deeply, in building a tableau you are trying to describe a
possible situation with respect to which all of the sentences in a
particular set are true. Whether they really are true with respect to
your favored situation, and even whether your favored situation is
really possible, may be no easier to recognize than whether the set of
sentences under consideration is consistent. As we have often seen,
if we were perfectly clear-headed, we would need no techniques for
logic.

It is clear that care is required in replacing the quantifier with a
designator if our aim is to accommodate all possible situations truly
described by the "someone"-sentence. The expedient enjoined by the
rule is to pick what we call a **neutral proper name**, a proper name
that does not occur in the tableau and that does not commit us in any
way to any characteristic other than that expressed in the
"someone"-sentence. To serve this purpose we will provide a stock of
such neutral proper names, names that do not occur in the present
cast of characters, that are not likely to occur in other tableaux you
construct, and that are neutral even with regard to gender. The rule

suggests that we use the alphabetically next such name, and since this is the first application of the rule, we have "Alex."

√ Someone was a gang member
Someone was not a gang member

|

Alex was a gang member

Next we have "Bo."

√ Someone was a gang member
√ Someone was not a gang member

|

Alex was a gang member

|

Bo was not a gang member

Now both of the quantifier sentences have been checked, and there is nothing more to be done. The unchecked sentences form an obviously consistent set, so our verdict is that the original set is consistent. That is just the verdict we want. No inconsistency has been introduced by the "someone"-rule.

Now let's turn to an obviously inconsistent set of two sentences where applying our rules will make recognition of the inconsistency mechanical.

Everyone was a gang member.

Someone was not a gang member.

Even though we have an "everyone"-sentence, no application of the "everyone"-rule is permitted now because no designator yet occurs in the tableau. Applying the "someone"-rule to the "someone"-sentence, we introduce "Alex."

Everyone was a gang member
√ Someone was not a gang member

|

Alex was not a gang member

Having introduced a neutral name, we now have a designator in the tableau and can apply the "everyone"-rule.

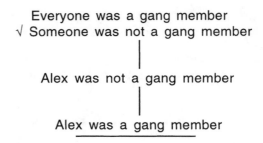

Everyone was a gang member
√ Someone was not a gang member

Alex was not a gang member

Alex was a gang member

Now the tableau closes because we have a sentence and its negation in the only path. Application of the "someone"-rule has enabled us to bring out the conflict between the original sentences, in particular by enabling us to specify a relevant instance of the "everyone"-sentence.

In this case the inconsistency of the original set was pretty obvious, so no objection arises to our introducing the neutral name under the "someone"-rule. But imagine another case where the "someone"-rule has been applied, and it is objected,

Who is this *Alex*, anyway? The sentence says, "*Someone* joined a gang." Who is to say it was Alex? That doesn't even sound like someone who would join a gang. Maybe it was someone else who joined the gang. "Someone joined a gang" occurred among a set of sentences, the "someone"-rule was followed, and the tableau closed. Maybe if you had named the right person we would have had an open path.

The reply is that the novelty of the neutral name is precisely what gives it the best chance of keeping the tableau open. If choosing this new designator results in a conflict with other sentences, perhaps spawned from other quantifier-sentences by means of other rules, choosing any other designator would have results just as bad. Put another way, if there is any possible situation with respect to which all of the sentences in the original set are true, including "Someone joined a gang," there will also be a possible situation with respect to which they are true in which it is Alex (perhaps among others) who joined a gang.

Simple Rule for "No one": If in any path of a tableau there occurs a simple sentence with the single one-word quantifier "no one," you may append to any branch below that occurrence the result of first replacing "no one" with any designator that already occurs in the tableau and then negating the outcome. Do not check off the sentence with "no one."

The rule for "no one" is as easy to justify as the rule for "everyone" and only a little harder to execute. Consider these two sentences, which we can easily see are inconsistent with one another.

> No one shot Maria.
>
> Chino shot Maria.

The problem with them is brought out by remarking that since no one shot Maria, Chino did *not*. The rule permits us to record this by introducing the negation of "Chino shot Maria," where this latter sentence is the result of replacing "no one" with "Chino."

No one shot Maria
Chino shot Maria

|

¬ Chino shot Maria
_____

Just as with the "everyone"-rule, restricting the instances to those designators already occurring keeps us within the bounds of the universe of discourse. It also helps keep us within the bounds of relevance to the objective of closing the tableau. Even with this restriction, we are permitted to append "¬ Maria shot Maria" since the designator "Maria" also occurs in the tableau. We refrain because the tableau closes without it, showing that indeed the original set is inconsistent. Notice in this rule the crucial feature of the quantifier "no one." When we say that no one shot Maria, we don't mean that some ghostly someone shot her, but rather that Chino did not, nor did Maria, nor did anyone else.

The "no one"-rule is equally effective in bringing out the inconsistency in a set of sentences where no relevant designator occurs.

> Someone warned Tony.
>
> No one warned Tony.

We could append "¬ Tony warned Tony," but it wouldn't contribute to closing the tableau. Instead we apply the "someone"-rule, introducing the first neutral name.

√ Someone warned Tony
No one warned Tony

|

Alex warned Tony

Now we have a designator that is relevant to closing the tableau, so we put it in place of "no one," not forgetting to introduce the negation symbol.

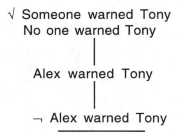

√ Someone warned Tony
No one warned Tony

Alex warned Tony

¬ Alex warned Tony

Of course the result is the negation of a sentence that already occurs in the path, and so the (only) path closes.

Our several applications of the three simple quantifier rules have had pretty obvious outcomes, but their purpose has been to portray the rules in action and to assure us that these rules represent sound principles of reasoning. We will soon employ the rules as we construct a rule-governed tableau for a difficult argument, but first we are reminded that the process of constructing counter-sets and—for some of the rules—the process of constructing tableau structures both result in negated sentences. What if the sentence in question is a quantifier sentence? To handle it, we will need rules for negations of simple sentences with single one-word quantifiers.

Negation Rule for "Everyone": Append the result of replacing "everyone" with a proper name that does not already occur in the tableau. (Use the next neutral name.) Check off the sentence with the negated "everyone."

The statement of this rule is very spare, but more is going on with it than appears. To appreciate how it works, let's keep in mind the smooth way of expressing the negation of an "everyone"-sentence, for example,

(1)   Not everyone was a gang member.

In saying (1), we are committed to there being a **counterexample** to the universal generalization that everyone was a gang member. That is to say, we are committed to there being someone who was *not* a gang member, though we may well not know who that counterexample is, or even if there is more than one. Again we make use of our neutral names, again choosing one that does not so far appear in the tableau. The wording of the rule presumes that the negation is expressed with the rule-governed "¬," as in,

(2)   ¬ everyone was a gang member.

With that set-up, what we can do is simply replace the "everyone" with the chosen neutral name:

¬ Alex was a gang member.

When we do so, the negation—which had wide scope—fortuitously remains to make for the counterexample.

It is important to recognize that the negation rule for "everyone" applies not only to negations introduced in the course of building a tableau, but to ordinary formulations as well, negative sentences that may have appeared in the original set of sentences. One example is the ambiguous sentence,

(3)   Everyone was a not gang member,

when it is understood as denying that everyone was a gang member. So understood, it should have been rewritten as (2) so that it falls under the rule we are discussing. In short, the negation rule for "everyone" applies to any grammatically simple sentence in which "everyone" has narrow scope, within the scope of "not."

The negation (2) leaves it open how many counterexamples there are, so a conflict will arise in the case of one counterexample if it will arise at all; for that reason, the negation can be checked off once the rule is applied. Alex, whoever he or she may be, serves as the representative counterexample. There lies the contrast with reading "everyone" in (3) as having wide scope. Under that reading, (3) denies of everyone that he or she was a gang member, so not only is Alex not a gang member, but also Riff is not and Bernardo is not and Tony is not. The wide-scope reading of (3) can never be checked off; it falls under the "everyone"-rule itself, not under the negation rule. That is the essence of "everyone" having wide logical scope.

Negation Rule for "Someone": Append the result of dropping the negation and replacing "someone" with "no one." Check off the sentence with the negated "someone."

Negation Rule for "No one": Append the result of dropping the negation and replacing "no one" with "someone." Check off the sentence with the negated "no one."

The remaining negation rules are particularly easy, for as we have already recognized, the negation of,

Someone killed Maria,

is naturally expressed as,

No one killed Maria.

And the negation of,

Tony fought with no one,

is naturally expressed as,

Tony fought with someone.

We take advantage of the close relationship between "someone"-sentences and "no one"-sentences by simply dropping the negation and switching to the other quantifier word whenever the negated "someone" or the negated "no one" occurs. Since the new sentence is simply the more natural formation of the original, the original can be checked off.

§33   THE SIMPLEST QUANTIFIERS IN TABLEAUX

The tableaux we looked at in the last section did not surprise us with their outcomes. Their purpose was to illustrate the quantifier rules and confirm their effectiveness. But there are many quantifier arguments that are confusing to follow and to assess. It is with them that tableaux have their importance. Several one-word quantifiers occur in the argument below, contributing to its difficulty. All of them occur in complex sentences, within the scope of Subordinate Conjunctions.

(1)

If someone pulls a knife, then everyone will be drawn in.

No one will stop the fight if Tony is drawn in.

Bernardo will kill someone unless someone stops the fight.

If either Tony or Bernardo is drawn in, Maria will be heartbroken unless no one gets hurt.

Maria will be heartbroken if Riff pulls a knife.

First we introduce rule-governed connectives. Since we have an argument—to be assessed for validity—we construct the counter set, which forms the trunk of our tableau. As the tableau develops, we see that the one-word quantifiers turn up in shorter sentences where our new rules apply. Remember that the simple quantifier rules are restricted to sentences that have a single one-word quantifier and that are grammatically simple—Noun Phrase followed by Verb Phrase. The negation rules apply to the negations of those sentences, whether they occur naturally formulated in the original sentences, or they arise as the tableau unfolds.

Someone will pull a knife → everyone will be drawn in

Tony will be drawn in → no one will stop the fight

√ Bernardo will kill someone ∨ someone will stop the fight

√ (Tony will be drawn in ∨ Bernardo will be drawn in) →

(Maria will be heartbroken ∨ no one will get hurt)

√ ¬ (Riff will pull a knife → Maria will be heartbroken)

Riff will pull a knife

¬ Maria will be heartbroken

√ ¬ Someone will pull a knife   Everyone will be drawn in

No one will pull a knife

¬ Riff will pull a knife
_____

¬ Tony will be drawn in   No one will stop the fight

Tony will be drawn in
_____

√ Bernardo will kill someone   Someone will stop the fight
_____

Bernardo will kill Alex

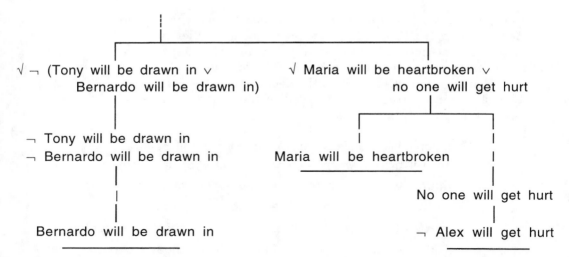

A few remarks will clarify the workings of the tableau. It is a peculiarity of the sentences in the counter set that in every case the rule-governed connectives have wider scope than the quantifiers. But the appropriate rules for connectives break these sentences down ultimately to simple sentences where the simple quantifier rules do apply. The "everyone"-rule and the "no one"-rule have been applied quite selectively, always with the aim of closing branches. Thus "¬ Riff will pull a knife" was spawned by "No one will pull a knife." Though lots of other instances were permitted by the "no one"-rule, this is the one that conflicts with "Riff will pull a knife" in the trunk. By contrast the "someone"-rule was applied to "Bernardo will kill someone" once and for all as soon as that simple sentence appeared. The rule introduced *Alex*, who was unmentioned in the tableau till that point. Alex is mentioned again at the lower right, where from "no one will get hurt" we get "¬ Alex will get hurt." This latter sentence makes no sense in concert with "Bernardo will kill Alex" higher in the path. Thus the path closes.

Finally, notice a short-cut that has been taken. In §31 we recognized that "No one will stop the fight" is the natural expression for the negation of "Someone will stop the fight." Since no situation is possible with respect to which both of these are true, the branch on the (center) right has been closed. A long route to the same effect would be to introduce a new neutral name via the "someone"-rule ("Bo will stop the fight") and then take that instance of the "no one"-sentence ("¬ Bo will stop the fight") and finally close the branch, which as a whole is unintelligible. It was this long route that we took in first introducing the "no one"-rule.

Since all of the paths have closed, the tableau shows that the counter set is inconsistent. Some readers might be surprised at the verdict of valid that our tableau has rendered. Perhaps to your ear the conclusion of argument (1) does not follow from its premises. Note that the conclusion does not mean that Maria will be heartbroken *over* Riff having pulled a knife, or even *because* Riff pulled a knife. From the given premises those conclusions indeed do not follow. Consistently with them, perhaps Maria doesn't know whether he will pull a knife, or afterward, whether he did. Rather the conclusion just means what it says, that if indeed Riff does pull a knife, Maria will be heartbroken for some reason or other.

Having seen our new rules in action, let's return to some cases that give rise to issues of logical scope. At the end of §31 we saw that in the sentence,

> Everyone was restrained by either Tony or Riff,

the one-word quantifier "everyone" has wide logical scope. What this means is that we cannot apply the rule for "∨," requiring either a situation in which everyone is restrained by Tony or a situation in which everyone is restrained by Riff. But we cannot apply the "everyone"-rule either since the sentence is not grammatically simple. The methods we have developed so far do not apply to this sentence.

On the other hand, the following argument has the active-voice sentence as its first premise; we decided that here "or" can be assigned wide logical scope.

> Either Tony or Riff restrained everyone.
> There was someone Riff did not restrain.
> ──────────────────────
> Tony restrained himself.

What this means is that not only is the premise syntactically derived from the underlying sentence, "Either Tony restrained everyone, or Riff restrained everyone," but it has the same meaning and thus the same logical force. Thus as we construct the counter set, we introduce the rule-governed connective "∨" into the first sentence.

As for the second premise, it illustrates a common transformation that introduces a so-called dummy subject "there." The effect is to insure that "someone" has wide logical scope, which might not be clear with "Riff did not restrain someone." We mark this in the tableau by leaving the "not" in the Verb Phrase of the second premise rather than introducing the rule-governed "¬." The upshot is that the "someone"-rule applies directly, introducing the neutral name "Alex"; the rule has been applied before any branching.

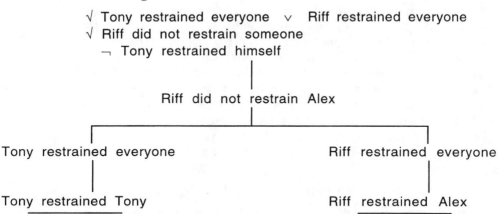

√ Tony restrained everyone ∨ Riff restrained everyone
√ Riff did not restrain someone
    ¬ Tony restrained himself

Riff did not restrain Alex

Tony restrained everyone   Riff restrained everyone

Tony restrained Tony   Riff restrained Alex

Note that it is the designator "Tony" that has been used with the "everyone"-rule to get the sentence "Tony restrained Tony" on the lower left. Of course the latter sentence conflicts with the earlier "¬ Tony restrained himself." This example emphasizes the license to bring any designator whatsoever into the "everyone"-rule, so long as it has already occurred in the tableau. When we say that Tony restrained everyone, we mean everyone in the universe of discourse, which obviously includes Tony himself. We often speak carelessly even though we have readily available a precise formulation that says what we might have wanted:

Tony restrained everyone but himself.

This means something different, namely that Tony restrained everyone other than Tony himself, that is to say, everyone who was not Tony. Making use of the relation of identity, we will be able to handle this different proposition in tableaux in Chapter IX. In the meantime, the conclusion of the argument does follow from its premises as written. The first of them does not say everyone but himself!

A second argument also illustrates some tricky cases with "not." Recall that sentence (8) of §31 ("Someone did not want to fight") is not the negation of (31.9) ("Someone wanted to fight"). In the first premise the dummy subject "there" emphasizes this, so we remember that "someone" in the subordinate clause has wider scope than "not."

If there was someone who did not want to fight, then everyone wanted to go home. Not everyone wanted to fight.

Bernardo wanted to go home.

Thus again, as we construct the counter set, we do not introduce the rule-governed "¬" in the subordinate clause of the first premise (i.e., the clause to the left of the "→"). On the other hand, "not" in the second premise does have wide scope, so we have the negation of an "everyone"-sentence, and for the first time we can see the rule for that combination in action.

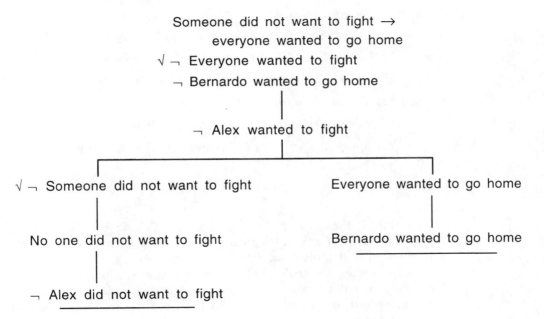

Since we don't have two of "¬," we do not apply the "¬¬" rule on the top of the left branch of the tableau, but rather the negation rule for "someone." With (10) and (11) of §31, we also saw that "No one did not want to fight" is not the negation of "No one wanted to fight"; "no one" has wide logical scope in both of them. Thus the last entry in the left branch is spawned by the "no one"-rule. We need not apply the "¬¬" rule at the bottom of the left branch because it is clear that the last entry conflicts with "¬ Alex wanted to fight" in the same path.

It is a crucial feature of our application of the simple quantifier rules that we do not apply them to sentences where the quantifier falls within the scope of another logical word. Thus where we have,

(1)   Tony didn't fight with everyone,

we don't apply the "everyone"-rule, getting,

(2)   Tony didn't fight with Bernardo.

Instead we recognize that (1) means,

It is not true that Tony fought with everyone,

and apply the negation rule for "everyone." And where we have,

(3)   If everyone is drawn in, then no one will stop the fight,

we don't apply the "everyone"-rule, getting,

If Bernardo is drawn in, then no one will stop the fight.

Rather we apply the rule for "→," getting a branching structure with,

¬ everyone will be drawn in,

on the left.

In both of these cases the logical scope of "everyone" is narrow, within the scope of another logical element. What that means in the construction of a tableau is that the "everyone"-rule does not apply, but rather some other rule applies, the one that is appropriate to the logical element that does have wide scope. Thus it is that the tableau rules bring out and confirm the real nature of the notion of logical scope introduced in §31. The question of logical scope is the question of which tableau rule to apply. We do not have a thoroughgoing grammatical account of logical scope, but we are working with enough cases to become adept at calibrating logical scope correctly and picking the appropriate rule.

There is another one-word quantifier in English whose logic differs from anything we have seen. Let's approach it by looking first at a sentence similar to (3).

(4)   If everyone shoots, the police will come.

Here again "everyone" has narrow scope, and it is the "→" rule that applies in a tableau. Now let's contrast (4) with,

(5)   If anyone shoots, the police will come.

What specifically is the difference between these two sentences? Only that "anyone" has replaced "everyone." What difference does that make? "Everyone" is a universalizing word, ranging over the entire universe of discourse. But so it seems is "anyone," as is emphasized by adding "whoever":

           If anyone whoever shoots, the police will come.

The answer as to the difference is one that we can understand only with this notion of logical scope that we have been carefully nurturing. "Anyone" is in fact universalizing, like "everyone," but the difference is that "anyone" automatically *has wide logical scope*. Thus, given that sentence (5) is true with respect to the situation in *West Side Story*, each of the following sentences is also true with respect to that situation.

(6) If Riff shoots, the police will come.

    If Bernardo shoots, the police will come.

    If Bernardo's sister shoots, the police will come.

    If the Shark who loves Maria shoots, the police will come.

    If he shoots, the police will come.

Precisely what was forbidden in the case of (4)—because there the quantifier "everyone" has narrow logical scope—should be licensed in the case of (5)—because "anyone" takes wide logical scope willy-nilly.

We have explained the difference between (4) and (5) in terms of the differing logical scope of the two universalizing quantifiers. This explanation can be tested against (1) above, in contrast with,

(7)   Tony didn't fight with anyone.

Whereas (1) is true with respect to *West Side Story*, sentence (2), which has a well-chosen designator in place of "everyone," is not true with respect to that same situation. This bears witness to our prohibition on applying the "everyone" rule to (1). But now consider a way of making sentence (7) true, the way of Maria's hopes. With respect to such a situation, sentence (2) indeed is true. Any other designator in place of "anyone" would also result in a sentence true with respect to Maria's hopes. Thus here also "anyone" has wide logical scope, despite the presence of the negating "didn't" in (7). With this confirmation in hand, we are led to formulate a rule for "anyone." Because "anyone" forces wide logical scope, this rule, unlike the earlier rules for one-word quantifiers, applies directly to complex sentences in which "anyone" occurs.

Simple Rule for "Anyone": If in any path of a tableau there occurs a sentence with the single one-word quantifier "anyone," do not apply the rule for another connective. Instead, you may append to any branch below that occurrence the result of replacing "anyone" with any designator that already appears in the tableau. Do not check off the sentence with "anyone."

We have already seen this rule in action. Presuming that the designators were already available in a tableau, the "anyone"-rule would permit us to append any of the sentences listed at (6) to a path in which (5) occurred. And it would permit us to append sentence (2) to a path in which (7) occurred. For an even more striking and useful application of the "anyone" rule, consider the following argument.

> If anyone killed Riff, he answered to Tony.
> Bernardo killed Riff.
> _____
> Bernardo answered to Tony.

It should be obvious that the argument is valid, but let's construct a tableau for it to see how the "anyone"-rule works in it.

Anyone killed Riff → he answered to Tony
Bernardo killed Riff
¬ Bernardo answered to Tony
|
Bernardo killed Riff → he (Bernardo) answered to Tony
|
┌──────────────────────────────┴──────────────────────────────┐
¬ Bernardo killed Riff   he (Bernardo) answered to Tony

Just as we expected, the tableau closed, showing that the counter set is inconsistent and thus that the argument indeed is valid. But pay special attention to the application of the "anyone"-rule in the tableau, which used the designator "Bernardo." In the resulting sentence (here with the rule-governed "→" spelled out),

(8)   If Bernardo killed Riff, he answered to Tony,

something wonderful has happened. Who does the pronoun "he" in the main clause refer to? Of course it refers to Bernardo. But what kind of pronoun is it? It's not an indexical pronoun, one that depends on the context for the salience of Bernardo. Bernardo is no more salient than Riff, who is lying on the asphalt mortally injured. No, it's an *anaphoric* pronoun, reaching back for its reference to the occurrence of "Bernardo" in the subordinate clause. But now consider the sentence,

(9)   If anyone kills Riff, he will answer to Tony,

from which (with a change of tense) sentence (8) was derived by means of the "anyone"-rule. Who does the same pronoun "he" refer to in (9)? Again to Bernardo? Not in particular. It could as well refer to Chino. In fact, though it also is an anaphoric pronoun, it is an anaphoric pronoun of a special kind. The pronoun "he" reaches back to "anyone," but since "anyone" is not a designator, the pronoun doesn't inherit any reference from that quantifier word. Instead this anaphoric pronoun awaits the application of the "anyone"-rule. Upon the replacement of "anyone" with a designator, "he" will refer to whoever that designator refers to. In fact, upon reflection it is clear that instead of (9), we should have,

(10)   If anyone kills Riff, he or she will answer to Tony,

because the instance,

If Anita kills Riff, she will answer to Tony,

is true with respect to the situation in *West Side Story* just as much as (8) is.

The propriety of a gender-neutral pronoun in (10) provides yet another confirmation of our principle that "anyone" forces wide logical scope. Suppose we flouted this principle and treated the "if" in (10) as having wide logical scope. That would lead us to apply the "→"-rule. On the left we would have,

¬ Anyone will kill Riff,

which seems okay. And on the right we would have,

He or she will answer to Tony.

But that simple sentence does not contribute to describing a situation at all. Who is "he or she"? Without an antecedent designator, the gender-neutral anaphoric pronoun simply dangles. What is needed is a prior application of the "anyone"-rule, providing a designator to serve as antecedent to the anaphor. When the "if"-clause is subsequently torn away, that designator can simply replace the anaphoric "he or she."

We have found that the "anyone"-rule together with the magic of natural-language anaphora gives the tableau technique a quite remarkable range, We will finish the chapter with one last example from our by-now familiar musical. In their bravado, the Jets sing,

> *"HERE COME THE JETS*
> *LIKE A BAT OUT OF HELL—*
> *SOMEONE GETS IN OUR WAY,*
> *SOMEONE DON'T FEEL SO WELL!"*

There is an inference here; the penultimate line provides the reason for the last one. But the inference has a suppressed premise. The premise that is needed can well be expressed with an "anyone"-sentence,

> If anyone gets in the way of the Jets, he or she will
> (subsequently) not feel so well.

At the risk of ruining the musical fun—perhaps to be repaid by some logical fun—let's use our simple quantifier rules to show that the inference is a valid one.

> √ Someone will get in our (the Jets') way
>   Anyone gets in the way of the Jets →
>   he or she will not feel so well
> √ ¬ Someone will not feel so well
>
> No one will not feel so well
>
> Alex will get in the Jets' way
>
> Alex gets in the way of the Jets →   he or she (Alex) will not feel so well
>
> ¬ Alex will get in the way of the Jets   Alex will not feel so well
>
>   ¬ Alex will not feel so well

Such a tableau marks the triumph of the special anaphoric function of "he or she" with "anyone." We don't even know who Alex is, or whether Alex is a he or a she. But the anaphor stands ready to inherit a reference to Alex and thereby to work in concert with the "someone"-rule. The tableau shows that "Someone don't feel so well," follows deductively from "Someone gets in our way," together with the suppressed "anyone"-premise. It establishes the validity of the inference implicit in the bragging chant of the Jets.

That final tableau also foreshadows an elaboration of our simple quantifier rules that will lift the restriction to one-word quantifiers. In the chapter to come we will see how to handle at least some of the complex and varied quantifier expressions of English. And we will see how to handle wide-scope occurrences of our simple quantifiers as they showed up in §31. The essential device to see us through will be the special kind of anaphoric pronoun we have just encountered.

Exercises for Chapter VIII

1. Identify the constituent quantifier expressions in the following articles of the Declaration of the Rights of Man and of the Citizen. Which of them are one-word quantifiers?

    A2.   The aim of every political association is the preservation of the natural and imprescriptible rights of man. . .

    A4.   Liberty consists in being able to do anything that does not harm others: thus, the exercise of the natural rights of every man has no bounds other than those that ensure to all other members of society the enjoyment of the same rights. . .

    A5.   The Law has the right to forbid only actions that are injurious to society. Nothing that is not forbidden by Law may be hindered, and no one may be compelled to do what the Law does not ordain.

    A6.   The Law is the expression of the general will. . . All citizens, being equal in its eyes, shall be equally eligible to all high offices, public positions, and employments. . .

A16. Any society in which no provision is made for guaranteeing rights
or for the separation of powers, has no Constitution.

2.   For each of the following sentences, identify the rule that could be directly
applied to the sentence in a tableau. If none of the rules can be applied, say so.

a.   Someone opened the door.

b.   Everybody knows herself.

c.   Everybody is either male or female.

d.   Someone is bald and snub-nosed.

e.   Nobody saw the Big Bang.

f.   Some are born great, some achieve greatness, and some have greatness
thrust upon them.

g.   God created everybody, or else God created nobody.

h.   If no one comes to her party, Mary will despise everyone.

i.   If it rains, no one will come to Mary's party.

j.   If everybody knows the answer, then the instructor will be surprised.

k.   If anybody knows the answer, then the instructor will be happy.

l.   If anybody knows the answer, she should speak up.

3.   As if in a tableau, apply the simple quantifier rules exhaustively to the
following set of sentences. (Seven additional sentences will be spawned.) Is
the resulting set of sentences a consistent set?

> God loves everyone.
> Someone does not love Abraham.
> Nobody loves himself.

4.   Show that the validity of this argument depends on the logical scope given to
"everyone" in the ambiguous third premise.

> The alarm was rung only if someone was awake.
>
> If the alarm was not rung, then the fire trapped everyone.
>
> Everyone was not awake.
> ———————————————————————
> Someone was trapped by the fire.

Determine whether the following arguments are valid by checking the consistency of their counter sets, using tableaux.

5.

> Either everyone will walk or everyone will ride with Ned.
>
> If Martha walks, she will arrive with Otto.
>
> If Martha rides with Ned, she will arrive with him.
>
> ───
>
> Martha will arrive with someone.

6.

> Someone will be captured only if the ambush is effective.
>
> The ambush will be effective only if no one makes a noise.
>
> Not everyone will be quiet.
>
> ───
>
> The ringleader will not be captured.

7.

> If anyone is found out cheating, then everyone will be penalized.
>
> If anyone cheats, he or she will be found out.
>
> ───
>
> If George cheats, Martha will be penalized.

8.

> If anyone is desperate, he or she will shoot.
>
> If anyone shoots, everyone will be afraid.
>
> If anyone is afraid, he or she will run.
>
> If everyone runs, everyone will be hurt.
>
> Someone will be desperate.
>
> ───
>
> George will be hurt.

9. Can you think of an exception to the "anyone"-rule? That is to say, can you think of a sentence with the single one-word quantifier "anyone" that is true with respect to some situation that you could describe, where the sentence that results from replacing "anyone" with a relevant designator is not true with respect to that same situation?

IX: Quantifier Expressions and Syllogisms

> *"WHEN YOU'RE A JET,*
> *YOU'RE A JET ALL THE WAY*
> *FROM YOUR FIRST CIGARETTE*
> *TO YOUR LAST DYIN' DAY.*
> *WHEN YOU'RE A JET,*
> *IF THE SPIT HITS THE FAN,*
> *YOU GOT BROTHERS AROUND,*
> *YOU'RE A FAMILY MAN!"*

The same brave song that we exploited in the last section of Chapter VIII begins with these lines. Having dwelt on pronouns—indexical and anaphoric—we naturally notice in these lines the several occurrences of "you," and almost instinctively ask who they refer to. If we categorize "you" as an indexical pronoun, we know it refers to whomever is addressed by the speaker, one or many. But on further thought this conclusion doesn't seem right. What the Jets of that day are saying in their singing is not restricted to those in their hearing. It goes for anyone. What they are saying is that when *anyone* is a

Jet, he or she is a Jet all the way. And recognizing this brings their lyrics within reach of the treatment of "anyone" and anaphoric pronouns that we just concluded. It also provides the opportunity to expand the boundaries of that treatment to encompass not only these lyrics but a great many other quantifier formulations in English and other natural languages, including complex quantifier expressions that so far have been beyond our reach. After all, the sentence,

(1)   When anyone is a Jet, he or she has got brothers around,

is tantalizingly close to the sentence,

> Anyone who is a Jet has got brothers around,

which begins with the recognizably complex quantifier expression, "anyone who is a Jet."

Rather than pursuing the connection with complex "anyone"-expressions now, let's revert to the pronoun "you" and try to understand it not as an indexical, referring to whomever is addressed, but as an anaphor, similar to the "he or she" of (1). What is meant by the words of the lyric,

(2)   When you're a Jet, you've got brothers around,

would more explicitly be expressed as,

(3) No matter who you are, when you're a Jet, you've got brothers around.

This use of "you" in English is quite familiar, for example, in all the following sentences.

> If you want to stop on a slick surface, you should pump your brakes.

> Sharing a needle increases your risk of AIDS.

> If you voted for Gore, you were disappointed at the Florida count.

> You are not allowed to read classified documents without a security clearance.

Embarrassed on account of the more central second-person use of "you," some writers pedantically use the pronoun "one."

> Sharing a needle increases one's risk of AIDS.

And German reserves a special pronoun "man" for this particular use.

We want to embrace this use of "you" and indeed to categorize it as an anaphor, but one of that special kind of anaphor that we saw in §34, one that reaches back to a quantifier, but does not secure a reference from that quantifier, which—remember—is not a designator.   With "anyone" the reference of this special kind of anaphor is secured only when the quantifier is replaced by a designator, spawned as a particular case by the "anyone"-rule.

What functions as the quantifier in (3) is precisely the introductory expression "no matter who," which is ordinarily unspoken. Another way of saying the same thing—more stilted, but more adaptable—obviously involves a quantifier word.

(4)   Everyone is such that, when he or she is a Jet, he or she has got brothers around.

Another alternative is somewhat more fluent.

(5)   Whoever he or she is, when he or she is a Jet, he or she has got brothers around.

Much in the spirit of the rule-governed connectives of Chapter VI, we take these alternative expressions—(1), (2), (3), (4), and (5)—as amounting to the same thing. And so we introduce a general purpose, rule-governed **universal quantifier**, using the abbreviatory symbol, "$\forall$."

(6) $\forall$ (when you are a Jet, you have got brothers around)

This is simply an abbreviation of the more cumbersome (3). Its advantage is that, unlike (2), it makes manifest that the pronoun "you" is anaphoric in the special way we have been studying, what we will call a universally quantified anaphoric pronoun. Thus it is characteristic of the universal quantifier "$\forall$" that it be used in company with anaphoric pronouns, which are said to be **bound** by it. The expression "no matter who you are" has a logical scope, extending to all of the occurrences of the anaphoric pronouns that it does bind, and it will be convenient for us to use parentheses to indicate that logical scope.

As before, this symbol carries with it a rule for use in tableaux. What the rule should be is pretty obvious from the "everyone"-rule and the "anyone"-rule, that we have already used.

Rule for the Universal Quantifier: Suppose that in any path of a tableau there occurs a sentence with a wide-scope universal quantifier. To any branch below that occurrence, you may append the result of deleting that quantifier, and replacing each anaphoric pronoun bound by that quantifier, with a designator that already occurs in the tableau. Do not check off the universally quantified sentence.

In effect, we have seen the rule in action already, so similar is it to the "anyone"-rule.

> If anyone kills Riff, he will answer to Tony.
> Bernardo killed Riff.
> ─────────────────────────────
> Bernardo will answer to Tony.

Just as our universally quantified sentence at (6) is equivalent to (1), the "anyone"-premise of the argument can be expressed with the universal quantifier as we build the counter set. Then we apply the more general tableau rule with the same effect as when we used the simple rule for "anyone."

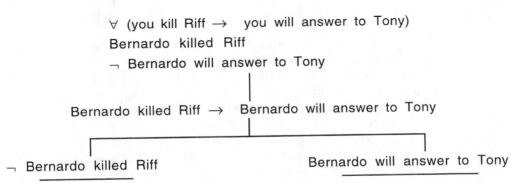

As long as we stick to sentences with one-word quantifiers there is no advantage to reformulating them using the universal quantifier. The advantage comes when we turn to complex quantifier expressions, as in the sentence,

Tybalt hates everyone who is a Montague.

The Noun Phrase that is the object of "hates"—as a whole—is the expression "everyone who is a Montague." Consisting as it does of more than the one word "everyone," it lies beyond the reach of the simple "everyone" rule of Chapter VIII. Even the somewhat simpler sentence,

Tybalt hates every Montague,

still has a complex quantifier expression, namely "every Montague." The two sentences are equivalent, so what we need to find is a formulation using the universal quantifier, one that will put them in the reach of the universal quantifier rule. The sentence,

∀ (you are a Montague → Tybalt hates you),

which is merely an abbreviation for,

No matter who you are, if you are a Montague, Tybalt hates you,

pretty clearly does the trick. With the help of this formulation that uses the universal quantifier, the following argument will succumb to our methods.

> Tybalt hates every Montague.
> Romeo is a Montague.
> _____
> Tybalt hates Romeo.

A tableau very similar to our prior tableau can be constructed on the counter set. As before, the tableau closes, indicating that the argument is a valid one.

In Chapters VI and VII we found it helpful to build rule-governed tableaux in two stages. First we resolved the reference of pronouns, recovered underlying sentences, and introduced rule-governed connectives and the identity sign. When we had more than one connective, there arose issues of scope, and we settled them in advance, using parentheses for grouping. After all of this was done for a given argument, we incorporated it in the counter set and went ahead to apply the appropriate rules for the various logical elements as we built the tableau in the second stage. Now we have another logical element to contend with, the universal quantifier. In combination with other connectives it also gives rise to issues of scope. It will keep us closer to idiomatic English if we change our practice and introduce rule-governed formulations more gradually. Let's see this new practice in action with an argument whose first premise not only has a complex quantifier expression but also the rule-governed "or."

> Every Jet was restrained by either Tony or Riff.
> Though Riff was a Jet, he did not restrain himself.
> _____
> Tony restrained Riff.

As we recognized in §31, the first premise is not synonymous with,

Either every Jet was restrained by Tony, or every Jet was restrained by Riff,

even though it might derive from it transformationally. The reason is that in the first premise, the quantifier expression has wide logical scope. We can secure the effect of that in a tableau by replacing the premise with a formulation using the universal quantifier. Of course the original can be checked off because it has been replaced by a reformulation. As we keep that in mind, our new practice is to begin by constructing the counter set, and then successively to reformulate sentences, gradually introducing not only the universal quantifier, but other logical elements as they become relevant to extending the tableau.

√ Every Jet was restrained by either Tony or Riff
√ Though Riff was a Jet, he did not restrain himself
¬ Tony restrained Riff
|
∀ (you are a Jet → you were restrained by either Tony or Riff)
|
√ Riff was a Jet & he (Riff) did not restrain himself
|
Riff was a Jet
¬ Riff restrained himself
|
Riff was a Jet → Riff was restrained by either Tony or Riff

¬ Riff was a Jet   √ Riff was restrained by either Tony or Riff
|
√ Tony restrained Riff ∨ Riff restrained Riff
|

Tony restrained Riff   Riff restrained Riff

Perhaps the resulting tableau is long-winded, but we have grown used to that. The advantage is that every step is small and transparent. We employ tableaux where the danger of confusion is great. To ensure accuracy and reliability, we pay a price in verbiage. Checking off sentences that we have used up keeps to a minimum the verbiage that continues to deserve our attention.

To confirm this advantage, it is worth contrasting the prior argument, which was valid, with another, which is not.

> Every Jet was restrained by either Tony or Riff.
>
> Though Riff was a Jet, he did not restrain himself.
> _____
>
> If Tony was a Jet, he restrained himself.

Confusion threatens because of the similarity of the first premise to one which would result in a valid argument:

Either Tony or Riff restrained every Jet.

Of course the difference lies in the scope of the quantifier expression. Following our new practice we come up with the following open tableau.

√ Every Jet was restrained by either Tony or Riff
√ Though Riff was a Jet, he did not restrain himself
√ ¬ If Tony was a Jet, he restrained himself
|
∀ (you are a Jet → you were restrained by either Tony or Riff)
|
√ Riff was a Jet & he (Riff) did not restrain himself
|
√ ¬ (Tony was a Jet → he (Tony) restrained himself)
|
Riff was a Jet
¬ Riff restrained himself
|
Tony was a Jet
¬ Tony restrained himself
|
Riff was a Jet → Riff was restrained by either Tony or Riff
|
Tony was a Jet → Tony was restrained by either Tony or Riff

¬ Riff was a Jet   √ Riff was restrained by either Tony or Riff
                        |
                        √ Tony restrained Riff ∨ Riff restrained Riff

Tony restrained Riff   Riff restrained Riff

¬ Tony was a Jet   √ Tony was restrained by either Tony or Riff
                        |
                        √ Tony restrained Tony ∨ Riff restrained Tony

Tony restrained Tony   Riff restrained Tony

Notably, the tableau is finished in that every rule that can be applied has been applied. In particular, the universal quantifier rule has been applied as much as possible to the (reformulated) first premise, using every designator in the tableau. Still a branch remains open, and the unchecked sentences in that path describe a possible situation which indeed exposes the argument as invalid, that is to say, one with respect to which the premises are true and in which indeed Tony was a Jet though he did not restrain himself.

With this new practice in hand, we are ready to extend our treatment of the universal quantifier to an argument whose conclusion can be reformulated using that mode of expression.

(7)

> Tybalt hates every Montague.
>
> Everyone related to Romeo is a Montague.
> _____
>
> Tybalt hates everyone who is related to Romeo.

This conclusion, like sentences (1) through (5) and, for that matter, like the premises of the argument, is an example of a **universal generalization**, or what is sometimes called a **categorical judgement**. In Chapter IV, when we first applied the tableau technique to arguments, we used the example of such categorical judgements most famous in writing about logic:

(8)   All humans are mortal.

What is characteristic of such judgements is that they brook no exception. *No matter who you are*, as we might emphasize, if you are human, you are mortal. It is the categorical, unqualified, character of these propositions that provides the key to negating them. To deny such a proposition is precisely to envision an exception to the generalization, what we have called a counterexample. Here a counterexample is a bit more complex. To revert to the conclusion of (7), a counterexample would precisely be someone who is related to Romeo but yet whom Tybalt *doesn't* hate. Since one counterexample serves as well as another, in building a tableau we introduce the next neutral name, confident that any inconsistency thereby made manifest has not been introduced by having chosen the wrong example. But what in general is it that makes the example a contrary one? Here the formulation with the universal quantifier is especially helpful. A counterexample to (8) is an immortal human, that is to say, a human who is not mortal. The formulation,

$$\forall \ (\text{you are human} \rightarrow \text{you are mortal})$$

shows how that arises. To serve as a counterexample, Alex (say) must be human, but it must not be true that Alex is mortal. With that explanation, we can formulate our rule.

Counterexample Rule for Negated Universal Categoricals: Chose a proper name that does not already occur in the tableau. Append the "if"-clause with all anaphoric pronouns replaced by the proper name. Then negate the main clause, replace all anaphoric pronouns with the proper name, and append the result. Check off the negated categorical.

With this rule to handle the negated conclusion, we can make short work of the argument in a tableau.

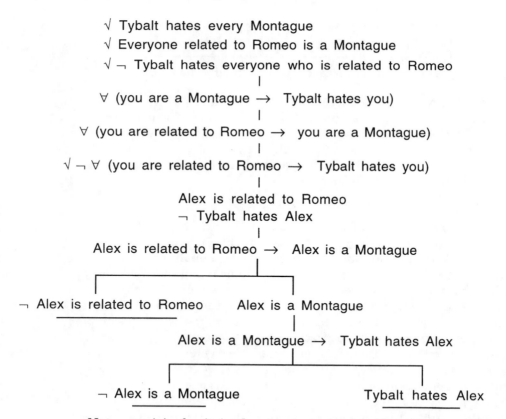

Not surprisingly, it is the counterexample, Alex, who provides the relevant instance of each of the universally quantified premises. It is his or her being related to Romeo and yet not being hated by Tybalt that makes for the inconsistency. In any case the tableau closes, showing that the argument is valid.

Argument (7) is an example of what traditional logic calls a syllogism in **Barbara**, which is exemplified in many textbooks with further elaborations on humanity and mortality. The method that we used on it can be applied to another syllogistic argument that is very similar. The subtle difference between them is important. In fact the following argument is fallacious. The conclusion does not follow from the premises.

> Tybalt hates every Montague.
> Every Montague is related to Romeo.
> ─────────────────────────────────
> Tybalt hates everyone who is related to Romeo.

A tableau will make the fallacy manifest by describing a situation with respect to which the premises are true but the conclusion is not. Of course the tableau is also quite similar to the one we constructed for (7), so we will concentrate on the differences.

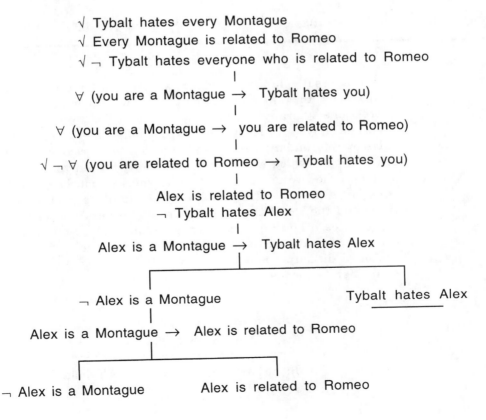

This tableau is by no means finished in that the universal quantifier rule could be applied four more times, resulting in four more conditional sentences, each of which would spawn two branches under the "→"-rule. But the story told by the unchecked sentences in the rightmost open path helps us to see that none of this would carry us to closing all of the paths. In this story Alex, who is the counterexample to the conclusion, is related to Romeo, but yet not hated by Tybalt. We see how this could be when we see in the path that he is not a Montague. This story becomes unmistakably intelligible if we add that he is a *maternal* relative of Romeo! No consideration of the premises as they apply to Tybalt and Romeo himself will be relevant. Though this would be manifest if the additional instances were actually written down and broken down by the appropriate rule, in this and other similar cases it is not worth going further in actual practice.

§36   RELATIVE PRONOUNS, AND THE EXISTENTIAL AND NIHILISTIC QUANTIFIERS

The universal quantifier, which we treated in the last section, enables us to reformulate sentences with complex quantifier expressions typically beginning with quantifier words like "every," "all," and "any." We bring these expressions under the control of our rules by reformulating sentences in which they occur in the manner of (3) of §35, which was abbreviated using the universal quantifier symbol. The two universal quantifier rules obviously generalize the rules in Chapter VIII for "everyone" and "anyone," so as to transcend the restriction to one-word quantifiers that characterizes those rules. The following argument illustrates another kind of complex quantifier expression that occurs very frequently in reasoned discourse and that is obviously related to the one-word quantifier "someone."

(1)

> Juliet loves a Montague.
> Every Montague hates Tybalt.
> _____
> Juliet loves someone who hates Tybalt.

Though the quantifier word "someone" does not occur in the first premise of argument (1), the same proposition might naturally be expressed with the "someone" present, as in,

> Juliet loves someone who is a Montague.

It might be expressed more briefly,

> Juliet loves some Montague,

or with the dummy subject "there,"

> There is some Montague whom Juliet loves,

or at more length,

(2)   There is someone who is a Montague and whom Juliet loves.

The telltale "someone" already appears in the conclusion to (1). That word could disappear in favor of "a"—although awkwardly—as in,

> Juliet loves a hater of Tybalt.

And the "someone" could acquire the dummy subject, as in,

(3)   There is someone whom Juliet loves who hates Tybalt.

Let us concentrate on the formulations (2) and (3), which both have the expression, "there is someone," which has a dummy subject. Though mildly verbose, this turns out to be the formulation that is most interesting grammatically and most adaptable to a variety of cases. As such it is most promising for a rule to be used in tableaux.

First, consider the word "who," which occurs repeatedly in (2) and (3), sometimes as the variant "whom." (Though not always used in ordinary speech, "whom" marks a grammatical distinction— what in English grammar is called objective case—that will be useful for our procedures.) What kind of words are these? Where do they arise in a syntactic derivation, whether by way of rewriting rules or transformations? (The only thing like this we saw in our laboratory grammar of Chapter V was the word "that," as in "cats *that* chase mice.") Traditional grammar calls these **relative pronouns**, and they are importantly similar to the anaphoric pronouns that we have studied in that they reach back, or even forward, to an antecedent. They occur in sentences with no quantifiers as well, as in,

(4)   Juliet loves Romeo, who is a Montague,

and,

> Romeo, whom Juliet loves, is a Montague.

In both of these cases the relative pronoun has as its antecedent the name "Romeo," which of course is a designator.   Notably, the fragment,

who is a Montague,

can be taken to express a true proposition so long as we take "who" to refer to Romeo in the manner of an anaphor.   It seems only a grammatical accident that the fragment does not qualify as a sentence in its own right.   In exactly this spirit, a transformational treatment might well take (4) to be derived transformationally from,

Juliet loves Romeo, and Romeo is a Montague.

When we turn to the quantifier version,

(5)   Juliet loves someone who is a Montague,

there are important similarities and important differences.   As before the relative pronoun "who" has a noun as its antecedent, but this time the antecedent is the quantifier word "someone," which is not a designator.   We cannot say that "who" refers to whomever "someone" refers to—because "someone" does not refer to anything. As for an underlying sentence, it may be that the grammaticality of (5) can be explained by way of transformation from an underlying sentence,

(6)   Juliet loves someone, and someone is a Montague,

but if so we have another exception to the Katz-Postal Hypothesis, for (5) and (6) are certainly not synonymous.

In the case of anaphoric pronouns, "he or she" and "you," that had quantifier words as their antecedents, we said that the anaphors stand ready to inherit a reference when the quantifier rule is applied and a genuine designator is introduced.   With relative pronouns whose antecedent is "someone" the situation is analogous.   Unlike with the universalizing quantifier words, not just any designator will do.   And an appropriate designator might not be recognizable.   (After all, it is a secret that Juliet loves Romeo!)   It was just this circumstance that led to the introduction of neutral names in the simple "someone"-rule.   If we do introduce such a name, say "Alex," we have an antecedent for the relative pronoun:

Juliet loves Alex, who is a Montague.

That maneuver happens to work with (5), but it does not result in a grammatical sentence when we begin with the dummy subject version:

There is Alex who is a Montague and whom Juliet loves.

Rather we can imitate the treatment of the anaphoric "you" in the universal quantifier rule. We should drop the entire expression, "there is someone" and replace all of the relative pronouns tied to that expression with the neutral name. Here the result will be,

Alex is a Montague and Alex Juliet loves.

But wait. What is this ungrammatical string, "Alex Juliet loves"? The objective case marker on "whom" comes to our rescue. In English, the object must follow the verb, and so the "whom" warns us to rearrange and we get,

Alex is a Montague, and Juliet loves Alex.

We have seen enough to justify abbreviating this adaptable expression, "there is someone," comprising the dummy subject, the copula, and the quantifier word. We use the symbol "∃," and we call it the **existential quantifier**. Just as with the universal quantifier, the existential quantifier has a scope, which we indicate with parentheses. Thus we abbreviate (2) as,

∃ (who is a Montague & whom Juliet loves).

What is important here is that relative pronouns within the parentheses are bound by the existential quantifier and that, in a tableau, if the scope of the quantifier is wide, we can apply a rule.

Rule for the Existential Quantifier: Suppose that in any path of a tableau there occurs a sentence with a wide-scope existential quantifier. To every branch below that occurrence, append the result of deleting that quantifier, and replacing all relative and anaphoric pronouns tied to that quantifier, with a new proper name. (Conventionally we choose the alphabetically next neutral proper name.) Adjust the word order and add "&" as necessary. Check off the existentially quantified sentence.

We have had enough explanation to enable us to formulate our rule for the existential quantifier, but we are not yet ready to take on argument (1) in a tableau. The conclusion of the argument should itself be reformulated with the help of the existential quantifier, but remembering the counter set, we recognize that we also need a negation rule. It will be easy to state, yet it will take us into new territory. The map of that territory has already been sketched for us in Chapter VIII; just as two simple quantifier rules, the one for "everyone" and the one for "someone," have already been adapted to complex quantifier expressions, so will the simple rule for "no one" be generalized using what we will call, in honor of its evocation of nothingness, the **nihilistic quantifier**.

What, after all, does it amount to to deny the conclusion of (1), that is, to assertively utter the following?

(7)   It is not true that there is someone whom Juliet loves who hates Tybalt.

More briefly the same assertion could be made with the sentence,

(8)   There is no one whom Juliet loves who hates Tybalt.

Supposing something like this generally to hold for existentially quantified sentences that are negated, we need a new abbreviation and a new rule. The new abbreviation, applied to (8), will be,

(9)   Й (whom Juliet loves (&) who hates Tybalt).

As for the rule, we need think no further than to remember the "no one" rule and to extend our new practice of replacing—by any designator—the relative pronouns that reach back to the quantifier word "no one" itself.

Rule for the Nihilistic Quantifier: Suppose that in any path of a tableau there occurs a sentence with a wide-scope nihilistic quantifier. To any branch below that occurrence, you may append the result of deleting the quantifier, negating what is left, and replacing all relative and anaphoric pronouns tied to that quantifier with any designator that already occurs in the tableau. Adjust the word order and add "&" as necessary. Do not check off the nihilistically quantified sentence.

Applied to (9), the rule for the nihilistic quantifier gives us such instances as the following—assuming that the designator in question already occurs in the tableau.

¬ (Juliet loves Tybalt & Tybalt hates Tybalt)

¬ (Juliet loves Alex & Alex hates Tybalt)

¬ (Juliet loves the Montague heir & the Montague heir hates Tybalt)

¬ (Juliet loves her father & her father hates Tybalt)

Like the rule for the universal quantifier, this rule is a permission. In practice, only the instances that are likely to cause branches to close should be written down. And because the instances might keep coming, the nihilistically quantified sentence cannot be checked off.

We recognized the nihilistic quantifier by considering argument (1), whose conclusion is an existentially quantified sentence, to be negated in the counter set. And so we need a negation rule for the existential quantifier, and while we are at it, a negation rule to handle nihilistically quantified conclusions. We have already anticipated the first of these, and the second will be equally easy.

Negation Rule for the Existential Quantifier: Append the result of dropping the negation and replacing the existential quantifier with a nihilistic quantifier. Check off the sentence with the negated "someone."

Negation Rule for the Nihilistic Quantifier: Append the result of dropping the negation and replacing the nihilistic quantifier with an existential quantifier. Check off the sentence with the negated "no one."

Armed with the full complement of rules for three rule-governed quantifiers, we are ready to investigate argument (1) by way of a tableau.

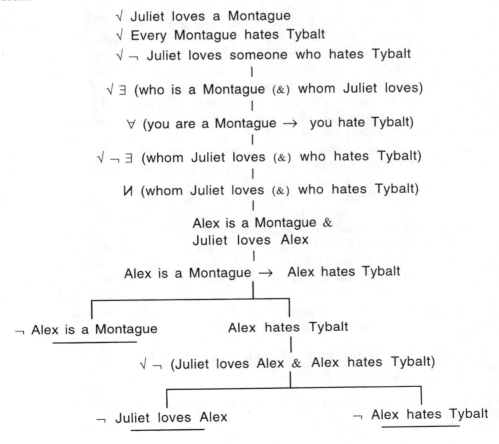

As you would expect, the tableau closes. In fact this valid argument is also an example of a traditional syllogistic form. In the next section we will see our quantifier rules applied to another form of syllogism. But we also will see them applied to a much more wide-ranging argument.

§37   TABLEAUX FOR SYLLOGISMS AND OTHER ARGUMENTS

We have occasionally used the term "syllogism," which might not be familiar to you. It applies to a range of arguments which were intensively studied in the tradition of logical inquiry that began with Aristotle and flourished with the recovery of Aristotle's writings in medieval philosophy. By definition a **syllogism** is an argument with two premises and, of course, a conclusion. Each of the three sentences includes exactly one quantifier expression. As with the argument (35.7), each sentence must either be grammatically simple ("Tybald hates every Montague") or have very limited grammatical complexity ("Tybald hates everyone who is related to Romeo), confined in fact to the quantifier expression. The quantifier expressions in question are limited to those beginning with the quantifier words, "all," "some," and "no"—or variants like "every," "a," and "none." It should be clear by now that such sentences can be reformulated using the universal, existential, and nihilistic quantifiers, respectively.

Though narrowly circumscribed, syllogistic arguments are very common, and they have an honored place in the history of logic. For these reasons, it is worthwhile to see the application of our six rules for quantifiers to syllogisms of a variety of forms. We saw in (35.7) the form traditionally called Barbara, and argument (36.1) is called **Datisi**. But equally it is essential to see that our rules enable us to establish the validity of a much wider range of arguments. Before doing so, let's consider one more syllogism, this one of the form called **Festino**.

Tybalt was killed by someone who loves Juliet.

No one who loves Juliet wanted to hurt Tybalt.

Someone who did not want to hurt Tybalt nonetheless killed him.

There follows the tableau for this syllogistic argument. Notice the unusual reformulation where "someone who loves Juliet" is the Noun Phrase that goes with the "by" of a passive-voice sentence. (Something similar would be done for "Tybalt sat by someone who loves Juliet," where "by" is a Preposition.) As before, "whom" in the objective case helps us rearrange when we apply the rule.

√ Tybalt was killed by someone who loves Juliet
√ No one who loves Juliet wanted to hurt Tybalt
√ ¬ Someone who did not want to hurt Tybalt nonetheless killed him
|
√ ∃ (by whom Tybalt was killed (&) who loves Juliet)
|
И (who loves Juliet & who wanted to hurt Tybalt)
|
√ ¬ ∃ (who did not want to hurt Tybalt (&) who killed Tybalt)
|
И (who did not want to hurt Tybalt (&) who killed Tybalt)
|
Tybalt was killed by Alex &
Alex loves Juliet
|
√ ¬ (Alex loves Juliet & Alex wanted to hurt Tybalt)

    ¬ Alex loves Juliet   ¬ Alex wanted to hurt Tybalt
          ————— |
              √ ¬ (Alex did not want to hurt Tybalt & Alex killed Tybalt)

√ ¬ Alex did not want to hurt Tybalt   ¬ Alex killed Tybalt
|
√ ¬ (¬ Alex wanted to hurt Tybalt)
|
Alex wanted to hurt Tybalt
—————

The traditional syllogistic treatment would render a verdict of valid, and our closed tableau reaches the same verdict. If you keep your head straight, you actually can close the path on the bottom two steps earlier. (The conflict is with "¬ Alex wanted to hurt Tybalt.") But spelling out the double negation and then eliminating it leaves no doubt as to the inconsistency.

Having exercised our quantifier rules on several syllogistic arguments, we are ready to apply them to more complex arguments. The earlier argument (36.1) had the conclusion that Juliet loves someone who hates Tybalt. That conclusion might lead us to go back on its premise that *every* Montague hates Tybalt.

> Juliet loves a Montague.
> Every Montague other than Romeo hates Tybalt.
> Juliet doesn't love anybody who hates Tybalt.
> _____
> Juliet loves Romeo.

The weakened second premise takes advantage of the relation of identity, for "every Montague other than Romeo" means "every Montague who is not Romeo," with "is" in the sense of "is one and the same as." (Similarly "Tony restrained everyone but himself" should be understood as "Tony restrained everyone who is not Tony.")

In its treatment of the third premise, the tableau below recalls a lesson about "anybody" from Chapter VIII. Even where the quantifier is complex, "any" differs from "every" in taking wide-scope. Thus the third premise is correctly formulated as a wide-scope universal quantification, with the negation confined to the clause, "Juliet doesn't love you." If the sentence had said, "Juliet doesn't love everybody who hates Tybalt," the reformulation would have a wide-scope negation.

√ Juliet loves a Montague
√ Every Montague other than Romeo hates Tybalt
√ Juliet doesn't love anybody who hates Tybalt
¬ Juliet loves Romeo
|
√ ∃ (who is a Montague (&) whom Juliet loves)
|
∀ (you are a Montague other than Romeo → you hate Tybalt)
|
∀ (you hate Tybalt → Juliet doesn't love you)
|
⋮

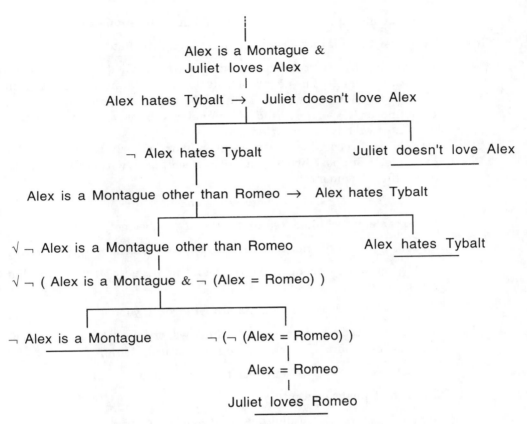

It is at the end of the tableau that an identity sentence occurs in one branch. Applying Leibniz's rule to the sentence, "Juliet loves Alex," which appears earlier in the path, yields "Juliet loves Romeo." But that has been denied to form the counter set, and so the path closes. The argument has been shown to be valid.

"ANYONE" AND LOGICAL EQUIVALENCE   §38

If you have persisted in reading our symbolic quantifiers as abbreviations and kept your ear tuned to the formulations that we have utilized, there was an earlier sentence that you may have found awkward. Sentence (7) of §36 is rewritten here.

It is not true that there is someone whom Juliet loves who hates Tybalt.

Your ear may have urged you to formulate the sentence as,

(1)   It is not true that there is *any*one whom Juliet loves who hates Tybalt.

It was only by resisting that urge that we were led to the nihilistic quantifier and to the negation rule for both it and the existential quantifier. But now we will indulge the urge, taking advantage of it to define an important kind of equivalence between sentences that until now we have only flirted with.

We can recognize the urge even more clearly with a simpler example. Suppose we begin with a sentence with the one-word quantifier "someone":

Juliet loves someone.

If the tableau technique requires us to negate, we get,

(2)   It is not true that Juliet loves someone,

and even more strongly do we feel the urge to transform that sentence to,

(3)   It is not true that Juliet loves anyone.

The urge becomes irresistible when we try for the more fluent internal negation. The nearly ungrammatical string,

Juliet doesn't love someone,

has to be transformed into,

Juliet doesn't love anyone.

However natural it may be to call these transformations, they don't seem to be syntactic transformations of the sort we introduced in Chapter V. Explaining these urges would take us deep into grammatical theory, and in fact into semantics, an area that we have avoided.

What we can say, making use only of the quantifier rules that we now have, is that (2) and (3) are **logically equivalent**. If our linguistic competence pushes us to use (3) rather than (2), at least part of the explanation must lie in that logical relation. What is meant by saying that the two sentences are logically equivalent is that they are equivalent with respect to their behavior in logical settings. We have seen three distinct logical settings in which a sentence might occur: (a) as one among a set of sentences; (b) as one among the premises of an argument; and (c) as the conclusion of an argument. To say that sentence (3) is logically equivalent to sentence (2) is to say that the logical verdict will remain the same if sentence (2) is replaced by sentence (3) in any of those settings. In short, there is no logical context in which our linguistic preference for (3) over (2) will lead us astray.

Rather than defending these claims about logical equivalence, let's turn to a practical test for the relationship. If two sentences are logically equivalent, each entails the other. That is to say, *two* arguments are valid, namely the argument that has the one as premise and the other as conclusion, and the converse argument where premise and conclusion are switched. Practically speaking, a better test issues from thinking of the counter sets.

> **Two sentences are logically equivalent if, and only if, the negation of each is inconsistent with the other.**

This test for logical equivalence can be applied to (2) and (3) in tableaux—not to be shown here—that have some interest of their own. They require not only a disciplined application of the one-word quantifier rules, but also an innovative maneuver with "anyone."

The full quantifier rules of this chapter are required to apply the test to the following sentence, which is one of the premises appearing in an argument in §37. (It may well be merely a syntactic variant of (1) above.)

(4)   Juliet doesn't love anybody who hates Tybalt.

As your ear probably tells you, this premise is logically equivalent to,

(5)   There is nobody who hates Tybalt whom Juliet loves.

Both of the tableaux in the test will close. Since they are logically equivalent, (5) can be substituted for (4) as a premise in the earlier (valid) argument. The resulting argument is also valid, as a reconstituted tableau would show. The original counter set was inconsistent. When one of its sentences is replaced by a logical equivalent, the resulting counter set remains inconsistent.

The one-word quantifier rules of Chapter VIII—including the "anyone"-rule—are explicitly restricted to sentences with only one quantifier expression of any kind. Yet there are lots of sentences in which occur multiple one-word quantifiers.

> Someone loves someone.
>
> No one loves anyone.
>
> Everyone loves someone.
>
> Someone is loved by everyone.

The quantifier rules of this chapter have been designed to handle quantifier expressions of the sort that occur in the categorical sentences found in syllogistic arguments.

> Some students admire George.
>
> No student admires Mary.
>
> Every student admires Martha.
>
> Some professor is admired by Tony.

But these rules have also been designed to handle multiple occurrences of such quantifier expressions, like those found in these analogous sentences.

(6)   Someone loves someone else.

> Some students admire a professor.
>
> No student admires any professor.
>
> Every student admires some professor.
>
> Some professor is admired by every student.

In the universal, existential, and nihilistic quantifier rules, there is no restriction to sentences that have only one quantifier expression. Rather there is the requirement that the quantifier under consideration have wide logical scope. Whether or not it does have the required wide logical scope turns out to be the same question as how to reformulate sentences like those at (6), in each case using either the universal, existential, or nihilistic quantifier. Should the fourth among those sentences be reformulated with the universal quantifier?

∀ (you are a student → you admire some professor)

Or should it be reformulated with the existential quantifier?

∃ (who is a professor (&) whom every student admires)

This is a particularly difficult example, perhaps an ambiguous one. But a choice must be made, in this and every case, as to which pattern of reformulation to utilize. Illustrating these choices and applying our rules to an illuminating selection from the huge variety of multiple quantifier arguments are tasks that we must leave for another occasion.

Those tasks will be complicated by the transformational urges that we have discussed in this section. In constructing a tableau, we may be led to the negation of one of our multiple quantifier sentences, for example,

>It is not true that someone loves someone else.

We feel the linguistic urge to move to a logical equivalent,

>It is not true that anyone loves anyone else.

Whether we resist or acquiesce will make a difference as to which quantifier rule we will apply. Exploring the ramifications of that choice is not just a matter of rehearsing our basic procedures as they apply to various cases. Rather it is an investigation of those deeper linguistic issues mentioned above.

§39

THINGS, TIMES, AND PLACES

Having worked in these chapters to tame a wide variety of quantifier expressions that range over a domain of persons—"everyone," "someone in our classroom," "no one who loves Romeo," etc.—it would be a pity not to look briefly at an easy generalization to quantifiers for things, times, and places. The one-word quantifiers that we began with have their parallels in each of these categories.

(1) One-Word Quantifiers of English

Persons	Things	Times	Places
everyone	everything	always	everywhere
someone	something	sometime	somewhere
no one	nothing	never	nowhere
anyone	anything	ever	anywhere

In any stretch of text or conversation each of these categories has a proprietary universe of discourse. But of course these universes differ from one another as to their characteristic inhabitants. There are substantial and interesting philosophical problems concerning the nature of these entities. What sort of things are times and places anyway? Are there really any such things as virtues or tones, characters or situations?

Even when we set aside these metaphysical problems to concentrate on more characteristically logical issues, we are faced with some uncertainties. The universe of discourse for the personal quantifiers pretty clearly can include people like George and Martha and characters like Romeo and Juliet. The universe of discourse for temporal quantifiers can include *times*, but it may be uncertain whether these are instants of time or also periods of time. It will be *places* or locations that make up the universe of discourse for the locational quantifiers, but again it may be unclear just how extensive a place can be. Finally, the most accommodating quantifiers are those with the ending "thing," and so the universe of discourse for these can include any *thing*. Examples will show that things generally must not only include concrete individual things like shoes and ships, rocks and rills, but also substances like sugar and water and abstract things like faith, hope, and charity. More indeterminate is the question whether things also include persons and times and places. Since these have their own categories of quantifier, it might seem unnecessary to include them among things. (And it is often remarked that no person likes to be treated as a thing.) On the other hand, there are logical contexts ("God created everything") that seem to require a comprehensive universe of discourse—that is, to require speaking of everything whatever.

Rather than treating these uncertainties independently of particular discursive contexts, we should be guided by the designators that may happen to occur. Whether it is an instant of time, like 8:00 sharp, or a period of many weeks, like autumn, if a temporal designator occurs in one of a set of sentences, the temporal quantifiers occurring in those sentences must include that time in their temporal universe of discourse. After all the one-word quantifier rules permit replacing "everyone" with any designator already appearing in the tableau in question. We would expect to modify the rule similarly to permit replacing the temporal one-word quantifier "always" with any temporal designator already appearing in the tableau. All of our quantifier rules can be analogously modified for the various categories of quantifier and their proprietary designators.

Decisions remain even when these modifications are made in a natural way. First we must be able to sort designators into the appropriate categories. It is perhaps most obvious with descriptions as to whether they are personal, temporal, locational, or just descriptions of things of a general sort. And just as we have proper names for people, so do "noon," "Christmas Day," and "July" seem to be names for times, as do "the North Pole," "Africa," and "Ottawa" for places. There are proprietary pronouns for persons. But "it" and "they" must serve for all of the categories. More interesting are demonstratives. "This" and "that" serve for things generally. "Now" and "then" are parallel demonstratives for times; "here" and "there," for places.

The expressions abbreviated by our existential and nihilistic quantifier symbols can easily be adapted to other categories. Thus the sentence,

> ". . *SOMETHING GREAT IS COMING!*"

can readily be reformulated as,

> There is something that is great that is coming,

with the repeated "that" recognizable as the relative pronoun relevant to the rule for existential quantifiers. Similarly,

> "*WE'LL FIND A NEW WAY OF LIVING,*
> *WE'LL FIND A WAY OF FORGIVING,*
> *SOMEWHERE.*"

can be reformulated as,

> There is a place where we'll find a new way of living, and
> where we'll find a way of forgiving.

The locational relative pronoun is "where." And finally the lyric,

> "*Never've I once looked back to sigh,*"

can be reformulated as,

> There is no time when I have looked back to sigh,

with the temporal relative pronoun being "when." We can abbreviate all these cases, as appropriate, with the existential and nihilisitic quantifier symbols, taking the cue from the relative pronoun for what kind of designator to use in each case, as the tableau unfolds.

Of course with some of the quantifier rules we must introduce new names, and we want these names to seem natural and to introduce no prejudice. Neutral names were our expedient for personal quantifiers, but no such ordinary names come to mind to serve us for the other categories. It is this pressure that leads us to go technical, to use **constants** in the manner of mathematics:

$a, b, c, \ldots$	for things generally
$t_1, t_2\ t_3, \ldots$	for times
$p_1, p_2, p_3, \ldots$	for places.

It would be infelicitous to try to adapt the universal quantifier expression, "no matter who you are," with its associated anaphoric "you," to the universal quantifier expressions for things, times, and places.   Fortunately, we have an alternative universalizing expression, "whoever he or she is," which can easily be adapted.

> *"EV'RYTHING FREE IN AMERICA*
> *FOR A SMALL FEE IN AMERICA!"*

can be reformulated in the manner of a universal categorical:

> Whatever it is, if it is in America, it is free, but it carries a small fee!

The repeated anaphoric pronoun "it" clearly reaches back to the quantifier expression and must be replaced in every occurrence by the chosen designator.   Universal quantifiers in the temporal and locational categories usually are simple.   But this complex case,

> *"ALWAYS THE HURRICANE BLOWING,*
> . . .
> *AND THE MONEY OWING,*
> *AND THE BABIES CRYING,*
> *AND THE BULLETS FLYING."*

can be reformulated as:

> Whenever it is, the hurricane is blowing then and the money is owing then and the babies are crying then and the bullets are flying then.

Presuming that the designator "tonight" occurs in the tableau in question, the universal quantifier rule would license the following instance.

> the hurricane is blowing tonight &
>
> (the money is owing tonight &
>
> (the babies are crying tonight &
>
> (the bullets are flying tonight)))

Perhaps the most interesting parallel is to the wide-scope universalizing "anyone."   It is not surprising that "anything" and "anywhere" behave similarly.   But we can finish our treatment of things, times, and places by switching musicals.   In the lines,

"IF EVER I WOULD LEAVE YOU,
IT WOULDN'T BE IN SUMMER,"

the word "ever" means "anytime" and constitutes a one-word
universal quantifier forcing wide scope and serving as the antecedent
for "it," which here means "that time." Of course the anaphoric "it"
will take its reference to a particular time only when the quantifier
word is replaced by a temporal designator. Let's make our final
farewell an invitation that you construct a tableau for the following
romantic, academic inference.

> If ever I would leave you, it wouldn't be in summer.
> I am leaving you now.
>
> ---
>
> It is not summer now.

Exercises for Chapter IX

1. Reformulate each of the following using rule-governed sentence connectives
    and the universal, existential, and nihilistic quantifiers.

    a. You will receive a form only if you filed last year.

    b. You are eligible for a refund precisely if your withholding exceeds
        your total tax.

    c. Every logic teacher confuses me.

    d. Some students like logic.

    e. No philosophy student received Departmental Honors.

    f. A student that I had met was on the bus.

    g. At least one of the invited guests did not attend.

    h. George outran all of the runners in the next lane.

    i. George outran none of the runners in the next lane.

    j. Only females bear children.

k.   I could not remember all of the guests.

l.   I could not remember any of the guests.

2.   Show that this syllogistic argument is valid by constructing a closed tableau on its counter set.

> No prudes like dancing.
> Some school teachers like dancing.
> _____
> Some school teachers are not prudes.

3.   This argument is two syllogisms combined. Easily show that it is valid using our methods.

> None but the diligent will graduate with honors.
> No friend of mine is diligent.
> Tom's sister is a friend of mine.
> _____
> Tom's sister will not graduate with honors.

4.   Here is a problem adapted from Quine. Since there are so many designators, blindly spawning all the instances from uncheckable quantified sentences results in a mess. The trick with it is to foresee which instances will be inconsistent with one another.

> Everyone who knows both George and Martha understands Martha.
> Her doctor knows Martha but does not understand her
> _____
> Some who know Martha do not know George.

5.   This problem involves identity and mixes one-word quantifiers with quantifier expressions.

> Whoever drove down his lane was going to visit Ortcutt.
> If anyone visited him, then Ortcutt is the Soviet spy.
> Ortcutt knows the Western-front defense strategy.
> The lady in the black Mercedes drove down Ortcutt's lane.
> _____
> The Soviet spy knows the Western-front defense strategy.

6.   Apply the test for logical equivalence to sentences (38.4) and (38.5).

7.   This problem tests our rules against multiple quantifier expressions. You
        should be able to make them work to show that the argument is valid.

Romeo, who is a Montague, loves Juliet, who is a Capulet.

Not every Montague hates every Capulet.

APPENDIX: Truth-Functional Logic

The standard sentence connectives are negation, "¬"; conjunction, "&"; disjunction, "∨"; the conditional, "→"; and the biconditional, "↔." In developing the method of tableaux, we distinguish them from other ways of forming complex sentences because they are governed by very simple rules. For this reason we call them **rule-governed connectives**. Since negation applies only to a single sentence, it is a connective only in a degenerate sense. In order to mark the distinction, let us agree to call the others **proper connectives**. Now we can explain precisely what it is for all these connectives to be rule-governed. First consider any complex sentence S that can be paraphrased as the result of joining two simpler sentences S_1 and S_2 with a proper rule-governed connective. In any tableau, S can be broken down in accordance with the appropriate rule on the left of table (1), below. Next consider any sentence S that is a negation of a sentence S', where S', as before, can be paraphrased as the result of joining S_1 and S_2 with a proper rule-governed connective. S can be broken down in accordance with the appropriate rule on the right of table (1). Finally consider any

248

sentence S that is the negation of a sentence S', which is itself the negation of a sentence S_1. S can be simplified in accordance with the rule on the bottom of table (1).

(1) Tableau Rules for Sentence Connectives

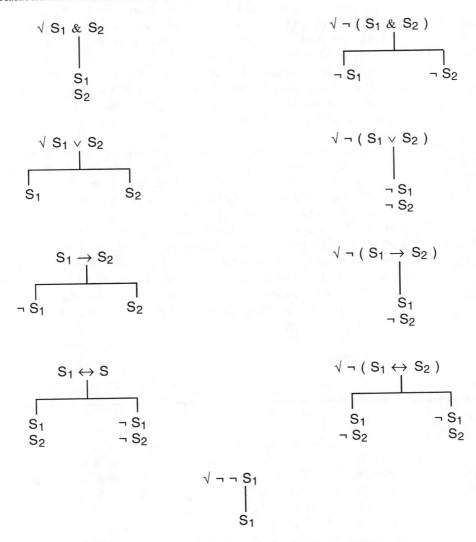

A sentence that is grammatically complex may have been formed through introducing a co-ordinating conjunction like "or," "and," or "but." Or it may have been formed with a subordinating conjunction,

like "if ," "although," or "unless."   Or it may have been formed
through some other sentence-forming operation. Of sentences that
are grammatically complex in any of these ways, many can be
paraphrased, more or less accurately, by operating on one or more
simpler sentences with rule-governed connectives. Under an idealization commonly adopted in propositional logic, such paraphrases
are embraced, and complex sentences that resist paraphrase by way
of the standard connectives are excluded from logical treatment.
Under the idealization, a given set contains only simple sentences
together with complex sentences built up from simple sentences
using the standard connectives. Consider the construction of a
tableau on a set like this. The sentences divide into four categories:
(1) simple sentences; (2) negations of simple sentences; (3) sentences
whose main connective is a proper (rule-governed) connective; and
(4) negations of sentences that are themselves complex. Sentences in
the fourth category will have a subsidiary, rule-governed connective.
In the case of any sentence in the third or fourth categories, exactly
one of the nine rules in table (1) can be applied in order to extend the
appropriate branches of the tableau with one or more simpler
sentences. Sentences in the first and second categories cannot be
further broken down; they passively await the chance to contradict
other sentences, as the latter make their appearance in one or more
subordinate branches of the developing tableau. The crucial fact is
that the entire tableau can be constructed in accordance with the
rules in table (1). It is this that makes the set of sentences in question
an ideal one to work with.

§41   THREE LEVELS OF SYMBOLIZATION

For purposes of logical analysis and assessment, sentences can be
treated at any of three, successively more abstract, levels of
symbolization. The first level is reached by introducing the symbolic
sentence connectives which are governed by tableau rules. Each
sentence is paraphrased, insofar as possible, using symbolic
connectives that have the same logical force as the conjunctions or
other grammatical constructions which composed the complex
sentence out of its constituent sentences. Of course it is common for
words like "either" and "both" to occur in complex sentences as
indicators of scope. In other cases, the effect of transformations

leaves no doubt as to the scope of the various underlying operations that formed complex sentences out of simpler constituents. At this level of symbolization, parentheses are introduced along with symbolic connectives; they serve to indicate grouping and scope.

We have noted that the ideal case is for the complex sentences in a tableau to have these symbolic connectives, and none others, joining their simpler constituents. In this case, the process of constructing the tableau becomes entirely systematic, a matter of applying the rules for the various connectives. A **sentence tableau** is a tableau constructed from sentences containing symbolic connectives in accordance with tableau rules.

A second level of symbolization is reached by recognizing that simple sentences appear and reappear as constituents of various of the complex sentences. A significant efficiency in constructing the tableau results from introducing **sentence letters** to stand for each of the simple sentences in question. We might regard the sentence letters as abbreviations of the respective simple sentences, and we do well to choose letters that are naturally abbreviatory. The tableau is much briefer in that whole sentences do not have to be written over and over again. A price to be paid for this brevity is that some sources of inconsistency will be masked. In effect, we will be able to close a branch only when there occurs in the path both a sentence and the negation of that very sentence. The simplest instance would be a path containing both a sentence letter and the same letter negated.

The result of symbolizing a sentence in this way is called a **formula**. It consists only of sentence letters, symbolic sentence connectives, and parentheses serving to indicate scope. So far we count the formula as merely an abbreviation of the complex sentence from which it originated.

A third—more abstract—level of symbolization comes when we consider a formula in its own right. A **scheme of interpretation** is an assignment of simple sentences to the sentence letters in the formula. As a matter of convention, formulas to be considered in this abstract way incorporate the letters "P," "Q," and so on, for sentence letters. (The convention was originally motivated by "p," in *proposition*.) When it is assigned to a sentence letter, a particular simple sentence is no longer regarded as spelling out what was only abbreviated, but rather as providing an interpretation for what was uninterpreted. Two complex sentences, entirely different in their subject matter, result from differently interpreting the sentence letters in a single formula. What the two complex sentences have in common is the structure portrayed by the formula itself. For obvious reasons this structure may be called the **logical form** of the complex sentence.

A **symbolic tableau** is one constructed on a set of formulas. Symbolic tableaux have the two virtues, first, of being governed by tableau rules and, second, of brevity in using sentence letters rather than full sentences. But a more significant virtue emerges with multiple schemes of interpretation. Distinct sets of complex sentences result from introducing distinct schemes of interpretation for a given set of formulas. A single symbolic tableau addresses the question of consistency for any such set of complex sentences. Not only is a given argument analyzed and assessed by a symbolic tableau constructed on its counter set, but every argument is simultaneously assessed, whose premises and conclusion have respectively the same form as those of the given argument. It must be granted that hidden sources of inconsistency may lurk in the simple sentences themselves, introduced by the scheme of interpretation into an otherwise consistent set of formulas. But a verdict of inconsistency is final, even when delivered by a symbolic tableau. It applies to any interpretation of the formulas in question.

§42   SYMBOLIC LANGUAGES FOR ALGEBRA

In symbolizing sentences using sentence letters and the symbolic connectives, we have constructed formulas that bear a close resemblance to the formulas used in ordinary algebra. In fact a phrase-structure grammar can be specified for these formulas as follows.

(1) A Phrase-Structure Grammar for Sentential Formulas

Formula $\Rightarrow$ ¬ Formula

Formula $\Rightarrow$ **(** Formula   Sentence Connective   Formula **)**

Formula $\Rightarrow$ Sentence Letter

Sentence Connective $\Rightarrow$ **&** | **v** | $\rightarrow$ | $\leftrightarrow$

Sentence Letter $\Rightarrow$ **P** | **Q** | **R** | **S** | **T** | ...

Though the principles involved are not usually made explicit, there is a sharp distinction to be made between strings of variables, operators, and parentheses that make for intelligible algebraic expressions and strings that are just nonsense. In the case of our symbolizations of complex sentences, exactly that distinction is effectively made by the phrase-structure grammar in (1). Even though all of the symbols in the string,

$$\neg\,(\,)\,R\,\rightarrow\,\leftrightarrow\,S\,R\,(\,\vee\,\rightarrow\,Q\,\neg\,\neg\,($$

are terminal symbols of the language defined by the grammar, the string itself is not grammatical. No phrase-marker with this terminal string can be constructed using the rewriting rules of the grammar. (It is enough to note that parentheses are introduced only in the second rewriting rule, but that rule would produce a right parenthesis at the end of the formula to match the left parenthesis after the first occurrence of the negation sign.)

By contrast, the formula,

$$(\,\neg\,(\,R\,\rightarrow\,Q\,)\,\leftrightarrow\,(\,P\,\&\,(\,R\,\vee\,\neg\,Q\,)\,)\,)$$

even though complicated, is indeed a grammatical string. We show that it is grammatical by constructing a phrase-marker whose terminal string is exactly the given formula.

(2) A Phrase-Marker for a Sentential Formula

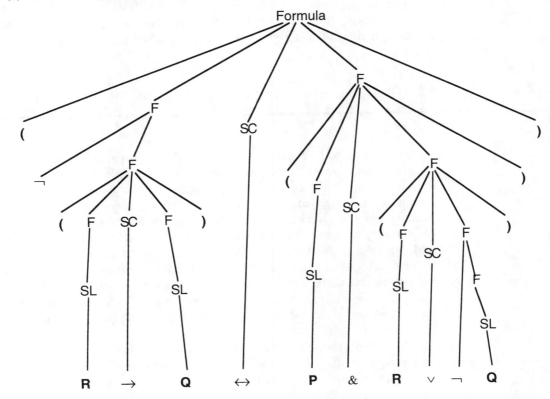

Like those governing ordinary algebraic formulas, but unlike those of English grammar, the recursive rules of the grammar for sentential formulas invite unlimited embedding in actual practice. Thus our formula seems to have outstripped in complexity any English sentence likely to be formulated. Actually a choice of simple materials and care in expressing the relevant connectives will yield a sentence that comes close to being intelligible to our ears. Suppose we take as a scheme of interpretation,

P :   It is blowing.

Q :   It is quiet.

R :   It is raining.

The sentence that results from our formula is,

That it is raining only if it is quiet is not true if, and only if, it is both blowing and either raining or not quiet.

While not something you are likely to hear on the weather report, this is recognizable as a sentence of English, and with a little effort you can get a rough idea of what it means. Determining whether it is true, even with the kind of information you can get by looking out the window, is another matter—a matter to be taken up in §44.

§43   TRUTH-FUNCTIONS AND THEIR COMPUTATIONAL TABLES

In §40 we specified an idealization of the meanings of central conjunctions of English that enables us to build tableaux governed by simple rules. The conjunctions in question are replaced by sentence connectives, each of which is governed by two rules, one for affirmative sentences whose constituents are joined by the assigned connective, and one for negations of such sentences. Presently we will extend that idealization, leading to a dramatic simplification and theoretical systematization that is called truth-functional logic. We introduce truth-functional logic in connection with the logical analysis of complex sentences; as we will see in later sections, truth-functional logic can be reinterpreted to yield applications far from this current topic.

We adopt the idea, deriving from John Stuart Mill, that the fundamental entity of interest to logic is the **proposition**. Propositions are independent of any particular linguistic formulation, and are identifiable by three features. (1) Propositions are the objects of belief. (2) Propositions are expressed by complete declarative sentences. And (3) propositions are susceptible of truth and falsity. What is meant by the third point is that propositions are the sorts of things to which truth and falsity are primarily attributed. Insofar as truth and falsity are attributed to sentences, it is by way of the propositions that they express. We speak of truth and falsity as **truth-values**. The condition of being true is the truth-value **True**, and the condition of being false is the truth-value **False**. There are no other truth-values. Where it is determinate what proposition is expressed by a particular sentence, the sentence inherits whatever truth-value is enjoyed by that proposition.

The crucial idealization leading to truth-functional logic requires the assumption that every proposition *has* a truth-value, that every proposition is either true or false. Since propositions are expressed by declarative sentences, the idealization applies to them as well: every declarative sentence that expresses a proposition has one of the two truth-values. This assumption applies to complex sentences and also to the constituent sentences that make them up. But more is required. We must consider other situations than the actual one. Different propositions are expressed by given sentences with respect to different situations. Is each of the propositions either true or false in the situation at hand? We must assume that each one is, that is, not only that every proposition has an actual truth-value, but also that any proposition that is expressed by a given sentence with respect to a given situation has a truth-value in that situation. Since the letters in our formulas are to be interpreted by sentences, we must go even farther. Each sentence must be presumed indeed to express some definite proposition with respect to a given situation, in order for the sentence to inherit the truth-value that turns up. All of this can be summed up as the powerful assumption, required by our idealization, that every sentence, whether simple or complex, has a truth-value with respect to every possible situation.

Truth-functional logic proceeds from the recognition that this idealizing assumption is sufficient for the rule-governed sentence connectives to comprise **truth-functions**. A truth-function is a function in the mathematical sense of determining a unique value on the basis of one or more arguments supplied to it. Both the domain and the range of these functions (to use the standard mathematical terminology) are simply the two truth-values, True and False.

The simplest truth-function of interest is negation. Our symbol "¬" is short for the phrase, "it is not true that." The result of applying it to a sentence S is the complex sentence,

$$\neg \, S.$$

What is the truth-value of "¬ S" when S is true? Let us take the phrase at its word. Since S is true, what the complex sentence says is not true. We must choose from the two truth-values, so nothing is left for us but to assign "¬ S" the value False. When the sentence that we negate is false, the result—since it says that it is not true that S— is surely true. For if S *were* true, it would be both true and false. We summarize these results in the following simple table.

(1)

S	¬ S
True	False
False	True

Notice that table (1) bears out the tableau rule for double negation. In effect the negation sign simply switches us from one truth-value to the other. But then the effect of doubly negating will be to leave the truth-value as it was. So the one way for ¬ ¬ S to be true is for S itself to be true.

The other truth-functions we will consider have two arguments. To take a central example, consider the conditional, i.e., the sentence connective we have symbolized as "→." Suppose we have a complex sentence of the form,

(2) $S_1 \rightarrow S_2.$

With two constituent sentences, there are four combinations of truth and falsity, each represented by a line in the table that follows. Early on we recognized that sentence (2) rules out any situation in which S_1 is true and S_2 is false. This much insures that the value on the third line will be False.

S_1	S_2	$S_1 \rightarrow S_2$
True	True	
False	True	
True	False	False
False	False	

In order to find values for the other three combinations, we turn to the controversial negation rule for conditionals. According to that rule the only way for a sentence of the form ¬ $(S_1 \rightarrow S_2)$ to be true, is for S1 and ¬ S2 both to be true. This means that the third line of the table is the *only* one with the value False—because $S_1 \rightarrow S_2$ can be false only if ¬ $(S_1 \rightarrow S_2)$ is true. Our idealization requires that the other lines be filled in, so we have no choice but the following table for the truth-functional conditional.

(3)

S_1	S_2	$S_1 \rightarrow S_2$
True	True	True
False	True	True
True	False	False
False	False	True

The tableau rules governing the other three connectives—"&," "∨," and "↔"—similarly determine what truth-function is defined for each one. The affirmative rule gives all the different ways (in the case of "&," there is only one) in which the complex sentence can be true. It thereby determines that those lines of the table that fall under none of the favored ways will be False. Here it is crucial that the ways in which the sentence can be true were all specified in terms of the truth of one or more of S_1, ¬ S_1, S_2, and ¬ S_2; the truth-value of each of the lines in question is thereby determined by the truth or falsity of just S_1 and S_2, that is to say, by the truth-values of the two constituents of the original complex sentence.

As for the remaining lines, we can't rush to conclude that they should be assigned True. For all we know so far, the truth-value of a sentence falling on one of these remaining lines is as yet indeterminate. As we found with the conditional, it is here that the negative rule does its work. Ways for the negated complex sentence to be true are ways for its affirmative counterpart to be false. In setting out such ways the rule effectively counts out any other way for the affirmative sentence to be false; thus it is determined that ways that are not included make the affirmative sentence true—here enters the idealizing assumption that the sentence must have a truth-value. So long as the negative rule specifies its ways (for the affirmative sentence to be false) again in terms of the truth-values of the two constituent sentences, the ways that are not included will be lines of the table. All such lines must be assigned the value True. It so happens in the case of each of the three connectives under discussion that the lines to be assigned True are all the remaining lines.

By this kind of reasoning we are led to assign a truth-value to each line of the following table, under each of the connectives. (The entries for ¬ S₁, and S₁ → S₂ were already assigned in the specific discussions of negation, and of the conditional, leading to tables (1) and (3) above.) By assigning a truth-value to each line for a given connective, we effectively define a truth-function that the connective expresses.

(4) Computational Tables for Five Truth-Functions

S_1	S_2	¬ S_1	S_1 & S_2	$S_1 \lor S_2$	$S_1 \to S_2$	$S_1 \leftrightarrow S_2$
True	True	False	True	True	True	True
False	True	True	False	True	True	False
True	False	False	False	True	False	False
False	False	True	False	False	True	True

The significance of this table can perhaps better be realized by comparing it to a multiplication table, actually to several computational tables each analogous to a multiplication table. The analogy becomes clearer when a column of (4), say the column for the conditional, is rewritten in matrix form.

→	True	False
True	True	False
False	True	True

The function (or operation) of multiplication takes two arguments. A so-called times-table can be taken to define the function, at least for arguments up to 10, by entering into the cell of intersection the result of multiplying the value on the row by the value on the column. Similarly, the computational table here given for the conditional effectively defines the relevant truth-function. The cell of intersection exhibits the truth-value of a conditional sentence whose subordinate clause—the "if"-clause—has the truth-value on the row and whose main clause has the truth-value on the column. So understood, the entries under the connectives of (4) serve as computational tables defining five important truth-functions, namely, negation, logical conjunction, disjunction, the (truth-functional) conditional, and the biconditional.

Recall now our problem, from the end of §42, of determining whether the peculiarly complex sentence of English there considered is true or false in a given situation.

(1)   That it is raining only if it is quiet is not true if, and only if,
            it is both blowing and either raining or not quiet.

Remember that sentence (1) results from introducing the scheme of interpretation given below with respect to this complex formula.

(2) $(\neg (R \rightarrow Q) \leftrightarrow (P \ \& \ (R \lor \neg Q)))$

Suppose that we do look outside our window, and we see that in fact the wind is blowing very fiercely and noisily, but that the skies are clear. In that situation, the simple constituents of (1) have these truth-values:

> P :   It is blowing.   True
>
> Q :   It is quiet.   False
>
> R :   It is raining.   False

We may not be able recognize right off whether our sentence (1) is true or not, even with the benefit of peering out at the weather. But with the computational tables given in (43.4), determining a truth-value for the complex formula—and thus for sentence (1), which the formula symbolizes—becomes a matter of calculation. The calculation is analogous to calculating the value of a complex algebraic expression once numerical values have been assigned to its variables.

The necessary calculation is indicated at (3) below. We begin on the left with the truth-values to be assigned to each of "P," "Q," and "R." These were determined by observing the weather conditions. These values are then entered under each occurrence of the respective sentence letters. Our calculation proceeds as indicated by the arrows below the truth-values. Note that it goes from inside, out; in other words, it proceeds upward with respect to the phrase-marker for the formula, given in (42.2). Each step of the calculation is determined by the relevant entry in one of the computational tables in (43.4). For example, the calculation labeled "1" is given by the fourth line of the table for the conditional, which says that a sentence of the form $S_1 \rightarrow S_2$ has the value True when S_1 and S_2 both have the value False.

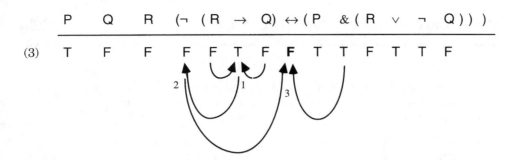

(3)

Next, as indicated by "2," we consult the first line of the table for negation, which says that if S_1 has the value True, then $\neg S_1$ has the value False. The main connective of the formula is the biconditional, the Sentence Connective introduced by the top rewriting rule in the phrase-marker (42.2). So, naturally enough, the last step in the calculation is the one labelled "3" (presuming that the calculations to the right of the "↔" have been done analogously to "1" and "2"). Consulting the table for the biconditional, we see on the second line that the value of $S_1 \leftrightarrow S_2$ is False when S_1 is False and S_2 is True. The bold-face "**F**" represents that truth-value of False, given to the sentence as a whole.

The truth-value that results from the calculation is False. What that tells us is that in the situation we imagined, where the wind was loudly blowing, but no rain was falling, our complex sentence (1) is false. That is to say, we learned from this calculation that, in the weather situation described, it is not true that that it is raining only if it is quiet is not true if, and only if, it is both blowing and either raining or not quiet!

In determining whether sentence (1) is true or false, we have taken advantage of the truth-functional character of the grammatical conjunctions that occur in it, or speaking more accurately, of the idealization that provides for our truth-functional treatment of them. Bear in mind that this idealization requires the assumptions (1) that every proposition is either true or false, and (2) that, with respect to any given situation, every sentence expresses a proposition that is either true or false in that situation. The latter assumption enables us to carry further the kind of calculation we have used. Under the idealizing assumption, the sentences assigned to "P," "Q," and "R" each have one of the two truth-values no matter what situation we envision.   Since the grammatical conjunctions have been paraphrased by truth-functional connectives, the truth-value, with respect to any situation, of the complex sentence as a whole will be determined by the truth-values of its constituents. Thus its truth-value, with respect to each situation, can be calculated, just as we calculated the truth-value of (1). If we consider all of the possible combinations of truth-value assignments to "P," "Q," and "R," we can systematically survey the truth-value of the complex sentence (1) with respect to every possible situation. Such a systematic survey is called a **truth table**.

In constructing a truth table, the primary thing to be sure of is that the survey is well-organized and complete. We achieve this by constructing lines of the table as follows. To begin we construct two lines, first assigning True to "P" and then assigning False. Since "Q" can be either true or false as well, we assign True to "Q" on these two lines and then construct two more lines exactly like the first two, except that on them we assign False to "Q." We proceed to double the number of lines in the table for each additional sentence letter, assigning the additional letter True on the original lines and then assigning it False on the duplicate lines. We continue this process until all of the sentence letters in the formula have been included. (In our example, there is only the one additional letter, namely "R.") It is not hard to see that the result of this doubling for each letter after the first one will be a table with 2^n lines, given a formula with n sentence letters.

P	Q	R	(¬ (R → Q) ↔ (P & (R ∨ ¬ Q)))
1	1	1	
0	1	1	
1	0	1	
0	0	1	
1	1	0	
0	1	0	
1	0	0	
0	0	0	

Obviously, something new has appeared in this table. To represent the truth-value, True, we have used, not "T," but the digit "1." Similarly we have represented False with "0." One reason for this is manual efficiency. In truth-tables, lots of entries need to be recorded, and digits require only one written stroke. But another, more theoretical reason becomes relevant when truth-values are reinterpreted in computational terms.

After securing the truth-values to be assigned to each of the sentence letters on each line of our systematic survey, we enter these respective values under each occurrence of each of the sentence letters in the formula.

P   Q   R   (¬ (R → Q) ↔ (P   & (R   ∨   ¬   Q)))

P	Q	R	¬	R	Q	P	R	Q
1	1	1	1	1	1	1	1	1
0	1	1	1	1	0	1	1	1
1	0	1	1	0	1	1	0	—
0	0	1	1	0	0	1	0	—
1	1	0	0	1	1	0	1	—
0	1	0	0	1	0	0	1	—
1	0	0	0	0	1	0	0	—
0	0	0	0	0	0	0	0	—

(Values appear under the occurrences of the sentence letters R, Q, P, R, Q in the formula.)

Now come the calculations, making use of the computational tables in (43.4). In the table below attention is fixed on what can be the first of these calculations, negating on each line the truth-values there assigned to "Q." We have chosen this particular column because the calculation proceeds from inside, out—from bottom, up in phrase-marker (42.2).

P   Q   R   (¬ (R → Q) ↔ (P   & (R   ∨   ¬   Q)))

¬	Q
0	1
0	1
1	0
1	0
0	1
0	1
1	0
1	0

The calculation just completed—negation—was pretty obvious. Calculating the value of the conditional "R → Q" (on the left below) may require you actually to consult the defining column of (43.4). For each value to be calculated, find the appropriate line of the defining column. Since the conditional is somewhat odd in its definition, it will be worthwhile to make an effort to commit it to memory. To find the values of "R ∨ ¬ Q" (on the right) we must make use of the values of "¬ Q" previously calculated. Though the left of these bold-face columns could have been calculated earlier, the right-hand one had to wait its turn.

P	Q	R	¬	R	→	Q	↔	P	&	R	∨	¬	Q
				1	1	1				1	1	0	
				1	1	1				1	1	0	
				1	0	0				1	1	1	
				1	0	0				1	1	1	
				0	1	1				0	0	0	
				0	1	1				0	0	0	
				0	1	0				0	1	1	
				0	1	0				0	1	1	

Proceeding up the phrase-marker, in effect, we negate "R → Q" and we apply the definition of logical conjunction to the values of "P" and of "R ∨ ¬ Q."

P	Q	R	¬	R	→	Q	↔	P	&	R	∨	¬	Q
			0		1			1	**1**		1		
			0		1			0	**0**		1		
			1		0			1	**1**		1		
			1		0			0	**0**		1		
			0		1			1	**0**		0		
			0		1			0	**0**		0		
			0		1			1	**1**		1		
			0		1			0	**0**		1		

At last we are able to utilize the defining column for the biconditional to enter the truth-values in what turns out to be the **main column** of the truth-table. The main column falls under the **main connective**, i.e., that connective introduced first as the formula is generated in its phrase-marker. The main column is the most important one in that here are recorded the truth-values of the formula as a whole under the respective assignments of truth-values to its sentence letters.

P	Q	R	¬	R	→	Q	↔	P	&	R	∨	¬	Q
			0				**0**		1				
			0				**1**		0				
			1				**1**		1				
			1				**0**		0				
			0				**1**		0				
			0				**1**		0				
			0				**0**		1				
			0				**1**		0				

In practice, all of these entries can be recorded, or calculated, in a single table, as follows. But it is crucial that they be entered in the inside-out order derived from the phrase-marker for the formula. With a little practice, you will be able to tell the order of the connectives by the seat of your pants and not actually need to consult a phrase-marker.

P	Q	R	(¬	(R	→	Q)	↔	(P	&	(R	∨	¬	Q)))
1	1	1	0	1	1	1	**0**	1	1	1	1	0	1
0	1	1	0	1	1	1	**1**	0	0	1	1	0	1
1	0	1	1	1	0	0	**1**	1	1	1	1	1	0
0	0	1	1	1	0	0	**0**	0	0	1	1	1	0
1	1	0	0	0	1	1	**1**	1	0	0	0	0	1
0	1	0	0	0	1	1	**1**	0	0	0	0	0	1
(*) 1	0	0	0	0	1	0	**0**	1	1	0	1	1	0
0	0	0	0	0	1	0	**1**	0	0	0	1	1	0

If you have understood the point of constructing this truth-table, you will realize that it includes among its lines the calculation that we earlier made on the basis of peering out at the weather. Included in the exhaustive survey is a line representing the meteorological situation on that blustery, clear day. It is the line with the asterisk (*) that reproduces the calculations of (3) above. In fact whatever the weather report, the complete truth-table will include a line telling whether the complex sentence (1) is true or false on that day. Why? Whatever the weather report, it will be either true or false that it is blowing, either true or false that it is quiet, and either true or false that it is raining. This is guaranteed by our idealization that every sentence is either true or false with respect to every situation. Having that guarantee, we need only find the line with the appropriate combination of truth-values for the letters "P," "Q," and "R." The entry in the main column will be the truth-value assigned to the formula, and thus to sentence (1), in that situation.

On the basis of truth tables and the systematic survey that they represent, we can define several important notions. A formula, and the sentence that it symbolizes, is a **tautology** if the main column of its truth table has all True entries. Such a sentence is true with respect to every possible situation. A formula, and the sentence that it symbolizes, is **inconsistent** if its truth table has all False entries in its main column. Here we recall a term which we earlier applied to sets of sentences. The current notion of an inconsistent *formula* (or sentence) is connected to the notion of an inconsistent set of sentences in two ways. In the first place, a tableau constructed on an inconsistent formula will close. That outcome is guaranteed by the relation between the truth-functions as defined in (43.4) and the tableau rules for the connectives. And so the *set* whose only member is an inconsistent sentence will be an inconsistent set. In the second place, suppose a set of sentences is inconsistent and can be shown to be inconsistent by means of a symbolic tableau. Construct a single sentence by taking the logical conjunction of the sentences in the inconsistent set. The resulting complex sentence will be inconsistent in the current sense, i.e., the main column of its truth table will show all False.

Finally, by way of truth tables we can define another kind of equivalence between sentences. Two formulas, and the sentences they symbolize, are **logically equivalent** if the main columns of their respective truth tables are the same. Here are two important examples of logically equivalent pairs.

(4a)   It is neither raining nor snowing.

(4b)   It is not raining, and it is not snowing.

(5a)   If it is snowing, then it is quiet.

(5b)   Either it is not snowing, or else it is quiet.

Sentences (4a) and (4b), if you think about what they mean, describe the same weather conditions. That realization, deriving from our understanding of English, is confirmed by the following truth table. Every situation with respect to which the left-hand formula is true is a situation with respect to which the right-hand formula is true, and vice-versa. And so the weather conditions that the one sentence truthfully describes are exactly those that the other does. In short, sentences (4a) and (4b) are logically equivalent.

R	S	¬	(R	∨	S)	(¬	R	&	¬	S)
1	1	**0**	1	1	1	0	1	**0**	0	1
0	1	**0**	0	1	1	1	0	**0**	0	1
1	0	**0**	1	1	0	0	1	**0**	1	0
0	0	**1**	0	0	0	1	0	**1**	1	0

Sentences (5a) and (5b) do not quite so readily strike our ears as each amounting to the same thing as the other. Still, when we consult the truth table, they turn out to be logically equivalent as well.

S	Q	(S	→	Q)	(¬	S	∨	Q)
1	1	1	1	1	0	1	1	1
0	1	0	1	1	1	0	1	1
1	0	1	0	0	0	1	0	0
0	0	0	1	0	1	0	1	0

The explanation is that here the truth-functional idealization is operating. Remember what a strain it was to settle on the defining table for the arrow. Even so, further reflection (under the idealization) will confirm the equivalence. Since if it's snowing it must be quiet, either it's quiet or else it must not be snowing. That is, either it is not snowing or else it *is* quiet after all.

Two formulas can turn out to be logically equivalent even though they do not have the same sentence letters. The formula on the left below lacks the letter "R." Even so, when we carefully arrange lines for all three letters, as indicated in the left three columns, and go on to record truth-values under each sentence letter in the proper way, the main columns for the left-hand (very simple) formula and for the right-hand (quite complex) formula are the same. See if you can see through these formulas to their English versions. Do the English sentences seem, to your ear, to have the same logical force?

P	Q	R	P	→	Q	((P	→	Q)	&	R)	∨	((P	→	Q)	&	¬	R)
1	1	1	1	1	1	1	1	1	1	1	1	1	1	1	0	0	1
0	1	1	0	1	1	0	1	1	1	1	1	0	1	1	0	0	1
1	0	1	1	0	0	1	0	0	0	1	0	1	0	0	0	0	1
0	0	1	0	1	0	0	1	0	1	1	1	0	1	0	0	0	1
1	1	0	1	1	1	1	1	1	0	0	1	1	1	1	1	1	0
0	1	0	0	1	1	0	1	1	0	0	1	0	1	1	1	1	0
1	0	0	1	0	0	1	0	0	0	0	0	1	0	0	0	1	0
0	0	0	0	1	0	0	1	0	0	0	1	0	1	0	1	1	0

Making use of the notion of logical equivalence, we can understand why, as speakers of English, we recognize no difference between the following two sentences:

Either it is blowing or quiet, or else it is raining.

Either it is blowing, or else it is quiet or raining.

We can symbolize these two, using the established scheme of interpretation, and using parentheses to reflect the grouping indicated by the word "either" and by transformational ellipsis. Doing truth tables on the two formulas shows that they are logically equivalent.

P	Q	R	(P	∨	Q)	∨	R	P	∨	(Q	∨	R)
1	1	1	1	1	1	1	1	1	1	1	1	1
0	1	1	0	1	1	1	1	0	1	1	1	1
1	0	1	1	1	0	1	1	1	1	0	1	1
0	0	1	0	1	0	1	1	0	1	0	1	1
1	1	0	1	1	1	1	0	1	1	1	1	0
0	1	0	0	0	1	1	0	0	1	1	1	0
1	0	0	1	1	0	1	0	1	1	0	0	0
0	0	0	0	0	0	0	0	0	0	0	0	0

The logical force of either of the earlier sentences might more briefly and less misleadingly be expressed this way:

It is either blowing or quiet or raining.

The appropriate formula, which we can consider an abbreviation for either of the two logically equivalent formulas in the truth table, is one with no parentheses:

(6)   P ∨ Q ∨ R

In fact there can be arbitarily many disjuncts without parentheses, and ambiguity never threatens; however you associate the disjuncts to satisfy the pairwise definition of disjunction in its computational table will result in the same main column. Obviously there is an easier specification of the truth-value of such a formula: it is True if any of the disjuncts are True. Only in the case that all of the disjuncts are False is the long disjunction False.

It may be illuminating to compare the formula (6) with this arithmetic expression:

5 + 7 + 4

Even though addition is fundamentally defined as an operation on two numbers, we have no trouble understanding a summation of many. No parentheses are needed because it doesn't matter whether you start adding from the left or from the right; you will get the same answer either way.

A similar equivalence holds with respect to logical conjunction. There is no difference in meaning as between,

It is both blowing and quiet, and it is raining,

and,

It is blowing, and it is both quiet and raining.

Either of them might better be expressed as,

It is blowing, quiet, and raining.

And so with a formula involving arbitrarily many conjunctions, no parentheses are required. Any of the three sentences can be symbolized indifferently as,

(7)   P & Q & R.

Each of the formulas (6) and (7) has been freed of parentheses. Though the phrase-structure grammar of (42.1) requires parentheses of a strict speaker, we regard the simpler formulas as abbreviations of formulas that are grammatical in the strict sense. It is time to introduce additional abbreviations that are motivated by the need to simplify formulas and make them more readable, while maintaining the principle that no formula be syntactically ambiguous, except as between logically equivalent alternatives. In general parentheses serve the grouping function in the symbolic language. In the process of symbolizing an English sentence that was syntactically ambiguous, we had to choose one syntactic structure in preference to the other and to introduce parentheses accordingly. We also used parentheses to match the disambiguating effects of words like "both" and "either" and of selectively applied transformations. But in cases like (6) and (7), the parentheses can be left out. Similarly, the outermost parentheses of a formula, the ones that surround the whole remainder, are not necessary. So by convention, we drop them.

There are additional conventions of abbreviation worth adopting in anticipation of an even more algebraic employment of the language of §42. Lower-case letters are more compact than upper-case, so let's begin using them throughout. This practice will permit a more compact and readable expression of negation, particularly when it applies to a single sentence letter; we will use an apostrophe *after* a sentence letter rather than the usual negation sign *before*. The familiar

$\neg Q$

becomes the more compact

q' .

When a subformula is negated, we may choose to use the unabbreviated "¬," as before. In ordinary algebra a significant efficiency is achieved by dropping multiplication signs, so that contiguous variables are taken to be factors. Analogously, in our formulas we drop the "&," that is, the sign for logical conjunction. Our formula (7) becomes,

pqr .

It is with this abbreviation that our convention about negation signs really pays off. Using all of these conventions, a complicated formula like,

((P & ¬ Q) & (R & (S & ¬ T))

has the transparent—and brief—abbreviation,

pq'rst' .

Carrying the analogy with ordinary algebra all the way, we had as well replace the disjunction sign with the more familiar plus. So where we had (6), now we will write,

p + q + r .

One last abbreviatory convention may now be added. It really goes almost without saying once we decide to drop the conjunction sign. Consider these two formulas:

p + (qr)   (p + q)r .

In unabbreviated form,

(P ∨ (Q & R))   ((P ∨ Q) & R),

they have the parentheses that differentiate

Either it is blowing, or it is both quiet and raining.

from

It is either blowing or quiet, and it is raining.

In unabbreviated form, all the parentheses seem equally necessary, but when we look at the abbreviated formula on the left, the parentheses seem superfluous. What else would we mean by

p + qr ?

With these abbreviatory conventions in place, certain English sentences correspond to particularly simple formulas. The doubly complex sentence,

Either it is raining but not snowing or else
it is not raining but snowing,

is symbolized without need for parentheses as

rs' + r's.

In its simplicity this is an example of a normal-form formula. Explaining the idea of normal form is a task for the next section.

§45   CONSTRUCTING AN ARBITRARY FUNCTION; NORMAL FORM

It may have occurred to you to ask why we have picked only five truth-functions to define by way of particular computational tables. Even within the natural expressive range of English there are other obvious truth-functions. One example is the exclusive "or," thought by many to be expressed in sentences like, "Either you will eat your spinach, or you will have no dessert." The computational table for the exclusive "or" is easily specified: it will be just like that for "∨," except that it will have the value False on the top line, where both constituent sentences have the value True. However obvious the definition of this truth-function, it is not obvious how to represent it in the algebraic language that we have been developing. Do we need to add a connective? Or can some combination of the connectives that we already have express this function? The answer is implicit in the following procedure. It enables us to construct a formula for any truth-function whatever, making use of the familiar truth-functions of negation, logical conjunction, and disjunction.

A Procedure for Constructing a Formula to Express an Arbitrary Truth-Function

(1) Write down the truth table with the main column you want.

(2) Identify the True's in the main column.

(3) Construct a disjunction with a disjunct for each True line.

(4) For each disjunct, construct a conjunction of sentence letters and negations of sentence letters, according to whether the sentence letter in question is True or False on that line.

Before discussing this procedure further, let's see how it works in practice, starting with the case of the exclusive "or." We are to enter, into a column of a truth table, the target truth-values for the various combinations of two sentence letters. These truth-values serve to specify the truth-function in question, in this case, the exclusive reading of the English conjunction "or."

p	q	p exclusive-or q	
1	1	**0**	
0	1	**1**	⇐
1	0	**1**	⇐
0	0	**0**	

It is the lines with the value True in the main column to which we are to pay special attention. They have been identified with "⇐." There are two lines so identified; the following disjunction has been set up with a blank space for each of them.

_____ + _____

The second line of the table has the value True; the first disjunct corresponds to this line. It is to be a conjunction. The value of "p" on this line is False, so we enter into the conjunction the letter "p" negated.

p'q + _____

On this same second line, the value of "q" is True, so "q" is entered into the conjunction without being negated.

p'**q** + _____

The same rule applied to the third line of the table, which also has the value True, finishes our formula. In this second disjunct, "p" is affirmative (since "p" has the value True on the third line), but "q" is negated (since it has the value False).

p'q + **pq'**

To verify the efficacy of this procedure, we do a truth-table on the formula we have constructed. (In a truth table on an abbreviated formula, we use connectives and parentheses as needed for clarity. Also notice the short-cut treatment of the negated sentence letters.)

p	q	(p	&	q')	+	(p'	&	q)
1	1	1	0	0	**0**	0	0	1
0	1	0	0	0	**1**	1	1	1
1	0	1	1	1	**1**	0	0	0
0	0	0	0	1	**0**	1	0	0

For a more interesting case we can apply the construction procedure to the truth-function expressed by the complex formula (2) from §44—which has here been abbreviated. Its main column has been transcribed from the truth table in §44; the True lines have been indicated; and the appropriate conjunction has been constructed for each True line.

p	q	r	¬ (r → q) ↔ (p (r + q'))		
1	1	1	**0**		
0	1	1	**1**	⇐	p'qr
1	0	1	**1**	⇐	pq'r
0	0	1	**0**		
1	1	0	**1**	⇐	pqr'
0	1	0	**1**	⇐	p'qr'
1	0	0	**0**		
0	0	0	**1**	⇐	p'q'r'

All that remains is to construct a disjunction of the five conjunctions on the right above. The result is the following formula. If the procedure indeed works as advertised, this formula will turn out to be logically equivalent to the complex formula we began with.

(1)   p'qr + pq'r + pqr' + p'qr' + p'q'r'

There is one degenerate case for which our procedure does not work. What if the main column you want has no True entries? Proceeding with this recipe will result in no disjuncts. Of course a formula with no True entries—that is, with its main column all False's—is inconsistent. Any inconsistent formula whatever will do for yielding such a main column. We can standardly use the most familiar example:

(2)   pp'

It is no accident that the formulas produced by our procedure have no parentheses. Our abbreviatory conventions were chosen with that result in view. Formulas of this sort, lacking parentheses and lacking both the arrow and the double-arrow, are in normal form, or what is more formally called **disjunctive normal form**. A normal form formula is a disjunction of conjunctions, each of whose conjuncts is either a sentence letter or the negation of a sentence letter. (By courtesy, we call a single sentence letter, or the negation of a single sentence letter, a conjunction with only one conjunct. And we call a single conjunction a disjunction with only one disjunct. Thus both (2) above and (3) below count as normal formulas. In fact the formula consisting of the letter "p" alone counts as a normal formula.) Our procedure works, for any formula that is consistent, to produce a formula that is logically equivalent to the original. It produces normal formulas willy-nilly. For inconsistent formulas, we can take refuge in formula (2) above, which—happily—is normal itself. Thus we have proved the following.

Normal-form Theorem: Any formula has a logical equivalent in (disjunctive) normal form.

Despite its normal form, (1) above is none too simple. It is characteristic of our procedure to produce rather long formulas. The worst case comes when the main column of the original formula has all True's. The procedure yields a normal form equivalent with eight disjuncts—supposing that the original has three sentence letters. Such a formula is a tautology. Of course there is available another normal formula,

(3)   p + p' ,

that is equivalent to the one in question, since they have identical main columns. And (3) is much simpler.

Calling our attention to simplicity raises the question in general whether there can be found simpler normal form equivalents, simpler than the formulas produced by our procedure. The answer is that, through manipulations of an algebraic character, the following normal formula,

(4)   p'q + pq'r + p'r' + qr' ,

can be derived from (1). Of course (4) is much simpler than (1), and the two formulas can be shown to be logically equivalent by constructing a truth table for (4). As you would expect, the manipulations in question have been chosen to preserve logical equivalence. They must be governed by appropriate principles, principles that turn out to be different from—though analogous to—those of ordinary algebra. The required principles are those of an abstract algebra developed originally by the mathematician and logician George Boole. If you wish to learn about them further, consult an appropriate mathematical source under the heading of Boolean Algebra.

Exercises for Appendix

1.   Rewrite the following formulas in explicit notation, eliminating abbreviatory
      conventions. Construct a truth table for each one.

      a. $p + q \rightarrow (q'r \leftrightarrow p)$

      b. $p' + pq'r$

      c. $pq + p'q + pq' + p'q'$

      d. $(q \leftrightarrow pr') \neg (p + q + r \rightarrow (r' \leftrightarrow pq))$

      e. $p'q' + p'(q + r') + pq'r$

      f. $(\neg (pqr) \rightarrow (p \leftrightarrow q' + r')) + p'(q \rightarrow r')$

      g. $\neg (p + q') + \neg (s \rightarrow q)$

2.   Specify which of the formulas in problem #1 are tautologies, which ones are
      inconsistent, and which ones are logically equivalent to which others. Which
      ones are in normal form?

3.   For each of the formulas in problem #1 that is *not* in normal form, use our
      recipe to construct a normal-form equivalent.

4.   By means of our recipe, construct a formula in "p," "q," and "r," using only
      "¬ ," "& ," and "∨," which comes out true whenever exactly two of the
      sentence letters are true, and otherwise comes out false.

For Reading and Reference

These books are appropriate for those who wish to further explore various aspects of the material introduced in the present book. Since our approach is unusual, most of them complement this book in one or another dimension. Currently in print are a great many textbooks of informal logic, of formal or symbolic logic, and of linguistics, particularly syntactic theory. This list selects from them. Others listed are out of print, but have enduring influence.

What is called informal logic in courses and textbooks is concerned with investigating argumentative and persuasive discourse in such vehicles as editorials, polemical essays, and of course philosophical treatises and dialogues, identifying premises–particularly suppressed premises–and conclusions, and classifying the kinds of reasoning involved. Thus such books develop and extend the topics of our §4, in Chapter I. They continue a tradition, dating from Aristotle, of recognizing and categorizing fallacies–unreasonable inferences masquerading as reasonable ones–commonly made in such discourse, whether wittingly or not. Two of the best of these books are mentioned below.

Formal logic textbooks typically are restricted to what is called first-order logic (growing from the territory of our chapters VI, VIII, and IX) and the logic of identity (our §§28 - 29, in Chapter VII). But within those bounds they develop fully rule-governed methods for showing validity that are demonstrably complete in a precisely defined sense. Included below are those most nearly compatible with the approach of this book.

Textbooks in syntactic theory have been hampered by the constant churning in that discipline, with its central practitioners frequently repudiating the theories both of each other and of their former selves. Those mentioned below either give perspective on the fray or promise to endure despite the dislocations and controversies.

Also included below are trade books and accessible monographs and handbooks that represent other topics that have been introduced in our pages. A small number are flagged as advanced sources that provide access to current research.

Baker, Mark C., *Atoms of Language: The Mind's Hidden Rules of Grammar* (New York: Basic Books, 2001). Attempts a taxonomy of the world's languages, making use of the "principles and parameters" perspective, and emphasizing universal grammar and explanations of language acquisition.

Barwise, Jon, and John Perry, *Situations and Attitudes* (Cambridge, Mass.: MIT Press, 1983). Their "situations" are similar to our "possible situations," but are given a metaphysical foundation and exploited in a theory of propositional attitudes.

Bell, John L., David DeVidi, and Graham Solomon, *Logical Options* (Peterborough: Broadview Press, 2001). Adapts the method of formal tableaux not only for first-order logic but for alternatives and extensions including second-order logic, modal logic, intuitionistic logic, and fuzzy logic.

Bergmann, Merrie, James Moor, and Jack Nelson, *The Logic Book* (New York: McGraw-Hill, 1980, 1990, and 1998). One of the best of current comprehensive textbooks of first-order logic, including chapters using the method of tableaux (there called "truth-trees"). In three editions.

Chomsky, Noam, *Aspects of the Theory of Syntax* (Cambridge, Mass.: MIT Press, 1965). Chapter I is the definitive statement by Chomsky of the methodology of linguistics.

_____, *Language and Mind*, 2nd ed. (New York: Harcourt Brace Jovanovich, 1972). Chomsky's classic statement of his view that the study of linguistics, particularly syntactic theory, provides our best avenue for understanding the nature of the human mind.

_____, *New Horizons in the Study of Language and Mind* (Cambridge: Cambridge U. Press, 2000). In its echo of Chomsky's earlier title, the book acknowledges the need for a latter-day treatment of the same topics. The lengthy polemics of this book make it a less than ideal fulfillment of that need.

_____, *Syntactic Structures* (The Hague: Mouton, 1957). Our introduction in chapter V draws from the treatment in Chomsky's widely influential early book, much of which he now disavows. Despite the disavowal, the book provides a very accessible introduction to what was the revolutionary conception of linguistic theory called generative grammar.

_____, *The Minimalist Program* (Cambridge, Mass.: MIT Press, 1995). A comprehensive statement of the program for linguistic theory that Chomsky currently champions. Though the technical material is difficult even for advanced students, the programmatic and polemical sections can be profitably surveyed by a novice.

Culicover, Peter W., *Principles and Parameters: An Introduction to Syntactic Theory* (Oxford: Oxford U. Press, 1997). A comprehensive textbook that provides perspective on Chomsky's changing theories.

Enderton, Herbert, *A Mathematical Introduction to Logic* (San Diego: Academic Press, 1972 and 2001). A full mathematical treatment of first-order logic, with a bit on second-order logic, in two editions. At the level of upper-level undergraduate mathematics.

Gabbay, Dov M., and F. Guenther (eds.), *Handbook of Philosophical Logic* (Dordrecht: D. Reidel, 1984-1989). State-of-the-art formal treatment of the logic of the various kinds of constructions that we sample, especially in our Chapter IV. In five volumes. An even more exhaustive second edition is underway.

Haegeman, Liliane, *Introduction to Government and Binding Theory* (Oxford: Blackwell, 1991 and 1994). In two editions; despite its outdated title, it remains a valuable introduction to syntactic theory in the Chomsky tradition.

Heim, Irene, and A. Kratzer, *Semantics in Generative Grammar* (Oxford: Blackwell, 1998).

Hodges, Wilfrid, *Logic* (Harmondsworth: Penguin, 1977). In many ways the parent of the present book. Uses semantic tableaux in natural language, with some grammatical foundations, and then develops formal versions of the same methods.

Jackson, Frank (ed.), *Conditionals* (Oxford: Oxford U. Press, 1991). A collection of influential papers on the logic of subordinate clauses beginning with "if." This is a central and much discussed topic, on which we have adopted a moderately unorthodox stance.

Jeffrey, Richard, *Formal Logic: Its Scope and Limits* (New York: McGraw-Hill, 1967, 1981, and 1991). In three editions; the classic treatment of first-order logic by way of semantic tableaux in tree form.

Kahane, Howard, *Logic and Contemporary Rhetoric* (Belmont, Cal.: Wadsworth, 1971 - 1988). In at least five editions; the paradigm of informal logic books.

LePore, Ernest, *Meaning and Argument* (Oxford: Blackwell, 2000). Much in the spirit of the present book, but quick to move to a formal treatment of each of various logically important constructions found in natural language. Good preparation for advanced work in the logic of natural language.

Loux, Michael (ed.), *The Possible and the Actual* (Ithaca: Cornell U. Press, 1979). This collection includes papers by Kaplan, Lewis, Plantinga, Adams, Stalnaker, and others, that discuss possible worlds, a metaphysical notion related to our possible situations and preferred by some as a conceptual basis for logic.

Ludlow, Peter, *Readings in the Philosophy of Language* (Cambridge, Mass.: MIT Press, 1997). A collection of papers that includes not only those most influential from twentieth-century philosophy of language, but also several that incorporate insights from linguistic theory.

Lyons, John, *Chomsky* (Harmondsworth: Penguin, 1970 and 1977). Though dated, it presents a highly readable treatment of the classic transformational grammar and a still relevant presentation of Chomsky's ambitions with respect to the nature of the human mind. Two editions; in the Modern Masters series.

Pinker, Steven, *The Language Instinct* (New York: William Morrow, 1994). A popular exposition of the lore of generative grammar. Chapter IV provides a succinct update of our introduction, including an introduction to the principles and parameters approach by way of so-called X-bar theory.

Quine, Willard Van Orman, *Methods of Logic* (New York: Holt, Rinehart and Winston, 1950, 1959, and 1972; Cambridge, Mass.: Harvard U. Press, 1982). In four editions; though its methods are quite different from ours and its philosophical view of the nature of logic is diametrically opposed to ours, its discussion of "words into symbols" is linguistically sensitive and helpful.

_____, *Word and Object* (Cambridge, Mass.: MIT Press, 1960). Though he despairs of the logical coherence of natural language, here Quine extends his sensitive treatment of the logic of natural language constructions to great length.

Radford, Andrew, *Syntactic Theory and the Structure of English: A Minimalist Approach* (Cambridge: Cambridge U. Press, 1997). Recommended by many linguists as an introduction to current Chomskian theory.

_____, *Syntax: A Minimalist Introduction* (Cambridge: Cambridge U. Press, 1997). An abridged version of the preceding entry.

Read, Stephen, *Thinking about Logic* (New York: Oxford U. Press, 1995). Canvasses many of the philosophical issues about logic that lie just beneath the surface of our treatment.

Sag, Ivan, and Thomas Wasow, *Syntactic Theory: A Formal Introduction* (Stanford: CSLI Publications, 1999). A reliable introductory textbook representing a part of the syntactic mainstream that maintains its independence from Chomsky's influence. Its perspective has been especially useful for computer processing of natural language.

Salmon, Merrilee, *Introduction to Logic and Critical Thinking* (New York: International Thomson Publishers, 1994). A reliable informal logic textbook that includes some formal methods, currently in print.

Smith, Neil, *Chomsky: Ideas and Ideals* (Cambridge: Cambridge U. Press, 1999). Includes a survey, endorsed by Chomsky, of the foundations of current linguistic theory. Helpful for seeing how early Chomsky evolved to minimalist Chomsky.

Van Benthem, Johan F., and Alice Ter Meulen (eds.), *Handbook of Logic and Language* (Cambridge, Mass.: MIT Press, 1997). Encyclopedic treatment of the state of the art of many of our topics. Mathematically demanding, often oriented toward computer processing of natural language.

Index

The page where a term is defined or explained is listed in **boldface**.

abbreviated phrase-marker, 116-117
abbreviatory conventions, 267-270
adjectives, 61
adverbs, 82-83
"Alex", 226
"although", 124, 128
"always", 241, 244
ambiguous, **27**-31, 43-44; *see also*
    anaphoric ambiguity, lexical
    ambiguity, structural ambiguity,
    syntactic ambiguity
anaphora, **31**, 43, 76
anaphoric ambiguity, **30**, 76-80, 92
anaphoric pronoun (or anaphor), 76,
    178, 180, 213-215, 219-220, 229, 230,
    231, 232
"and", 124, 128-129, 136-137, **139**, 193-195
"and"-transformation, 137
"and/or", 131
"And/Or" Transformation, **138**
annotating pronouns, 76-77
antecedent, 31
"anyone" (or "anybody"), 211-215, 219,
    236, 238, 244
arbitrary truth-function, **270**
argument, **11**-19, 68-72
arithmetic, 190

Barbara, **227**
"because", 74-75, 87-88, 124
belief, 3
Beth, Evart, 49
biconditional, 134
Boole, George, 273
Boolean algebra, 273

"both . . . and", 138
bound, **220**
branch, **50**
branching structure, 50
"but", 124, 128
"by", 2, 109-110, 235

calculation, 259-260
Carnap, Rudolf, 96
categorical judgement, **225**
checked sentence, 51, 85-91; *see also*
    unchecked sentence
Chomsky, Noam, 95-96
clause, 110-111, 114
clause-switching, 125
closed path, **53**
closed tableau, 60-63, **64**, 71, 73, 78, 83-
    84, 89, 130-131, 152-153, 168, 169-170,
    177, 200, 201, 202, 205-206, 208, 209,
    212, 214, 221, 223, 226, 232, 235, 237
closing rule, 135, 153
common nouns, 158; that do not take
    the plural, **159**
complex sentence, **110**
Computational Tables for Five Truth-
    Functions, **258**
computer-screen tableaux, 85, 90
conclusion, **11**
conditional, **127**, 256-257; negated, 146-
    149
conditionalization, **146**-149
conjunctions, 123-124, **125**, 136, 193-195
consistent, **42**, 49, 58, 69, 199; *see also*
    obvious consistency, obvious
    inconsistency

constant, **243**
constituent, **105**, 118, 181
conventional style, **12**, 20-21
converse, **133**
coordinating conjunction, 123
copula, **174**
count noun, **159**, 160, 187-188
counter set, **68**, 69, 70, 146-149, 178
counterexample, **202**
Counterexample Rule for Negated
    Universal Categoricals, **226**-228

data, 100
Datisi, **234**
declarative sentence, **5**, 9-12
deductive argument, *see* argument
deductive validity, *see* valid
deep structure, **110**
definite article, 188
definite description, 158, **160**
deletion rule, **110**
denial, 75
derived phrase-marker, **108**, 109
description, definite, 158, **160**
descriptive indexical, **25**, 43, 188-189;
    see also definite description
descriptive sentence, **7**
designator, **158**-161, 171-174, 181, 184,
    186, 188, 189, 196, 198, 200, 201
disjunctive normal form, **272**-273
dominate, **104**, 105
double "not", 74, 128
Doyle, Arthur Conan, 35, 36
dummy subject, 106

efficiency, 58-60; rules of thumb for, 59,
    64
"either . . .or", 138
entails, 15
"equals", 176
equivalence, 106; *see also* logical
    equivalence, transformational
    equivalence
equivalence class, **169**
equivalence relation, **169**
"even if", 136
"ever", 187, 241, 244-245
"everyone", 70-71, 187, **190**, 194-195, 196-
    197, 199, 210

exclamatory sentence, 5, 7
exclusive "or", 131, 270-271
existential quantifier, **231**-233
expresses with respect to, **37**, 41, 45
Extraposition, **113**, 114, 119

False, **255**, 259-260, 261
falsity, 3
Festino, **234**
follows logically, 14
formula, **251**
Freeman, Mary E. Wilkins, 44

general term, 187
Generalized "And/Or"
    Transformation, **138**
generative grammar, **96**
gradual introduction of rule-governed
    formulations, 222
grammar, **95**; *see also* generative
    grammar, school grammar

"he or she", 213, 219

"identical to", 174-175
identity, 171-180, 246
"if", 55-56, 82, 124, 127, 132-134
"if, and only if", 133-134
imperative, 5, 7
inconsistent, **9**-10, 31-32, 34-37, **42**-43,
    71-72, 73, 199, 205-207
inconsistent formula, **264**, 273
indexical, **23**, 43; descriptive, **25**, 43,
    188-189
inductive logic, 16
inference, reasonable, **15**, 21; to best
    explanation, 18
infinite clause, 114
infinite range of sentences, 96-97
initial symbol, **98**
intelligibility, 9, 32, 44-45
interrogative, 5, 7

Jefferson, Thomas, 4, 5
Joule, James Prescott, 3

Katz-Postal Hypothesis, **194**-195
Kelvin, Lord (William Thomson), 3

Leibniz, Gottfried Wilhelm, 171
Leibniz's Law, **171**-176, 182, 186, 189
Leibniz's Rule for Tableaux, **177**-180,
    237
"lest", 124
lexical ambiguity, **27**
Lincoln, Abraham, 3, 94, 96
locational relative pronoun, 243
Locke, John, 3
logical consequence, 15
logical equivalence, *see* logically
    equivalent
logical form, **251**
logical scope, **194**-196, 203, 207-209, 210-
    212, 216, 222
logically equivalent, **238**-239, 246, **265**,
    273

main column, **263**
main connective, **263**
meaning, 2, 26-31, 95
Mill, John Stuart, 3-5, 254
mixed tableaux, 153-**154**, 156
Moore, Clement C., 32-34
multiple quantifiers, 239-241, 247

narrow scope, **141**
negated conditionals, 146, 148-149
negation, **127**, 191, 193, 202, 255-256,
    268-269
Negation Rule, for "Everyone", **202**-203,
    209; for "No one", **203**-204; for
    "Someone", **203**-204; for the
    Existential Quantifier, **233**; for the
    Nihilistic Quantifier, **233**
neutral proper name, 197, **198**-200, 202-
    203
"never", 241, 243
nihilistic quantifier, **232**-233
"no one" (or "nobody"), 84, 187, **191**, 232
nominative case, 158
non-terminal string, **108**
non-terminal symbol, **98**
normal form, 272-273
Normal-Form Theorem, **273**
"not" transformation, 192
"nothing", 185-186
number, grammatical, **112**
numbering, **59**, 66

numeral, 158-**159**
numerical induction, 16, 17

objective case, 158
obvious consistency, 57-58, 199
obvious inconsistency, 46-49, 200
"one and the same as", 175
one-place predicate, **161**
one-word quantifier, **187**
One-Word Quantifiers of English, **241**
"only if", 132-133
open path, 57
open tableau, **64**, 79-80 179, 199, 224, 227
"or", 70, 74, 92, 124, 129-131, **139**, 193-
    194, 207-208
"or"-transformation, 138
overlapping branches, 52, 55

parentheses, 141-142, 267-268
parse, **104**
Passive Transformation, **108**, 110-114,
    119, 122, 195
path, **53**
performative sentence, **7**
phrase-class, **104**
phrase-marker, **98**, 99, 100, 102, 103,
    107, 115, 116, 117, 191, 192, 253
phrase-structure component, **110**
phrase-structure grammar, **98**-105
Phrase-Structure Grammar for
    Sentential Formulas, **252**
places, 243
possible situation, 32, **35**-37, 44-45, 48-
    49, 53, 57-58, 198
Post, Emil, 96
predicate 157, **161**-164
premise, **12**-14
Principle of Substitutivity, **172**
probability, 17
procedure, 270
proper connective, **248**
proper name, **158**, 197; *see also* neutral
    proper name
property, **161**-162, 164
proposition, **2**-8, 11, 19-20, 22-26, 119,
    254
propositional attitude, **112**
"provided that", 135
pruning, **108**

Putin, Vladimir, 171, 190

quantifier, *see* existential quantifier, nihilistic quantifier, quantifier expression, one-word quantifier, simplest quantifiers, universal quantifier
quantifier expression, **187**-188, 189-190, 196-198

Raising, 119
reasonable inference, **15**, 21
recursive grammar, **102**
recursive rule, **101**, 122
reference, 22-26, 75-80
relation, 139-140, **163**-169; equivalence, **169**; reflexive, **171**; symmetric, **165**-166, 168, 181-182, 183; transitive, **166**-169, 181-182, 183
relative pronoun, **229**-232
rewriting rule, **98**, 101, 103-104, 111, 112, 122
Rousseau, Jean-Jacques, 3
Rule, for the Existential Quantifier, **231**; for the Nihilistic Quantifier, **232**; for the Universal Quantifier, **220**
rule-governed connective, **127**-136, 143-146, 194, 195, 204, **248**; standard for, 145
rules for sentence connectives, **150**, 249

scheme of interpretation, **251**
scope, **105**, 118, 140-142, 193, 206; *see also* logical scope
selection restrictions, **113**
semantic tableau, **49**, 58, 69
sentence, **1**-2, **104**; *see also* declarative sentence, set of sentences
sentence letter, **251**
sentence tableau, **251**
set of sentences, 8-**9**, 19-20, 22-26, 40, 46-49, 50, 94-97
Shannon, Claude, 96
Simple Rule, for "Anyone", **212**-214, 217; for "Everyone", **196**-197, 206, 208, 221; for "No one", **200**-202, 206; for "Someone", **197**-200, 206
simplest quantifiers, 189-193, 196-209

"since", 81, 88, 124
singular noun phrase, 160
singular pronoun, **158**
"someone" (or "somebody"), **190**, 194-195, 196, 197-200, 229-231, 238
"something", 187
"somewhere", 187
statistical reasoning, 16-17
structural ambiguity, **27**, 114; *see also* syntactic ambiguity
subordinating conjunction, 123, 125
substitute, **172**
Substitutivity, Principle of, **172**
surface string, **109**
syllogism, 227, **234**-235
symbolic tableau, **252**
symbolization, 250-252
symmetric relation, **165**-166, 168, 181-182, 183
syntactic ambiguity, 114-120, 141-142, 191-193
syntactically ambiguous, **115**

tableau, *see* semantic tableau
Tableau Rules for Sentence Connectives, **150**, 249
tautology, **264**, 273
Taylor, Zachary, 130-131
temporal relative pronoun, 243
terminal string, **99**, 115
terminal symbol, **98**
things, 242
"though", 124, 128
times, 242-243
"Tough"-Movement, 119
transformation, **108**, 113, 118-120, 121, 136-142, 155-156, 207
transformational equivalence, **107**, 191-196, 207-208
transitive relation, **166**-169, 181-182, 183
True, **255**, 259-260, 261
true in a situation, **37**-39, 42, 45
true with respect to a situation, **38**-43, 45, 53, 69
trunk, **50**
truth, 3, 22, 23, 26, 42
truth table, **261**-264, 265-267, 271-272
truth-functions, **255**-258, 270-273
truth-value, **255**

two-place predicate, **162**

unchecked sentence, 54, 57, 86, 145
underlying constituent, 120
underlying phrase-marker, 108, 110, 120
underlying sentence (or underlying string), **107**, 207
unit of language, 1
unit of logic, 2
universal generalization, **225**
universal quantifier, **220**-228
universe of discourse, **190**, 197
"unless", 74, 124, 131-132,

valid, **14**, 69, 71, 75, 204, 207
verdict, **58**, 65, 75

"while", 124, 128
"who", 229
wide scope, **141**
Wittgenstein, Ludwig, 6

"yet", 124, 128
"you", 219, 231

Errata

p. xiii natural-¹language ᵖ

p. 155 swooshes

p. 155 4e no solution?

p. 130 √ S₁ ∨ S₂

p. 150 S₁ ↔ S₂
↖ missing

p 144 sentences?